WITHDRAWN

P9-DFD-392

IMAGES OF
WELFARE

ASPECTS OF SOCIAL POLICY

General Editor: J.P. Martin
Professor of Sociology and Social Administration, University of Southampton

361.942
G569i

PETER GOLDING and SUE MIDDLETON

IMAGES OF WELFARE

Press and Public
Attitudes to Poverty

The Library
Saint Francis College
Fort Wayne, Indiana 46808

MARTIN ROBERTSON · OXFORD

86-322

© Peter Golding and Sue Middleton 1982

First published in 1982 by Martin Robertson & Company Ltd., 108 Cowley Road, Oxford OX4 1JF.

Reprinted 1983

All rights reserved. No part of this publication may be reproduced, stored in a retrieval system, or transmitted, in any form or by any means, electronic, mechanical, photocopying, recording or otherwise, without the prior written permission of the copyright holders.

Except in the United States of America, this book is sold subject to the condition that it shall not, by way of trade or otherwise be lent, re-sold, hired out, or otherwise circulated without the publisher's prior consent in any form of binding or cover other than that in which it is published and without a similar condition including this condition being imposed on the subsequent purchaser.

British Library Cataloguing in Publication Data

Golding, Peter
   Images of welfare. - (Aspects of social policy)
   1. Social service
   2. Public welfare
   I. Title   II. Middleton, Susan
   III. Series
   361.   HU40

ISBN 0-85520-447-8
ISBN 0-85520-448-6 Pbk

Typeset by Pioneer in 10 on 11 point English
Printed and bound in Great Britain
by Billing & Sons Limited, Worcester.

Contents

Acknowledgements

The empirical research that forms the basis for Parts II and III of this book was originally undertaken as a project funded by the Nuffield Foundation. We are grateful to the Foundation and to Professor J. D. Halloran at the Centre for Mass Communication Research, University of Leicester who arranged and supervised the funding. Leicester University generously provided a small award to assist the research on which chapters 2 and 5 are based.

Many people assisted with the arduous mechanics of the survey and content analysis, and we would like to acknowledge the splendid work of the interviewing and coding teams in Sunderland and Leicester, with a special word for our field supervisors, Edna Rafferty and Carol Leivers. Paul Croll, Phil Harris, Paul Hartmann, Robin McCron and Barry Troyna, all of Leicester University, gave invaluable advice on the survey design and analysis, and Steve Pearce in particular provided crucial assistance with data analysis.

Much useful advice was gained from seminar presentations of aspects of the research in various academic and non-academic gatherings. We are also very grateful for the detailed comments provided by Ann Davis on the original research report. To the journalists, named and unnamed, who assisted with chapter 5, our particular thanks, in the hope they will not find the description of their work and views unrecognisable.

Edward Elgar, formerly of Martin Robertson, deserves special thanks for his encouragement and interest, and to Michael Hay our gratitude for continued support and considerable patience.

Last, but not least, our thanks to Mary Coldicott for her timely and productive return to the typewriter, and for an excellent typescript produced against many odds.

Peter Golding
Sue Middleton
May 1981

For Ben, despite whom this book was written.
                                        P.G.

For Dave, with love and thanks.
                          S.M.

1 Introduction: Images of Welfare

The sufferings of the poor are, indeed, less observed than their misdeeds; not from any want of compassion but because they are less known; and this is the true reason why we so often hear them mentioned with abhorrence, and so seldom with pity . . . They starve, and freeze, and rot among themselves, but they beg, and steal and rob among their betters. [Henry Fielding, A Proposal For Making an Effectual Provision for the Poor *1753*]

CHAPTER 1

Crisis and the Welfare Backlash

In November 1976 a Yorkshire villager became the target of repeated attacks by his neighbours. Tiles were ripped from his roof, squibs were posted through his letterbox, and in the street he was subjected to constant abuse. The villager, who was crippled with rheumatoid arthritis, had made the mistake of doing some light gardening in full public view while, as his neighbours well knew, he was receiving unemployment benefit. He was just one of thousands who became victims of a mounting hysteria that in the ensuing period created a welfare backlash of cruel and massive proportions.

The apparently smooth progress of the welfare state had run into choppy waters. As the economic slump bit deeper into daily life, venomous hostility to the supposedly protected and coddled charges of welfare and social security schemes returned the welfare state to the centre of the political stage. The British became more doubtful and looked around to find the whole world, as it seemed, indicting welfare and convicting the poor for the crisis of economic fortune.

The mood seemed universal. In Australia the crimes of 'dole bludgers' were a prominent feature of the 1975 election campaign, and newspapers were filled with outraged tales of 'dole dollies' shamelessly exploiting the largesse of the state. The new Prime Minister, Malcolm Fraser, got much mileage from accusing the Labour government of being soft on welfare cheats, and told Australians 'life wasn't meant to be easy'. Opinion polls showed that nearly half the Australian population thought the rise in unemployment was due to indolence among the young. In Canada in 1978 the government announced a million dollar advertising campaign to expose dole cheats. As Canadian unemployment hit peaks unprecedented since the Great Depression, television and newspaper commercials rammed home the message that welfare abuse was rife and had to be stamped out. In the United States in

3

1978 Howard Jarvis' Proposition 13 got massive acclamation from a Californian public sick of paying taxes for government services they were persuaded were unnecessary. By 1980 second thoughts crept in, but as a bemused public watched vital services being dismembered they reserved no regrets for cuts in welfare or social services. The new federal administration under Ronald Reagan came in announcing that 'the war on poverty has been won except for a few mopping up operations'. The new President's Senior Domestic Policy Adviser wrote that these would include enforcing 'support of dependants by those who have the responsibility and are shirking it'.

In the European welfare states the story was the same. In Denmark, Mogens Glistrup's Progress Party stopped being a joke and became the second largest party, with a populist, tax-cutting platform that asked questions of the welfare state little heard in Scandinavia for a generation. Veikko Vennamo's Small Farmers Party in Finland had a similar successful appeal. In Switzerland, James Schwarzenbach received massive support for the same tax-cutting, anti-welfare message.

The diffuse waves of public anxiety that rippled out from the storm centre of economic recession were closing in over the poor and the welfare systems on which they depended. In focusing these anxieties the mass media were to play a significant part in identifying targets and amplifying public indignation in a deep-cutting and highly effective welfare backlash. In this book we seek to examine the origins, nature and mechanisms of this backlash in Britain, as well as its impact on social policy and public attitudes, paying particular attention to the role of the mass media. To do so we have extended the usual method of mass communication research, which frequently examines content, or audiences, or more rarely production, each in isolation, less commonly investigating two of these in conjunction. We have tried to investigate all of these facets of mass communication and also to relate them to the history and political economy of relevant areas of social policy. Obviously this is an ambitious project, and we present our findings as a tentative beginning to the task of filling in some large gaps in theory and research.

Chapter 2 examines the history of social policies for the poor and discusses the assumptions and imagery that have framed these policies, particularly as they have appeared in the press. Our concern is to demonstrate the deep roots and ideological pedigree of the ideas and rhetoric we describe later in the book. In Part II we look at the picture of the welfare state and its clients that is painted by the mass media, and begin to examine the processes that lie behind the emergence of the finished product. Part III turns to popular attitudes and, using survey research findings, probes the comprehensions of the wider population of the apparatus of the welfare state and those who depend on it. Finally we try to draw together some of the themes that emerge from our research, and offer some preliminary suggestions to explain how the crisis in the British economy has become the occasion for a social derision of the poor so punitive in its impact as to threaten the very props of the modern welfare state.

CHAPTER 2

God's Poor and the Devil's

Buried beneath the surface of attitudes about the welfare state lie centuries of experience and imagery. How to deal with the poor has always been the central policy issue for the state, and before the state for the church and feudal authorities. For centuries the poor laws provided the foundation on which other social policies were built. As feudalism gave way to capitalism the problems of economic management and political order were solved in new ways, creating new institutions and new ideologies that have continued to frame explanations of poverty through succeeding shifts in economic and social structure.

In this chapter we do not attempt to chart this complex and detailed history. We do, however, attempt to isolate some of the major ideological taproots beneath welfare and social policy. These provide the raw materials from which the thicket of images and values investigated in the remainder of this book has grown. Neither are we attempting the foolhardy task of providing a condensed history of social policy. Our aim is the more modest and immediately pertinent one of isolating a few central ideas that have been fed into the mainstream of popular consciousness at key periods of economic and social development. In the latter part of the chapter we shall illustrate this more directly in the press reporting of the period. Two relationships will emerge as crucial in these key ideas. The first is that between the individual and the state. The second is that between the individual and the labour market. In other words, policy for poverty, like social policy in general throughout the development of capitalism, is about the twin problems of political and economic control.

The relationship between the individual and the state itself throws up two problems. The first is the issue of conditional citizenship—the extent to which political rights, including the franchise, could be extended to the propertyless and especially to those dependent for their existence on the organised charity of the rest of society. The second problem is the relative weight of state provision and individual self-help. The rationalisations and moral exhortations generated in balancing these two have provided much of the rhetoric about the poor from the earliest debates about the nascent centralisation of state power, through Victorian enthusiasm for self-help and into the period of the 'representative-interventionist' state created by modern capitalism.

Similarly, the relationship between the individual and the labour market will be seen to have two related aspects crucial to our interests. The first is the set of problems related to labour control; the maintenance of work discipline and the related issues of motivation of and incentives for the work force. The second aspect is the problem of social order outside the labour force; the control of those beyond labour discipline and the consequent criminalisation of certain forms of pauperism, most notably those that threaten the good order of the work force or exploit systems of income maintenance or subsistence provided by society for an impoverished minority.

These two central issues weave their way through the centuries of society's dealings with poverty. We can begin to detect their significance in the pre-capitalist origins of policies to contain or support the poor.

THE BEGGARS ARE COMING TO TOWN

The gradual shift from the comprehensive ecclesiastical altruism of feudal religious charity, alms-giving and monastic hospitality to the repressive and selective attitudes of pre-Elizabethan times is often starkly described. The Webbs, for example, in their mammoth and seminal history, viewed the earlier indiscriminate open-handedness (together with parochiality) as the distinctive feature of feudal charity. Indeed this was its weakness in their rigorously administrative view. 'How hard it is', wrote the Webbs in a characteristically stern aside, 'to become convinced that the spirit of love, if it is to be genuinely beneficent—and therefore really kind—must be disciplined, like the activities of the physician and the sanitary engineer' (1927, p. 5). A more likely summary of these times emerges from Tierney's work. Canon law certainly stressed the innocence of poverty—'*Paupertas non est de numero malorum*'—and did not make the easy equation between destitution and moral inadequacy. Nonetheless cupidity, voluntary poverty, was an identifiable malaise: '. . . idleness was condemned and poverty was not automatically equated with virtue . . .' It was the case, though, that 'It hardly ever occurred to the canonists that the law should seek to "deter" men from falling into poverty. Want was its own deterrent, they thought' (1959, pp. 11—12).

Charity was effectively a church monopoly, in a society that accepted a 'gift economy' as a normal method of subsistence for the voluntarily dependent—the Pauperes Christi. But, additionally, alms-giving not only helped the soul of the donor, it 'also guaranteed the continued existence of the labour market and the maintenance of a social equilibrium' (Lis and Soly, 1979, p. 23). The growing crisis in the feudal economy as production no longer adequately met the subsistence needs of the peasants and the surplus needs of land owners began to disturb this stable moral order. Between 1350 and 1450 there was a massive drop in population, and with it a growing labour shortage and, after 1380, rising wages, the whole turmoil being jolted further by the devastating effects of the Black Death in 1349. The nobles, under economic siege, needed desperately to get to grips with the labour market. The first obvious response was the Statutes of Labourers of 1349—57, 'among the most glacially explicit programmes of exploitation in the whole history of European class struggle' (Anderson, 1974b, pp. 201—2). Central to this campaign of social control was the containment of geographical mobility, a need met by a succession of vagrancy laws of increasing severity. The vagrancy laws capture, as do few other documents, the swelling anxieties generated by the mobile poor, together with the punitive response these anxieties provoked. Looking back from the no less censorious perspective of 1834, administrative historians could only conclude that 'The great object of our early pauper legislation seems to have been the restraint of vagrancy' (*Poor Law Report,* 1834, p. 73).[1]

The vagrancy laws (the first of which appeared in 1349) were intended to contain wage levels indirectly, 'to curtail mobility of labourers in such a way that labour would not become a commodity for which the landowners would have to compete' (Chambliss, 1964, p. 70).[2] Flight from the land to the towns, an alternative to serfdom or, increasingly, mercenary service, fed not only the needs of the embryonic weaving industry but also the fears of burghers. The corollary of labour market control was the limitation of unrestricted charity. In 1359 a proclamation in London forbidding begging heralded the much tighter controls of later decades.

The early vagrancy acts became the catalyst that produced a pre-industrial, propertyless and disciplined working class. But it took a further shift of gear into full-blown mercantilism to sharpen more clearly the discrimination between 'god's poor and the devil's'—the poor and the paupers—which was to be the crux of later legislation.

By the early sixteenth century vagrancy laws began to move from a narrow concern with labour to a greater interest in the criminality inherent in having no evident employment. The statute of 1530 provided for punishment of he who 'can give no reckoning how he lawfully gets his living' as well as 'all other idle persons going about', some of whom it warns use 'divers subtle crafty unlawful games and plays . . .' (Chambliss, 1964, p. 71). The rogues, vagabonds and sturdy beggars had entered the scene, and were to personify wilful poverty for decades, indeed centuries, to come.

A growing population, greater labour mobility and increasing economic activity built up a head of steam for the 'Tudor revolution in government' that fostered, among other things, the emergence of a centralised state administration, especially to back up parish operation of poverty relief. As Hill neatly portrays it, 'Leviathan had replaced the Good Samaritan' (1969, p. 262).

Three aspects of this emergent construction of social control are significant here. The first is the further secularisation of charity, and in 1536 its codification into systematic and compulsory form. Poverty was rapidly increasing. The fluctuating fortunes of the cloth industry, the enclosure of common lands and the conversion of arable land to pasture, a growing population (up 40 per cent during the sixteenth century), racking of rents, debasement of currency fuelling inflation, falling wages (down 50 per cent between 1500 and 1640), harvest failures, the ending of monastic hospitality and monastery-gate 'doles'; all these factors not only rapidly increased the numbers and suffering of the rootless poor, they also led to food riots and recurrent unrest.[3]

The second aspect of interest, then, is that the key to organised poor relief was the suppression of vagrancy.[4] The drifting population of ex-retainers (whose maintenance was outlawed by Henry VII) and ex-servicemen posed a serious threat to urban order. The 1547 Act noted that 'Idleness and Vagabondrye is the mother and roote of all thefts, Robberyes and all evil actes and other mischief'. Any vagabond and sturdy beggar caught 'given to loytringe' and not working within three days would be 'marked with an whott iron in the brest the marke of V'. If he ran away he would, if caught, be branded on the head or cheek to denote his slave status. The cycle of poverty thesis makes an early appearance in the observation that children 'brought up in idleness might be so rooted in it that hardelie theie maye be brought after to good twifte and labour' (1° Edward VII C.3). The Elizabethan Act of 1576 was more concerned with setting the poor to work, demanding the setting up of stocks of wool, hemp, wax or iron, so that none could 'have any juste Excuse in saying that they cannot get any Service or Worcke'. Idleness led to the houses of correction where 'no payne is limited for any ympotent person' if caught 'loyteringe and begginge' (18° Elizabeth C.3). Whipping, branding, pillorying and (in 1535) even death, as well as the many other grotesque cruelties of sixteenth-century jurisprudence, make the history of social policy in this period a singularly unattractive tale.

With the growing severity of punishment came the third aspect of relevance here—the discriminatory nature of both crime and punishment. It was the criminalisation of certain forms of poverty that formed the link to labour market regulation. Legislation in 1553 distinguished three groups of the poor: the impotent (chronic sick, orphans, the aged); casualty (war-wounded); and thriftless (rioters, vagabonds, the idle). The last group was the problem.[5] Crucial was the Statute of Artificers of 1563, which determined local wage rates, controlled employment conditions and restricted the mobility of labourers. In so doing it 'created the legal framework for English labour for over two centuries' (Woodward, 1980, p. 42). Chambliss notes how the vagrancy laws of this period very quickly broadened from poor relief to crime control, introducing the rogue as a distinct social type, a more dangerous outsider than the vagabond (1964, p. 74). But the imprecise distinction between criminality and destitution left a murky area of inexact morality that remained prey to centuries of special pleading. Classification of the poor into the necessarily and the voluntarily indigent became the central purpose of poverty relief, and the control of the labour market its primary function. The growing physical and psychological separation of the poor from other classes left free rein for the creation of a rich and only minimally informed mythology about the monstrous underworld of the wretched poor. Here was the birthplace of that misleading shorthand, 'the culture of poverty'. 'The sub-culture of beggars and vagabonds was in great measure the imaginative creation of an elite which chose the easiest way to remove the uprooted poor from society yet simultaneously to analyse the poor in terms sensible to that society' (Lis and Soly, 1979, pp. 82—3).[6]

POOR LAW AND POOR LORE

As England settled into a fruitful period of growth in the seventeenth century, with a flourishing agrarian and mercantile capitalism, a relatively peaceful rural labour force and the absence of an absolutist centralised state, poor law policy too was stabilised for over two centuries after a flurry of legislation in 1597—1601 (see, for example, Anderson, 1974a, ch. 5). The Poor Law Act of 1601, the famous '43 Elizabeth', consolidated earlier legislation. In sum it regulated relief for the impotent poor, employment for the able-bodied and correction for the wilfully idle. These triple aims of work discipline, deterrence and classification became the purpose of poor law policy for two centuries, until the institutions it created could no longer support the massive poverty and distress its inadequacies had produced. Much of the surface administrative tussle was over local autonomy, in part a tension between rural needs and urban fears. The enforcement of a local rate to maintain the poor added substance to the claims of rate-payers to regularise and control those they supported. Patrician concern for the poor touched by Christian morality now acquired the sharper flavour of the taxpayers' more pragmatic demands.

The engine driving social policy forward was the presence of an enlarging waged labour force, the defining characteristic of a maturing capitalist social order. In Marx's stark formula, 'Free labour: latent pauperism' (1973, p. 737).[7] The Puritan-influenced certainty that effort was duly rewarded and idleness the mark of the sinner became an obsession in a society with a free market and a labour shortage. There was, after all, the authority of St Paul's harsh injunction that 'If a man do not work neither do he eat'. The implicit theory of unemployment was thus a moral or psychological one equating lack of work with lack of effort. While containment of vagrancy continued to preoccupy legislators, a growing concern was to ensure that the sturdy poor should be working, a living example to the idle poor that poverty was the wage of sin, the avoidable result of individual indolence. When John Locke reported to the Board of Trade in 1697, he insisted that the root of poverty was no other than 'relaxation of discipline and corruption of manners'.[8] In the view of seventeenth-century theorists, economic expansion was being held back by the sloth of an ale-sodden pauper-class. Labour they understood as a factor of production, but the importance of adequate wage levels as a factor of consumption was ignored (see Garraty, 1978, pp. 40—3). In the early part of this period, then, philanthropy probably still outweighed organised relief, since the 'problem' was isolated instances of misfortune rather than endemic poverty.

Workhouses as the major institutional means of containing the idle and instilling the work ethic had been in existence since the original 'Bridewell' set up for sturdy beggars in London in 1555. Before long most towns had their Bridewell; perhaps 200 were built by 1690. As a source of production they were of decreasing importance, and before long their relevance as a moral corrective would be displaced by the factory discipline imposed on the rapidly increasing proletariat. The workhouses, and in turn the poorhouses, nonetheless remained, in different guises, the key institutions of poor law policy through three centuries. In 1723 the Workhouse Test Act facilitated the further building of workhouses by groups of parishes. Anyone refusing the offer of the workhouse would be 'put out of the book', that is removed from the relief register. The distinction between workhouses for the able-bodied paupers, poorhouses for the aged and sick and houses of correction for the vagrants began to dissolve. The result was the general workhouse, 'the dominant feature of the English poor law—as well as, in many places, of the English landscape' (Inglis, 1972, p. 50).[9]

Daniel Defoe had argued strongly in 1704 that workhouse production was pointless. It would merely create unemployment elsewhere, and all to 'feed Vagabonds and to set them to Work who would by choice be idle, and who merit the Correction of the Law' (Defoe, 1704, p. 17). There was certainly a labour shortage, but the answer was greater discipline for the work-shy. Charity merely exacerbated the problem: 'the reason why so many pretend to want Work is that they can live so well with the pretence of wanting work, they would be mad to leave it and work in earnest' (p. 12). The poor in any case ruined themselves through drink. 'The Crimes of our People, and from whence their Poverty derives, as the visible and direct Fountains, are 1. Luxury. 2. Sloth. 3. Pride' (p. 25). 'Tis the Men that wont work, not the men that can get no work, which makes the numbers of our Poor' (p. 27).[10] This emphasis on labour discipline for the poor became the keynote in policy, and fostered an increasingly intolerant attitude to poverty, until rising prices in the second half of the eighteenth century and growing social disturbance prompted fresh thinking. By 1751 when Fielding made his investigation into the proliferation of highway robbers the formula was clear. Idleness must be punished by labour; '. . . much the most numerous class of poor are those who are able to work and not willing' (Fielding, 1751, p. 59).[11] Parliament was not yet ready for the complex administrative schemes being drafted by such as Fielding, but as industrialisation and social unrest continued, more systematic provision for the lower orders was clearly required. As Coats remarks, 'their disposition to riot was certainly effective in persuading the rich to implement the machinery of parish relief and public charity' (1976, p. 110).[12]

From the mid-eighteenth century onward poor law policy becomes more and more transparently the appendage of employment policy. As the peasant economy dwindled, agrarian capitalism became more intensive and the industrial labour force, and indeed the overall population, increased, 'it is striking how the regulation of the labour market in nearly every city which experienced quick industrial growth after 1750 became the foremost purpose of poor law administration' (Lis and Soly, 1979, pp. 163—4).[13] There was thus a shift in emphasis from the correction of the idle poor to an anxious examination of the costs involved. The gaze of the munificent rich drifted from the blemished souls of the poor to the holes in their own pockets through which drained an ever-quickening flow of taxation for poor relief. The unemployed were now viewed as a burden, a drain on hard-won wealth, rather than simply as unused potential.

This was rational enough. Between 1784 and 1813 the cost of poor relief trebled, and hardship was massively extended by the dislocations of the industrial revolution, famines, war and an increasing population. Greater industry was understood as the cure rather than the cause of under-employment. The classical economists provided the theory to sustain the simpler axioms of an anxious and ambitious bourgeoisie. Smith's *Wealth of Nations,* published in 1776, did not argue that the work force was naturally idle by nature, but found it difficult to believe that poverty was particularly prevalent, and scarcely considered the possibility of endemic unemployment (see Garraty, 1978, pp. 64—6). Nature would abhor such an affront to the laws of supply and demand. The growth in the poor population became an object of particular concern. Ricardo's view was that the poor laws discouraged restraint and 'invited imprudence'. Poverty was a problem of overpopulation, a thesis given widespread and dramatic exposure by Malthus' *Essay on the Principles of Population,* published in 1798. Poor relief was unnecessary. It was sapping the will to work and encouraging imprudent breeding habits. A strong and virile nation should do away with poor relief, interfering as it did with the national balance between needs and resources.

By 1802, over one in ten of the population was on relief, and by 1815 there were over 4000 poorhouses containing more than 100,000 resident paupers (S. and B. Webb, 1927, p. 215). Nonetheless in the later eighteenth century earlier policy was being reversed, with a massive increase in outdoor relief. 'Gilbert's Act' of 1782 reorganised the 924 parishes into 62 unions for the easier establishment of workhouses. Gilbert's aim was to preserve the classification of the poor intended by the 43 Elizabeth, but by the 1790s it became clear that the general workhouse persisted. Rural impoverishment continued to increase, provoking widespread imitation of the Speenhamland system, introduced in 1795, of topping up agricultural labourers' wages from parish funds if bread prices rose.

Lurking behind the twists and turns of poor law policy was the grey spectre of insurrection. The unattached poor set loose by changes in the occupational structure were not yet uniformly subject to the new work disciplines of the factory system. While these new disciplines of time and indeed exhaustion, buttressed by the Combination Acts of 1798 and 1799, served to keep industrial dissension at bay, the unpredictable and increasingly riotous rural poor seemed less willing to behave as expected by the rosy predictions of classical political economy. No wonder that McCulloch wrote in his *Principles of Political Economy* (1825) that 'if we would preserve unimpaired the peace, and consequently the prosperity of the country, we must beware of allowing any considerable portion of the population to fall into a state of destitution . . . Without [the poor laws] the peace of society would not be preserved for any considerable period' (quoted in S. and B. Webb, 1927, p. 405). Poor relief was the insurance paid to control the reserve army of labour. Legislation, like the political economy that justified it, had no room for involuntary unemployment, and became increasingly entwined in a curious combination of punitive control and prudent relief. The post-Napoleonic War depression intensified distress, and widespread rioting only served to re-emphasise that the creaking machinery of the Elizabethan poor law was neither meeting the needs of the industrial poor nor assuaging the fears of the urban bourgeoisie. It was time to reinvent the machinery of poverty policy and to rewrite its moral rhetoric.

ENDING THE BOUNTY ON INDOLENCE AND VICE

Sporadic eruptions of riotous discontent, particularly in 1830—31, brought the crisis of the poor laws to a head. The new political economy was to be translated into legislation, in an admixture of Malthusian and Benthamite theory designed to withdraw poor relief back within its proper domain of pauperism. The Royal Commission on the Poor Laws was set up in 1832 and reported in 1834, in a 'brilliant, influential, and wildly unhistorical' document, as Tawney called it, which became the cornerstone of poor law policy, if not always of actual practice, for over a century, and indeed beyond. The Poor Law Amendment Act of 1834 which was its fruit rested on three principles. First, 'less eligibility': 'the first and most essential of all conditions', that the pauper 'shall not be made really or apparently so eligible as the situation of the independent labourer of the lowest class'. For 'Every penny bestowed that tends to render the condition of the pauper more eligible than that of the independent labourer, is a bounty on indolence and vice' (*Poor Law Report*, p. 335). Second was the ending of outdoor relief and the enforcement of the workhouse test. Third was centralisation of authority with uniformity of administration.

The judgement of history has been hard. In E. P. Thompson's verdict 'the Act of 1834, and its subsequent administration by men like Chadwick and Kay, was perhaps the most sustained attempt to impose an ideological dogma, in defiance of the evidence of human need, in English history' (1968, p. 295). The report was rich in justification, both moral and administrative, for its principles. The sleep of the rich was at last made easy by the comforting thesis that poverty was both inevitable and morally culpable, a somnolence disturbed only by the fear that this view might not be shared among the poor. Henceforth the political expediencies of a maturing capitalism would be vindicated in the language of moral theory.

Four tenets in this moral theory are of relevance here. First, the notion that what the poor needed was remoralisation, a key assumption that destitution was a judgement on the morally culpable individual, whose soul and spirit were as much in need as his pocket. The authors of the 1834 *Poor Law Report* were clear that theirs was a missionary task as much as an administrative one, aimed at 'the general diffusion of right principles and habits'. Their object was a scheme 'for elevating the intellectual and moral condition of the poorer classes' (p. 496). The individualism of the new moral economy lacked even the benign paternalism of the old. Excessive breeding, dependence on the ale-house and indolence were the traits to be eliminated.[14] Drink in particular served as a ready explanation of both poverty and work-shyness. Mr Huish, an assistant overseer in Southwark, assured the Poor Law Report inquiry that 'since the inquiry had been made, I have stationed persons at well known gin-shops to observe the number of paupers who came and the money they spend; and from all their statements I have drawn the conclusion that £30 out of every £100 given as out-door relief is spent in the gin-shops during the same day' (*Poor Law Report,* p. 118).[15] The pro-government *Morning Chronicle,* 'astonished' by opposition to the bill, noted quickly that, 'Of course the spending in the beer-shop and the public-house will be diminished', while *The Observer* was miraculously able to confirm this forecast as early as September 1834 when it reported that 'The most remarkable effect manifested where the changes have been made is the diminution of the custom of the gin-shops' (*The Observer,* 28 September 1834).[16]

The second key thesis behind the new legislation was the moral turpitude of the pauper, whose dependence on relief was matched only by his perfidious exploitation of the good intentions of benefactors. Indeed, the expansion of relief could be explained 'independently of any legitimate causes . . . to arise from the irresistible temptations to fraud on the part of claimants' (*Poor Law Report,* p. 377). Hence the importance of the third principle—that of deterrence, or what sometimes surfaces in more recent debate under the name of work incentives. The new Act was aimed not at the elimination of poverty but at the containment and repression of pauperism.[17] Benthamite principles reigned supreme. The workhouse test would sort out genuine indigence and encourage industriousness among the idle. Of course this might not work perfectly. To the able-bodied, 'relief in a well-regulated workhouse would not be a hardship: and even if it be in some rare cases a hardship, it appears from the evidence that it is a hardship to which the good of society requires the applicant to submit . . . he must accept assistance on the terms, whatever they may be, which the common welfare requires. The bane of all pauper legislation has been the legislating for extreme cases' (*Poor Law Report,* pp. 376-7). The logic was simple: 'If the claimant does not comply with the terms on which relief is given to the destitute, he gets nothing; and if he does comply, the compliance proves the truth of the claim—namely his destitution' (p. 378).

Central to these three tenets was a fourth—the need to classify the poor so as to distinguish the small minority of blamelessly indigent from the larger group of the 'vicious' and indolent. The underlying theory of how poverty arose among the able-bodied was simple: 'it has been found that the pauperism of the greater number has originated in indolence, improvidence, or vice, and might have been averted by ordinary care or industry' (p. 378). The separation of pauperism from poverty was at once the object of the new poor law and its empirical presupposition. Pauperism was not an extreme case of poverty but a qualitatively different condition. The distinction was to be detected in behaviour, attitudes and morality. Important too, therefore, was the distinction to be made, as social types, between the independent labourer and the pauper, since 'we do not believe that a country in which that distinction has been completely effaced, and every man, whatever his condition or his character, ensured a comfortable existence, can retain its prosperity, or even its civilization' (p. 333).[18]

With such cogent and principled justification behind the new poor law, opposition to it was bound to seem, in Tawney's words, 'a defiance alike of sound morality and of the teachings of science' (1964, p. 130).[19] Working-class opposition was directed at the workhouse, the dreaded 'Bastilles', while middle-class opposition railed rather more at the centralising powers of the Poor Law Commissioners, who replaced the old system of overseers. By 1839, 250 new workhouses had been built. By 1846 the 643 newly created poor law unions had 707 workhouses with an average of 270 inmates in each. The total number of inmates rose rapidly, from 78,000 in 1838, to 197,000 in 1843, and 306,000 by 1848 (Young and Ashton, 1954; Thompson, 1968, p. 297; Fraser, 1976, *passim*). The scandalous and often horrific excesses of workhouse discipline provided much of the imagery in popular opposition to the workhouse (see Edsall, 1971). Cases such as that of the infamous Andover workhouse, whose hapless inmates were found in 1845 to be supplementing their diet by getting what they could of raw potatoes, chicken feed and bone gristle, bored deeply into working-class lore, and resentment of the workhouse became a major stream in the gathering torrent of Chartist fervour. Indeed, the workhouse system was frequently honoured more in the breach than the observance, especially in the north where the harsh regimes of the new industrial order and the cruel fluctuations of trade were quite outside the understanding or investigations of the Poor Law Commissioners.[20] In these areas, outdoor relief continued extensively, while, as Ashforth points out, 'As a rule the only able-bodied applicants sent to the workhouse were those considered to be idle, troublesome, morally unsound, or Irish' (1976, p. 135).[21]

The new Act replaced overseers by elected Guardians, collected parishes into unions for the building of workhouses, and vested overall control in the Commissioners, the 'Three Bashaws of Somerset House', this control being rationalised into the Poor Law Board in 1847. The inchoate centralisation of the supervisory state was crucial in the mid-nineteenth-century efflorescence of public administration. The 1835 Municipal Corporations Act, the creation of the Registrar-General's Office in 1836, the various Factory Acts, and so on, provided an umbrella of state regulation to protect the social order from the new uncertainties of rapid industrialisation, urbanisation and population growth. This was not yet, however, the interventionist state of later decades. Although the population shot up by 57 per cent between 1801 and 1831 (from under 9 million to nearly 14 million), most parishes still averaged about 200 families. As Lubenow (1971) has argued, measures like the new poor law rationalised local administration rather more than they changed central—local government relations (p. 40 and ch. 2 *passim*).[22]

Criticism focused on the evils of centralisation nonetheless, with a power of rhetoric that has stamped itself on a continuing strain of conservative libertarianism prominent in more recent opposition to the welfare state, providing for a vocabulary that readily identifies collective or public provision with incipient totalitarian control by the state. Opposition to the new poor law coalesced a variety of forces: romantic Toryism, defending the traditional authority of parish self-government; the paternalism of the Tory radicals, deeply attached to 'the Throne, the Altar, the Cottage'; the provincial aristocracy, as well as those more cynically concerned with their own interests; the vestrymen and farmers worried about the supply of low-paid casual labour. Many of these groups reinvented an idealised bucolic past protected by an ancient constitution.

Most vocal among these voices were the provincial newspapers and some of the London papers, especially *The Times*. Nassau Senior vented his particular frustrations on the pernicious influence of the press, which was in the business of 'the production and sale of the opinions which can be got ready in the least time, and with the least trouble, and can be sold to the greatest number of customers'. In his estimate the Poor Law Bill had been 'attacked in all its provisions by four-fifths of the metropolitan journals, with unexampled virulence and pertinacity' (Senior, 1841, p. 66). Most papers, argued Senior, were either violently Tory or violently Radical, and thus bound to oppose a Whig measure. They also served the middle classes, the London shop keepers and artisans, the provincial middle classes, and others who were both against the new poor law in principle and also persons 'who delight in coarse and strong excitement' (p. 67). *The Times* was especially anguished by the tendency to 'amplifying the province of the legislature and asserting its moral prerogatives'; what it referred to as 'centralisation mania' (4 May 1847; 21 July 1834).[23]

The 1830s and 1840s were a key period of growth for the press, especially after the reduction of Stamp Duty and of Excise Duty on paper in 1836. Sunday newspapers like *Lloyds' Weekly* (1842), *Reynolds News* (1850) and the *News of the World* (1843) built up large circulations, grafting shrewd business techniques and commercial acumen onto the solid foundations laid by the unstamped and Chartist press. The number of English provincial papers rose from about 150 in 1830 to over 230 by 1851. In England and Wales as a whole the number of newspapers published rose from 267 in 1821 to 563 in 1851 (Asquith, 1978, p. 99). While throughout the Victorian period effort never ceased to keep the principles of 1834 aloft, a burgeoning newspaper press became available to give house room to the slogans, mythologies, passion and debate surrounding society's continuing bewilderment about what to do with the poor. A zeal for classification and moral exhortation of the poor could now find a ready outlet in the investigatory urges of a new journalism, released from political patronage and corruption by the expansion of the mid-century into new popular postures and repertoires by the commercialisation of the following decades.

IN DARKEST ENGLAND: LOOKING INTO THE ABYSS

Mid-nineteenth-century prosperity diverted attention from the troubles of the poor, and was partly responsible for the social quiescence that succeeded the never fully explained demise of Chartist radicalism. That laissez-faire, the pure doctrine of non-intervention by the state in the untroubled workings of an expanding economy, was more an ideal than a reality, has become a truism of much recent historiography (see, for example, Brebner, 1948). In fact there was both a growth and a rationalisation of state activity, particularly after the establishment of the Civil Service Commission in 1855. In 1871 the Local Government Board was set up to provide central direction of poor relief as well as sanitary and public health services. The development of poor law policy in the later nineteenth century saw, among other things, the successive removal of classes of claimant from the central institution of the workhouse to more specialised forms of supervision and support, including infirmaries for the sick, and separate provision for the elderly, children and lunatics. The administrative process was hard at work on that endless task of classification that continued to be both the object and the basis of poor relief.

Such classification required prior investigation, and the Victorian period furnished three forms of inquiry into the condition and manner of the poor, all brewing that curious mixture of apprehension, disgust and genuine concern that is the characteristic temper of Victorian social policy. In Ryan's terms, this became an age of 'savage discovery' (1971, ch. 1), lifting the splendidly textured carpet of Victorian gentility to peer anxiously at the moral and physical squalor beneath. The first form of inquiry was from within the state apparatus, with the proliferation of Royal Commissions, Select Committees, inspectorial reports, Blue Books, and the general evolution of an apparatus of statutory voyeurism of an increasingly rigorous and statistical nature quite different from the 'political arithmetic' from which it derived (see Shaw and Miles, 1979; Cullen, 1975).

Secondly came the professionals, not the social reformers like Louisa Twining and the rest, but the begetters of social science. As McGregor wryly observes, 'the stench of urban poverty drove thoughtful, vigorous, unsentimental middle class people—doctors, bankers, those experienced in insurance, and the like—to the study of social pathology' (1957, p. 147). Theirs was a far from disinterested quest. Disdain for aristocratic incompetence on the one hand and anxiety about the moral and physical condition of the lower orders on the other, led them to seek a more rational basis for social administration as the best sedative for insipient disorder. As Lord Brougham told the National Association for the Promotion of Social Science at its inaugural meeting in 1857, 'knowledge thus diffused . . . possesses the great, the cardinal virtue of ensuring the stability of the social system' (quoted in Ritt, 1959, p. 95). Much of their research was into the moral condition of the poor—how many books were to be found in the home rather than pounds in the pocket. Social discipline surveys far outnumbered investigations of poverty, at least in the 1830s and 1840s and in much of the later work of the Association (see Ritt, 1959, *passim*; Hennock, 1976, p. 77; Yeo, 1971, pp. 52—4).

With growing urban poverty and unemployment in the 1860s and 1870s, however, a third force came on the scene—popular journalism—which rose to a sensationalist crescendo in the 1880s. The ending of the taxes on knowledge, together with technical developments in printing and rapid advances in transport and communications, fostered a major growth in the middle-class press. The number of local dailies grew from 2 in 1850 to 196 in 1900, while the number of local weeklies rose from under 400 in 1856 to over 2,000 in 1900. Sunday newspapers, still the market leaders, developed six-figure circulations (Lee, 1978, pp. 120—2, and more generally Lee, 1976). Hardly revolutionary, this expanding press (mostly Liberal in the provinces, even though the metropolitan press was largely Whig or Tory) caught the tide of Victorian reformism and, in C. P. Scott's phrase, aimed to make 'readable righteousness remunerative'.

The wretched world of the workhouse had already provided the raw material for orchestrated indignation in the press before 1870. In the 1860s a campaign to remove sick paupers from the workhouse found ready support in many papers, including *The Times*, and also the *Daily Telegraph*, the major middle-class paper in the second half of the century. However, their campaigns tugged more at the purse-strings than the heart-strings of their readers. As *The Times* pointed out, separate the sick and 'it will at once be found a much easier task to deal with all other classes of poor . . . separate them, and let judgement go against idlers and imposters' (6 March 1866). The *Telegraph* was equally pragmatic, 'It is more expensive to keep a pauper in your sick room than to cure him—more expensive in the ratio of the cost of medicine to the cost of gruel' (6 March 1866).[24] Classification and separation—these were the watchwords. In the more punitive and turbulent times of twenty years later it was the seductive comforts of the workhouse that exercised the *Telegraph*, worried that

> the now dreaded 'Union' would become a sort of cooperative almshouse, where family life would blossom again, relieved from the chilling frost of penury, and where the state would step in like a good fairy to harbour and support everybody who had failed to make provision for a rainy day . . . It does not do to make these refuges too Elysian . . . they must not present too attractive a look to the lowly loafers and incorrigible idlers of society. [18 March 1866]

Without apparent irony the writer adds 'At all events it is better than it used to be; for a philosophically minded individual it offers unequalled opportunities for quiet meditation'.

Pioneer of this investigative journalism was Henry Mayhew, whose massive researches on 'London Labour and the London Poor' produced acres of material in the *Morning Chronicle* in 1849 and 1850. Thompson and Yeo, in their resurrection of Mayhew's reputation, show him to be a forerunner of meticulous social analysis rather than just the author of the colourful portrayals of street life for which he is better remembered (see the introductory essays in Thompson and Yeo, 1971). This 'higher journalism', particularly in Mayhew's hands, was a brief interlude of perspicacity. As Yeo notes, 'Mayhew's ability to see poverty in the round, as the product of an economic system, with devastating moral and social consequences and yet varied cultural manifestations, amounted to a unique and short-lived moment in middle class consciousness' (1971, p. 88). It was replaced by professional specialisation, paternalistic individualism and a more sensational style of investigatory reporting.

The pamphleteers and sensationalists of the 1870s and 1880s were all men whose primary outlet was journalism. These were not the 'literary adventurers' of the 1840s and 1850s (Thompson, 1971, p. 15), but men with a political mission, seeking their material in the murky, terrifying and uncharted territory of late-Victorian urban working-class squalor. They saw themselves as social explorers, penetrating a region of immorality, deprivation, disease and crime (see the introduction to Keating, 1976). Campaigning was good for circulation. As E. G. Salman commented sourly in 1886, 'Directly any abuse in the ranks of the masses is discovered, an article is secured on it in one of the papers, and an organisation started for its removal' (Salman, 1886, p. 109).[25]

One such discoverer was George Sims, author of 'Christmas Day in the Workhouse', whose articles on 'How the Poor Live' appeared in *The Pictorial World* in 1883. Sims was researching 'in a dark continent . . . as interesting as any of those newly explored lands which engage the attention of the Royal Geographical Society' (Sims, 1883, p. 5). Sims' work was quickly succeeded by the spectacular success of Andrew Mearns' *Bitter Cry of Outcast London,* given considerable publicity in the *Pall Mall Gazette,* which became a leader in the campaigns for housing reform (see Wohl, 1970). W. T. Stead, the editor of the *Pall Mall Gazette,* was a pioneer of the 'new journalism', aimed at an increasingly prosperous lower-middle class and making full use of the new design and presentational techniques being borrowed from American examples, made possible by advances in printing technology and made profitable by the massive increase in advertising revenue. Stead was quick to latch on to the attractive possibilities of using riveting insights into the sordid life of London's lower orders as material both for campaigning and for sensational copy. Taking up a challenge by H. M. Hyndman, 'the father of English socialism', to investigate distress in 1886, Stead grandly told his readers:

> We readily adopted the suggestion. Governments may, perhaps, wait to be convinced of the reality of distress, just as we wait to learn of the urgency of reforms, by the arguments of clamour and violence; but journalists cannot afford to live in fools' paradises or castles of indolence. The journalist is 'the watchdog of civilisation', and is not worth his bone if he waits to sound the alarm till the enemy is within the gates' |*Pall Mall Gazette* 24 February 1886|.[26]

Arising from this feverish agitation in the popular press came the systematisers of 'savage discovery'. Charles Booth's *Labour and Life of the People, London* was initially published in two volumes in 1889 and 1891, and attempted to chart in statistical detail the extent of metropolitan poverty.[27] Here was the beginning of a new style of exploration, begetting the ostensible detachment of Rowntree and his sociological successors. (Booth's 'surveys' were in fact based on second-hand impressions.) Research, like policy, was about classification, particularly distinguishing the 'residuum'—those who 'from shiftlessness, idleness, or drink are inevitably poor'—from the respectable working class—'decent, steady men paying their way and bringing up their children respectably'. As Brown puts it, 'Booth's immediate influence should be seen in the way it preserved a concern for character within an empirical approach to the problem of poverty' (1971, p. 111).[28] The poor in Booth's view were the victims of pressure from the very poor. The solution was to remove the latter. By the time we reach Rowntree, on whose surveys of York at the turn of the century Booth advised and commented, a more rigorous methodology and accounting system are in force, incorporating the recent discoveries of nutritional science and providing for a distinction between 'primary poverty', where 'total earnings are insufficient to obtain the minimum necessaries for the maintenance of merely physical efficiency', and 'secondary poverty', caused by 'Drink, betting, and gambling. Ignorant or careless housekeeping, and other improvident expenditure, the latter often induced by irregularity of income' (Rowntree, 1913, pp. 116-17, 176). Categories, especially in Booth, remained rooted in morals and behaviour as much as in material conditions. The 'culture' of poverty is as prominent as its causes, that 'whole social question' Rowntree felt unable to address.

Behind the Victorian fascination with the dismal yet titillating world of urban poverty lay fear; fear of the mob, fear of the unknown, and fear of socialism. The depression in the 1880s and increases in the numbers without work were forcing on to middle-class awareness the structural nature of unemployment. In February 1886 violent demonstrations by the unemployed in London sent a tremor of terror through the metropolitan upper classes (see Stedman Jones, 1976, pp. 291ff); the temper and potency of the mob provided a frightening confirmation of George Sims' words, published three years earlier:

> For very shame England must now do something, nay for self-preservation which is the most powerful of all human motives. This mighty mob of famished, diseased and filthy helots is getting dangerous, physically, morally, politically dangerous. The barriers that have kept it back are rotten and giving way, and it may do the state a mischief if it is not looked to in time. [Sims, 1883, pp. 28—9]

Writing at the same time, Howard Association reformer Francis Peek, using an image that has proved serviceable in more recent journalism, warned that 'It is no time to dream on in blind security while there is an army of more than three-quarters of a million of paupers at our gates' (Peek, 1883, pp. 19—20). Palliative measures were swift. A distress fund was set up by the Mansion House, and Chamberlain, President of the Local Government Board, issued his famous Circular authorising municipal schemes of public works to relieve unemployment—the first wresting of unemployment from the poor law.

Publicity had also fostered that fear of the unknown exploited by the social explorers. The strange and faintly disgusting morality of life in darkest England was held up at arm's length to reaffirm the need for clear distinctions between the casual and respectable poor, between the 'residuum' and the true working class. After all, as Sims wrote, 'The constant association of the poor and the criminal classes has deadened in the former nearly all sense of right and wrong' (1883, p. 10). Terrible tales of promiscuity, incest, violence, drunkenness and obscene entertainment kept a frisson of disgust tingling amidst the more philanthropic or pragmatic of political arguments. Not least was fear of contagion from the disease-ridden tenements investigated by the 1884—5 Royal Commission on the Housing of the Working Classes. The distinctions to be made were thus moral in tone if economic in origin.[29] The poor were being demoralised by indiscriminate charity and by the immorality of the undeserving residuum. This was the class, in the view of *The Times,* 'recruited from the incapable or immoral who have fallen out of the ranks of respectable labour . . . For the adult members of the class the old remedy would have been a sound whipping at the cart-tails; and it would be worth while to try one or two experiments of the kind on bodies proverbially suited to them' (6 February 1886).

Finally there was the fear of socialism, in its varied forms now taking tangible political shape in Britain, a generation or so behind the 'new unionism'. Hyndman's Social-Democratic Federation was formed in 1881. The Fabian's first pamphlet appeared in 1884 and 'asked the central question which troubled the conscience of the reforming middle class in late-Victorian England. It was called *Why Are the Many Poor?'* (MacKenzie and MacKenzie, 1979, p. 29). A major stimulus to much embryonic socialism at this time was the massive influence of the American journalist Henry George's *Progress and Poverty* (1883), arguing the cause of common land ownership and the Single Tax in a grandiloquent mixture of Christian and libertarian socialist language.[30] George's dire warnings of the impending decay of civilisation struck a chord in friend and foe alike. Terrible alarms were sounded about the growing power of the mob on the one hand and the character-sapping effect of creeping collectivism on the other.[31] Sims drew the moral plainly:

> In any other land but ours, the mighty mass of helots would long ago have broken their bonds and swept over the land in vast revolutionary hordes . . . It will be well to meet the movement half-way and yield to them that reform and humane recognition which some day they may all too noisily demand. [Sims, 1883, p. 55]

The lesson was well taken, most celebratedly by Chamberlain, who asked a Birmingham audience in January 1885, 'what ransom will property pay for the security which it enjoys? What substitute will it find for the natural rights which have ceased to be recognised?' Two weeks later the proposition was equally clear: 'What insurance will wealth find to its advantage to provide against the risks to which it is undoubtedly subject?' (see Gulley, 1926, pp. 213—14).[32] This Bismarckian strategy was echoed by Baldwin in 1895: 'Social legislation, as I conceive it, is not merely to be distinguished from Socialist legislation but is its most direct opposite and its most effective antidote' (quoted in Fraser, 1973, p. 129).

The increasing inadequacy of individual philanthropy and the obvious inability of the workhouse or charity to cope with urban poverty produced a new social policy, together with a change in attitudes to the poor. One level of response was 'practicable socialism', using the missionary zeal of decent middle-class reformers to spread education and soup among the denizens of London's East End. The settlement movement, Toynbee Hall (1884) and adult education all sought to restore the moral order that the physical separation of the rich from the poor had disturbed (see Abel, 1978; Stedman Jones, 1976).

A second practical response came in the variety of schemes to remove the troublesome unemployed to work colonies or overseas. Worried that 'the bulk of this human deposit of vice and poverty is hereditary', Samuel Smith suggested state-aided emigration of children, for 'there is a boundless field in the colonies for planting out these neglected little ones'. They would need to be depauperised though; 'Decent people cannot be expected to take repulsive children, using bad language and telling lies . . . they must be made loveable and attractive' (Smith, 1883, pp. 907—9).[33] A variety of fanciful, utopian, often punitive and rarely successful schemes were tried to furnish work for the unemployed in work colonies. General Booth's detailed plans in *In Darkest England* to solve the problem of the 'submerged tenth'—that 'population sodden with drink, steeped in vice, eaten up by every social and physical malady' (1890, pp. 14—15)—provided for a City Colony, a Farm Colony and an Over-Sea Colony (pp. 92—3 *et seq.*). Such a farm colony was started at Hadleigh in 1891, and by 1904 included William Beveridge among its supporters, since, as he wrote in *The Contemporary Review,* 'The mass of idlers and dependents who usually expect to reap an easy harvest from the opening of relief funds ceased to apply as soon as they found that work was demanded' (Beveridge and Maynard, 1904, p. 630).

The political solution was the extension of the franchise in 1867 and 1884. As we shall see below, this continued to exclude paupers, but it seemed that the masses had been enfranchised. The time for demonstrations was past, said the *Daily Telegraph* in February 1886; 'There was a time when the unenfranchised multitude had no power, and when dear newspapers very imperfectly reported the sayings and doings of the masses', but now workers comprised the majority of voters, and thus had no excuse for the loutish excesses of violent disturbance reported in the same issue (*Daily Telegraph,* 12 February 1886). In fact it was 1911 before even 59 per cent of adult males had the vote, and the palliative of franchise extension was a distant glimmer to those 'denizens of Darkest England' most feared by anxious reformers.[34]

Moral theory as it applied to the poor was certainly being changed. As Perkin has suggested, the aristocratic paternalism that spawned the Christian socialists, the settlement movement and individualist philanthropy was perforce being replaced by a more structural view of poverty as a social phenomenon (Perkin, 1969, pp. 262—4). The casework approach, stressing individual inadequacy, lived on, notably in the work of the Charity Organisation Society, set up in 1869 to introduce method and order into philanthropy by strict investigation of the poor, and their separation into the deserving and undeserving. But despite the Society's survival, and the persistence of a casework approach in subsequent social administration, the ideals and values of the COS, like those of the settlement movement, were already out of touch in the new situation of the 1890s.

Thus the individualism of Samuel Smiles' 'self-help' was, despite his book's frequent reprinting, being reinterpreted a generation after its first appearance in 1859. Smiles' call for 'better habits' rather than 'greater rights', his conviction that

> what we are accustomed to decry as great social evils will, for the most part, be found to be but the outgrowth of man's own perverted life . . . the highest patriotism and philanthropy consist, not so much in altering laws and modifying institutions, as in helping and stimulating men to elevate and improve themselves by their own free and independent individual action . . . [Smiles, 1910, pp. 2—3][35]

—these views were transformed by the new dimension of urban poverty in the 1880s and 1890s. The pathology of the poor was remade into the secularised Calvinism of the work ethic. The term 'unemployed' first appeared in the Oxford English Dictionary in 1882; 'unemployment' in 1888. With three-quarters of the population in waged labour, urban poverty had to be perceived in the context of the labour market. Hard work, thrift and organisation of the failures were what was required. Idleness was still the object of concern, but its causes were less often seen in the individual than in indiscriminate charity and a demoralising environment.

Inevitably the crude classifications of an earlier age underwent continual refinement. Mayhew had the poor in three groups 'according as they will work, they can't work, and they won't work' (quoted in Thompson and Yeo, 1971, p. 54). Social policy thrived on this distinction between, in Francis Peek's more sententious terms, 'the workless, the thriftless, and the worthless', so that 'the aim of all legislation must be to make the worthless classes realise that they must work, if not in freedom, then under compulsion' (Peek, 1888, p. 62).[36] Those in power, argued the *Daily Telegraph,* would 'have little difficulty in distinguishing the solid body of the working population from the scum of lazy brutality which floats upon its surface, and the mischievous residuum of crime beneath' (11 February 1888). For that residuum 'The interest was less in destitution in this world than in damnation in the next' (Gilbert's comment on the Salvation Army—1966a, p. 22). In 1900 the Local Government Board was still telling its Guardians that 'in every way deserving paupers should be treated differently from those whose previous habits and Character have been unsatisfactory' (Circular quoted in Young and Ashton, 1956, p. 62).

The importance of this moral theory for our concerns is that it was being developed in a period of rapid expansion of the press. Just as the new inequalities of urban wealth and poverty were being established, so were new ways of legitimating these inequalities being voiced in the increasingly widespread middle-class press. As Perkin puts it, 'The key to the triumph of the entrepreneurial ideal in formal education was its victory at the informal level of social education through the press' (1969, p. 302). A reworked accreditation of wealth, as of poverty, was given expression in this crucial period of social reconstruction by a medium perfectly designed to meet the need for a new form of hegemony. Reform might pay the ransom, but it was the press that stated the terms.

The fate of more radical or socialist thought and action has provoked continuing debate among historians. Pelling (1968) claims that working-class pressure and socialist ideas were largely absent from the forces that led to social policy reforms in the 1885—1914 period, and that socialist ideas on social policy were in any case the product of middle-class intellectuals. This view has been much disputed by historians who stress pressure from below. Clearly there was recognition, as the *Pall Mall Gazette* neatly put it, that 'To sit on the safety valve is not the best means of preventing an explosion' (12 February 1886). That the explosion never came has yet to be satisfactorily explained. What can be shown is the massive growth of a middle-class press expressing the reforming consensus of the age.

After the ending of press taxes, numerous technical advances in printing, graphic reproduction, paper manufacture, the introduction of linotype composing, as well as rapid extensions of transport and telecommunications, all facilitated major expansion of newspaper sales and titles. Between 1856 and 1900 the number of London dailies increased from 15 to 32, and in the provinces the increase was from 15 to 171. In the same period well over 4,000 new newspaper companies were founded, following the Companies Act of 1856 (Lee, 1978, pp. 121, 125).

The socialist press did not share in this bonanza however. In part this was because of the relative lack of commitment to building a socialist press among trade union and labour leaders. In part too it was due to the entrenched conservatism of the British working class, or at least of their reading matter after the radicalism of earlier generations. As Mountjoy has suggested, popular journals conveyed a simple message: 'The roads to riches of fictional and biographical heroes begin when they break their pipes, renounce the cup, wash, or read the bible. Hard and humble work—not politics and jealousy—are the key' (Mountjoy, 1978, p. 277). The state or, more commonly, royalty and the aristocracy were rather more the butts of criticism than the fundamental order of capitalism.[37] There were, of course, large numbers of small left papers, but never with the penetration or popularity of the heroic years before Chartism, and mostly dissipating into sectarian periodicals. There were no socialist dailies at all before 1911 (for more details see Hopkin, 1978). The massive rise in capital costs and the growing influence of advertising revenue confirmed the marginalisation of a left press.

The net result, as James Curran has explained, was that the new press of the Northcliffe revolution, commercial in design, purpose and origin,

> was also a powerful source of social cohesion. The values and perspectives that it mediated were at total variance with those mediated by early radical newspapers. A construction of reality as a system of exploitation gave way to a new definition of society in which even the existence of class conflict was denied . . . The stress on collective action gave way to a stress on individual self-improvement and the myth that anyone through his own efforts could become successful. [Curran, 1977, p. 223]

As the industry moved from being predominantly Liberal until the 1880s to increasingly Conservative thereafter, it acquired the apolitical tone that is the distinguishing feature of modern journalism, a commonsensical consensus couched in a rhetoric of shared values and common understandings by which ideology is masked behind the claims of objectivity and professionalism. By the 1890s, as Lee concludes, 'survival for the newspaper had come increasingly to involve compromise, to necessitate a bid for the middle ground, to entail the loss of party character, and the eschewal of party allegiance' (Lee, 1976, p. 162).[38] The evacuation of radicalism by market forces left a vacuum filled by a reformism explicitly anti-socialist in style and attack. While politics was becoming class-based, the language and arguments of class were replaced by an assumed national consensus voiced by a press that was, in Hobhouse's words, 'the sounding-board for whatever ideas commend themselves to the great material interests (cited in Lee, 1976, p. 196).[39]

The importance of this is twofold. It fixed an understanding of social reform and poverty in the moral rhetoric of late-Victorian liberalism firmly into the vocabulary and tone of popular journalism at its birth. At the same time it undoubtedly helped prevent the radicalisation of a Labour movement approach to poverty by confirming the divisions between casual and respectable poor, between the residuum and the deserving, in fact and in beliefs. The new journalism was a beneficiary but not a benefactor of darkest England, and was to become a major contributor to the energetic channelling of working-class demands away from the commanding heights of capital towards the safer pastures of the welfare state.

THE RANSOM PAID

Threats to Empire abroad and to the good order and condition of society at home were the progenitors of that period of Edwardian social policy now commonly described as the infant years of the modern welfare state. Two concerns among opinion of the time stand out: the efficiency of the industrial system and the labour market, and the physical condition of the work force. Chamberlain's ransom was to appear a shrewder, more essential and more productive investment than he might have imagined.

Poverty was increasing and becoming more visible with the surveys of Rowntree in York and other similar work. Per capita incomes were declining between 1895 and 1914 and Bowleys studies of poverty showed how great a proportion of those in poverty were in full-time work. At the same time, the cost of poor relief was soaring, by over 50 per cent from the 1870s to 1900 and from £11½ million to £14 million just between 1901 and 1906 (Gilbert, 1966a, pp. 233 *et seq.*; J. F. Harris, 1972, ch. 3). Indoor relief was costing four times as much as outdoor relief by 1913 and there was growing concern about the excessive sheltering of the able-bodied in work houses. In fact, as Crowther has shown, these concerns depended on a great deal of mythology and sophistry. Official figures suggesting an increase of over 20 per cent in able-bodied paupers between 1895 and 1905 were almost certainly exaggerated (Crowther, 1978, p. 48). It was nonetheless a powerful mythology, and a godsend to enthusiasts of work colonies. The 'comforts' of the workhouse came under constant attack, especially in the new popular press. Northcliffe's *Daily Mail,* for example, regaled its readers with the story of 'The Workhouse de Luxe', a 'poverty palace' in Camberwell, which 'haven of rest from worldly turmoil' made 'a paradise of this oasis in poverty's desert'. The relative advantages of pauperism were clear to the inmates who knew 'for a certainty that half the labouring world, penned in its little hutches in mean streets is never acquainted with anything so fresh and wholesome'. The writer concludes exasperatedly: 'and yet people say, "Heaven keep us from the workhouse" ' (*Daily Mail*, 12 April 1905).[40] Claims about the relative discomforts of unemployment outside the workhouse were of course not without foundation. It was the beginning of the end of the general workhouse (see Crowther, 1978).

Initiatives in social policy were in part facilitated by the drop in military expenditure after the Boer Wars, stimulated by the pragmatic reforming zeal of the 'new Liberalism', led by the arrival of Lloyd George and Winston Churchill in the Cabinet in 1908, and given particular urgency by industrial unrest after 1910. A Royal Commission on the Poor Law sat from 1905 to 1909, and a major burst of legislation between 1905 and 1911 restructured much of the basis of poor relief (and indeed made much of the Commission's initial sentiments and final reports redundant). This included the Unemployed Workmen's Act of 1905, which set up Distress Committees for the unemployed and allowed for labour exchanges, the introduction of school meals in 1906, pensions in 1908, and unemployment and health insurance in 1911.

Underlying this apparent explosion of legislative altruism were two obsessions: the condition of the people in the heart of the Empire, and the continuing refinement of methods of classifying the poor. The miserable condition of Boer War applicant recruits, three-fifths of them unfit for service, sharpened a growing awareness that the British race was no longer stocked by robust and rosy-cheeked yeomen, but by a pallid and sickly proletariat that was both an offence to racial stereotypes and a problem for imperial superiority. A diffuse militarism provided one answer in the form of boy scouts, physical education in schools and the Boys Brigade. The Interdepartmental Committee on Physical Deterioration, which met in 1903—4, showed the extent of racial decline, and linked inextricably the problem of poverty with the prospects of Empire.[41] Other countries, it was stressed (with Germany most prominently in mind), managed better. The *News of the World* was worried that children 'have none of the manly pride of their industrious fathers . . . No country, however rich, can permanently hold its own in the race of international competition if hampered by an increasing load of this dead weight' (21 February 1909). A further solution was the provision of school meals from 1906, albeit patchily and with considerable reservation. Enthusiasm for work colonies, and indeed eugenics, sterilisation and other measures, was also as much provoked by fears for the condition of the people as by hopes for their contribution to the employment problem. Country air and hard work would do the men good, argued William Beveridge, himself leader writer on the Conservative *Morning Post* from 1906 to 1908.[42] This would achieve the necessary 'maintenance of efficiency and the arrest of degeneration' (Beveridge and Maynard, 1904, p. 633).

Throughout this patchwork of reform ran the linking thread of classification, drawing firm boundaries around the rights and assistance accorded to different classes in the citizenry. Indeed the notion of citizenship lay at the heart of the 'New Liberalism', injecting into British political allegory the image of the decent working man—T. H. Green's 'better sort of labourer'—who was the ideal recipient of the new state benevolence (see, *inter alia,* Emy, 1973). By corollary, conditional citizenship or exclusion were the due of pauperism. Most formally this idea survived in the disenfranchisement of paupers, made statutory in the 1832 Representation of the People Act though unimportant until the Reform Act of 1884. The logic of disqualification had been lucidly argued in the name of liberty by J. S. Mill:

> I regard it as required by first principles, that the receipt of parish relief should be a peremptory disqualification for the franchise. He who cannot by his labour suffice for his own support has no claim to the privilege of helping himself to the money of others. By becoming dependent on the remaining members of the community for actual subsistence, he abdicates his claim to equal rights with them in other respects.

These stipulations would 'leave the suffrage accessible to all who are in the normal condition of a human being' (Mill, 1910, p. 282). These two ideas, that the franchise was a reward for labour and self-sufficiency and that the disenfranchised were those 'not in the normal condition of a human being', a sort of sub-citizenry, survived intact into later reforms and were widely expressed.[43] In less explicit form they became part of the standard idiom of welfare ideology right through the succeeding decades.

It was for such reasons that Dicey could oppose the vote for those in receipt of school meals. Bad enough that meals were provided,

> still less does it seem morally right that a father who first lets his child starve, and then fails to pay the price legally due from him for a meal given to the child at the expense of the rate-payers should, under the Act of 1906, retain the right of voting for a Member of Parliament. Why a man who first neglects his duty as a father and then defrauds the State should retain his full political rights is a question easier to ask than to answer. [Dicey, 1914, p. 50 of introduction][44]

The logic was equally clear to a reformer like Beveridge: 'In the first place men who cannot in ordinary circumstances support themselves in independence are not citizens in fact, and should not be in right . . . In the second place it is dangerous to let recipients of public relief elect its dispensers' (written in 1905; quoted in Brown, 1978, p. 130).

This was a language closely in tune with the massed voices of the middle-class press, now growing in size and confidence. The *Daily Mail* was quite certain in predicting that the public 'will view with concern the theory of the minority [report of the Royal Commission on the Poor Law] that a man who is not self-supporting, but a positive burden to the state, has the right to dictate its legislation and influence its destinies' (18 February 1909).[45] It was not difficult to link this popular mood to the increasingly volatile eruptions of xenophobia. The lingering rhetoric of the settlement laws had fed anti-Irish sentiment in the 1830s and 1840s, and indeed subsequently (Jones, 1977, pp. 56—7). Edwardian hostility to European anarchists plotting in London cellars and to Jewish refugees from the pogroms bringing an alien culture to our native shores was expressed not just in comic book jingoism but in the new vocabulary of citizenship and racial purity. The Aliens Act of 1905, conceded Balfour in a letter to the King in 1905, was at least in part intended to 'keep out destitute and other undesirable aliens who should become a burden on the State and a charge on the rates' (quoted in Middlemas, 1979, p. 45). The papers cheered any move to check 'pauper immigration'. The link between welfare dependency and the alien was solidly forged. Henceforth conditional citizenship was the lot of welfare claimant and immigrant alike, offering national mythology a serviceable and resilient scapegoat. Pauper disqualification was removed in 1918, but what was erased by constitutional amendment left a permanent mark in the popular imagination.[46]

The more important aspect of classification perhaps was its continuing derivation from moral judgement. The 1905 Unemployed Workmen's Act was intended, as Balfour told the House, 'to exclude loafers, workshyers, intermittent workers . . .' (H. C. *Hansard* 20 June 1905, Vol. 147, Col. 1116). The question of discrimination was 'the crux of the problem', since local authorities had been guilty of 'the absence of discrimination between those who were deserving and those who were undeserving of relief of this kind' (Cols. 1122—24). There would remain the problem, as Herbert Samuel stressed, of 'the unwilling, the wastrels and tramps' who 'ought to be employed on penal farm colonies' (Col. 1186). The *Daily Telegraph* expressed a common conditional support for the Act so long as its purpose was

> to distinguish between the cases of men unemployed through their own incapacity, intemperance, and thriftlessness, and those thrown out of work by the fluctuations of industries and manufacturers . . . There is a class which is hopeless through its own vice and incapacity, and there is a class which suffers through no fault of its own. The object of sensible legislation on the subject is to prevent the latter class, as Mr. Balfour earnestly pointed out, from falling into the state of demoralisation and despair from which the former can never be extricated. The victims of vice must pay the penalty; the willing, capable man who would gladly work if he could find employment must be saved from reduction to the level of the victims of vice. [*Daily Telegraph*, 5 August 1905]

The Royal Commission report was shot through with a similar rhetoric.[47] So too was the debate over Lloyd George's 'People's Budget' of 1909, raising money 'to wage implacable warfare against poverty and squalidness' but taking due note of the Commission's view that 'the leading principle of poor law legislation in future should be the drawing of a clear and definite line between those whose poverty is the result of their own misdeeds and those who have been brought to want through misfortune' (H. C. *Hansard,* 29 April 1909, Vol. 4, Col. 486).

The misdeeds of the undeserving were common knowledge. After all the Royal Commission could refer to 'A great weight of evidence' which 'indicates drink as the most potent and universal factor in bringing about pauperism', though it produced considerable evidence also on the evils of gambling and venereal disease (1909, paras 531—6). Vicious in life-style, unrepentant of temper, the pauper class was not to be trusted with the new statutory largesse. Stories in the papers stressed the cunning exploitativeness of beneficiaries. 'Pension Fraud—First Conviction Under New Act' headlined the *News of the World* in I-told-you-so tones (7 February 1909). Jack London's co-residents in the Whitechapel casual ward complained bitterly that 'This super'-tendent 'ere is always writin' to the papers 'bout us mugs'.[48]

The Liberal reforms were thus both conditional and supervisory. Pensions inaugurated by the 1908 Act were unavailable to those guilty of 'habitual failure to work' or who had been imprisoned in the previous ten years. The National Insurance scheme was introduced in 1911 with all kinds of qualifications to preserve 'less eligibility' and to check on malingering by the 'shirkers and shams' (see H. C. *Hansard,* Vol. 25, 4 May 1911, Col. 635; Vol. 26, 24 May 1911, Col. 331). National insurance was opposed by much of the press, and indeed by the Webbs since 'any grant from the community to the individual, beyond what it does for all, ought to be conditional on better conduct' (Webb, 1948, p. 417).[49] Churchill was more far-sighted: 'We seek to substitute for the pressure of the forces of nature', he wrote in 1909, 'operating by chance on individuals, the pressures of the laws of insurance'.[50] Discipline and efficiency were the keynotes of the new insurance scheme, as of employment exchanges, as some on the left of the Labour movement appreciated. They were the banners that won the war in the battle for institutional loyalty.[51]

There were thus three legacies from this outburst of social policy. First it successfully and intentionally deflected any thrust toward socialism. The press, overwhelmingly anti-socialist, was only too aware that 'In every society there exist the unsuccessful, the unfortunate, the discontented and the lazy; and these, together with the ill-balanced dreamer of dreams, are the material out of which socialist parties are formed' (R. D. Blumenfeld, editor of the newly established *Daily Express,* quoted in Middlemass, 1979, p. 53). The divisive force of the classificatory principles in the new social policy gave the 'decent working man' a confirmed contempt for the pauper regiments below him. As so often, a generation later the press was able to suggest that 'The genuine unemployed workman has a strong distaste for all these futile demonstrations, while the loafer probably prefers the full-blooded eloquence of Tower Hill . . .' (*Daily Express,* 15 February 1909).[52] At the same time it alerted its tax-paying readers to the burden placed on them by the creeping collectivism of state welfare provision. In a vocabulary to prove enduring and persuasive there was talk of 'a vast army quartered upon us unable to support themselves' (*Daily Mail,* 18 February 1909). 'Englishmen are no longer too proud to loaf, to "sponge", to beg. Of these wastrels there is an alarming army always with the colours' (*News of the World,* 21 February 1909). The burden model of welfare had been wheeled onto centre stage.

Secondly, having incorporated the working class into reformism, implicated the unions in the new welfare institutions and secured the wavering but largely dutiful adherence of the Labour Party, at least in Parliament, to the insurance system, the Liberal social policies successfully equated welfare with efficiency, as both its object and criterion. As Beveridge wrote, 'The ground on which it is suggested that the relief of the unemployed shall be made a public charge is that the deterioration of workers during periods of enforced idleness is a waste of national resources, which the nation will find it profitable, as well as just, to prevent' (Beveridge and Maynard, 1904, p. 635). The constant production of schemes to deal with the industrial reserve army reinforced the notions both of wilful poverty through indolence and of the burden model of assistance.

Thirdly, the Edwardian solution reconstructed, yet retained, the moral assumptions of Victorian welfare. Against a background of 'labour unrest', the limited Liberal welfare reforms acted as a temporary stabilising source of social control, though in due course it was the moral rhetoric that was more enduring than the social settlement itself. The often punitive and highly regulatory new schemes never forgot that 'every pauper is not only an economic or educational problem, he is primarily a moral and spiritual failure' (*Morning Post,* 16 February 1909). The collectivist surge had successfully rewritten an individualist morality into state provision for poverty. The poor would never improve on conditional citizenship.

GENUINELY SEEKING WORK: WATCHING FOR 'A DANGEROUS
UNDERCURRENT OF MISCHIEF'

The 'long weekend' between the wars has etched itself into living
memory as a mean and cheerless interlude of hunger and mass
unemployment. Indeed much of the potency of more recent
imagery has been drawn from the contrast of post-war 'affluence'
with the privations of the 'hungry years' of the 1920s and 1930s.
Unemployment dominated these decades, with never less than one
million unemployed, and one in five of the labour force out of
work in the early 1930s. Yet this was also a period of enormous
divergencies in social experience. The industrial workshop of the
world was in ruins, and the decline of traditional heavy industries
left much of the north of England a bleak wasteland of idle
factories and shipyards. But outside the 'depressed areas' output
and productivity rose, new industries thrived, the tertiary sector
expanded and domestic consumption soared.

For those who remained in work, standards of living improved,
with an average rise in real incomes of 1.7 per cent per annum
between 1920 and 1938. Wage rates did not in fact go up very
much in the period, and were level or falling in the 1920s. Even
with recovery after 1932 wages rose only slowly (Bain *et al.,* 1972,
p. 121). But the cost of living dropped steadily from 1921 to 1934,
and the benefits were magnified by the drop in the birth rate and in
average family size.[53] Real divisions appeared within the working
class as the glittering new spoils of working-class affluence were
very unevenly scattered.[54] Possibly, as George Orwell speculated,
'fish-and-chips, art-silk stockings, tinned salmon, cut-price choco-
late (five two ounce bars for sixpence), the movies, the radio,
strong tea and the Football Pools have between them averted
revolution' (1937, p. 190). Just as plausibly, demoralisation among
the unemployed was equally responsible.

The giant shadow benighting the whole period was unemployment. State concern with poverty was overwhelmed by the
regulation of unemployment benefits, and other causes of poverty
were largely left to the investigative or humanitarian urges of
campaigning academics or reforming trusts. The state remained
more interested in the moral than the social condition of the
unemployed, and prevailing attitudes to poverty became a mirror
of ruling definitions of its most apparent cause, unemployment.

This is clearly evident in the mass circulation popular national press that at last arrives in this period. Gestating since the late nineteenth century, the new papers now circulated among a wide working-class readership that had not previously subscribed to a daily newspaper. In 1918 national daily circulation was 3.1 million. In 1939 it was 10.6 million (Murdock and Golding, 1978, p. 130; Wadsworth, 1954/5, p. 28). Much of this growth was in the thirties when the popular dailies, notably the *Daily Herald* and *Daily Express,* bribed their way into the affections of millions with give-away sales gimmicks from tea-sets to bound volumes of Dickens or Shaw. The *Daily Herald* circulation rose from 1.12 million in 1930 to 2.03 million in 1937, while that of the *Daily Express* increased from 1.69 million to 2.2 million in the same period. By 1937 these two had 42.5 per cent of the national daily circulation between them and three other papers had daily circulations in excess of a million (Royal Commission on the Press, 1949, App. III, p. 190). Circulations were to continue their upward climb to a peak in 1947.

Increasing production and editorial costs, together with massive expenditure on the 'circulation wars', expanded the size of the minimum market needed for a title to survive. This extended the tendency to concentration of ownership already apparent before the war (Murdock and Golding, 1978). What prevented these costs from keeping cover prices too high for the new working-class readership was advertising, expenditure on which nearly trebled from £20 million in 1907 to £59 million in 1938 (Curran and Seaton, 1981, p. 73). Consumer expenditure rose by nearly a third in real terms between 1922 and 1938, especially on the new 'consumer durables' that began to appear in the display advertising of the popular press.[55] The result was to sever once and for all the party roots of national papers and replant them firmly in the richer soil of the entertainment industry. At the same time the threshold cost of entry to the market was raised high above the head of radical or fringe journalism. The new working-class mass circulation press found itself dependent on advertising revenue yet unable to secure the majority of its income from this source in the way that the smaller but up-market 'quality' papers were able to. Thus began its pursuit of even bigger circulations and of the centre ground in political discourse where fewest readers could be offended.

The more demotic tone this required sometimes suggests 'a

marked shift towards the left in the world of printed communications' in the 1930s (Addison, 1977, p. 151). Certainly the loyalties of the *Daily Herald* were in no doubt, though the *Daily Mirror's* transformation from a Conservative to a Labour daily was more cautious than its carefully planned redirection of style and market in 1933-4. However, this change of manner was more an 'irreverence for the sacred cows of the pre-war Establishment' (Edelman, 1966, p. 40) than a clarion-call for the socialist utopia. Brass-hats, bureaucrats, big-wigs and political fumblers were more likely objects of headlined diatribes than the inner sanctums of capitalism's higher echelons. Radicalism of a more consistent political pedigree was safely confined to Fabian pamphlets, the Left Book Club, the *New Statesman* and the new literati of the Communist Party.

Thus the period forged a tacit consensus between the major political parties, in practice if not in rhetoric, that became the political touchstone for the press. Baldwin's 1929 election slogan 'Safety First' got it exactly right. British politicians emerged from the First World War equipped only with Victorian ideals and Edwardian techniques in a world impatient to leave them behind. They clung to a stubborn faith in a balanced budget and sound money. Retrenchment was the order of the day, cutting government expenditure to remove the deficit in state accountancy.

'War socialism' had pushed government expenditure up from £184 million at the outbreak of war to £1,825 million in 1916. Public expenditure multiplied sixfold during the war and the National Debt mushroomed from £650 million to nearly £7,500 million. Interest on this debt increased from 11 per cent of public expenditure in 1913 to 24 per cent in 1924. By 1931 it was 41 per cent. This was exacerbated by Churchill's return to the gold standard in 1925 (it had been suspended since 1919) at pre-war parity, which also had the effect of further handicapping Britain's ailing export industries by increasing the cost of exports to buyers. The tax-paying classes, still amost exclusively middle class, were not happy, and the rising cost of social services was a prominent target for their anger.

The press readily joined the clamour for retrenchment. Northcliffe's papers railed at 'squandermania' and with his brother Rothermere gave support to the Anti-Waste League. In the *Sunday Pictorial* Rothermere predicted 'Pauperism for the Middle Classes' (30 January 1921), while in the *Daily Mirror* the cry was 'Voters Crushed by Taxation Determined to Save Country' (8 January

1921). Attacks on the 'lavish distribution of doles' were a piercing note in this chorus of outrage (*Morning Post,* 17 February 1922).[56] The voice of employers was important in forming this frugal mood. Initially willing to see the utility of welfare in maintaining stable social order, work incentives and labour control, they soon began to regret and resent the rising floodtide of public expenditure as industry trod water or sank (Hay, 1978). More influential, however, was the 'Treasury view', a pre- and indeed anti-Keynesian orthodoxy that unemployment was being inflamed by the twin bellows of excessive wage costs and public expenditure. The surface plausibility of this thesis was buttressed by the evident rise in living standards of those in employment following the deflationary effects of public spending cuts. Doing well by doing little seemed to work—if you ignored unemployment and industrial stagnation (Skidelsky, 1981; Middlemas, 1979, pp. 228—9).[57] In 1922 the Geddes Report showed that expenditure on education, health, labour and pensions had increased from £33 million in 1913/14 to £124 million in 1922/3. 'Geddes axe' hacked at all before it, especially education, to the rousing cheers of the press, which trumpeted about 'Waste in the Social Services' and suggested the 'Cuts Are Not Big Enough' (*Daily Mail,* 16 February 1922; *Sunday Pictorial,* 12 February 1922; *Daily Express,* 11 February 1922).

The general mood of antagonism needed to set its sights on a target, and in the 1920s it found one in the east London district of Poplar. In 1919 Labour had a clean sweep in council and Board of Guardians elections in Poplar. George Lansbury, editor of the *Daily Herald* and a popular figure among the socialist left, became Mayor. Defying a rates increase levied by the London County Council, Lansbury and his fellow councillors went to gaol demanding equalisation of rates among London boroughs. From 1922 the Poplar Board of Guardians provided outdoor relief on increasingly generous scales, now that the workhouse test had been swept away by the sheer scale of unemployment. Press propaganda was virulent. *The Times* saw Poplar's action leading to 'the destruction of the present social organisation of this country' (23 March 1922; quoted in Branson, 1979, p. 133). *The Morning Post* warned that in Poplar it was 'going to be more profitable to be out of work than to be in work' (1 February 1922). In the *Daily Telegraph* it was 'socialist Madness' (1 February 1922) and 'Communism at Poplar' (8 February 1922).[58] 'Poplarism' neatly linked a red scare with opposition to public expenditure and, when a commissioned report on Poplar was published in May 1922, with the burgeoning mythology of dole abuse and malingering (see Ryan, 1978; Branson, 1979).

Confusion about unemployment benefits between the wars is hardly surprising. No fewer than forty Acts relating to unemployment insurance reached the statute book between 1911 and 1938. The tortuous twists of unemployment relief parallel the meandering course of a policy caught among the pressures of humane concern, political expedience, moral judgement and economic necessity. Much of the story revolves round the measures invented to prevent abuse of or dependence on benefits. Between 1921 and 1930 nearly three million applicants for benefit were disqualified for one reason or another.[59] Servicemen returning to 'a land fit for heroes' after the war immediately overloaded the capacity of the insurance fund, necessitating a provisional 'Out of Work Donation' scheme. In 1920 unemployment insurance was extended to cover over eleven million workers, but the dramatic increase in unemployment (from 3.7 per cent at the end of 1920 to 18 per cent in June 1921) pulled the carpet from under the insurance principle. Fearful of civil disturbance, reported regularly to the Cabinet in the context of widespread revolutionary activity, a new scheme of uncovenanted (i.e. non-contributory) benefits was concocted. Throwing the unemployed on poor relief was no longer politically feasible, or even practicable as the results of the *Daily Herald's* 'Go To The Guardians' campaign proved. The sting was removed from a potentially violent swarm of unemployed. Unemployment slowly dropped from 1922 to 1929 while the real value of benefits increased. Though the two characteristics etched deepest into bitter memories of inter-war unemployment—the 'genuinely seeking work' clause and the means test—were introduced in March 1921 and February 1922 respectively, their most severe impact was delayed.

The 1924 Labour government extended uncovenanted benefit (renamed extended benefit) and removed the means test.[60] The quid pro quo was the tightening up of rules on abuse and the 'genuinely seeking work' requirements, which set in train a period of intensified pressure on claimants, as the unemployed became a major scapegoat for successive governments' frustrated attempts to keep a moribund economy alive.

With the return of the Baldwin government came the return of the means test. At the end of 1925 the Blanesburgh Committee was appointed to look into unemployment insurance, amid a thickening flurry of abuse stories in the press. As *The People* announced on its front page: 'Dole Frauds To Stop—Plans Being Prepared for Great Comb-Out' (3 May 1925). Churchill's budget speech, in which he remarked on the 'general habit of learning how to qualify for unemployment benefit' further fuelled the flames.

When the Blanesburgh Committee reported in 1927, abuse stories were still thick on the ground, and its deliberations were mainly reported in that context. The resulting Act created a single benefit, all claimants for which had to show that they were 'genuinely seeking whole-time employment'. The punitive application of this rule restored the full glory of the ethics and psychology of 1834 to the administration of relief. What was in question was 'the state of the applicants' mind' as a famous judicial decision of 1926 made clear (Deacon, 1976, p. 58). As the *Daily Telegraph* commented, when greeting a drop in out-relief, 'Much irreparable mischief has been done in breaking down the old attitude of independence. So long as out-relief is made easy, there will be ever-lengthening queues of persons lined up to receive it and grumbling at the inconvenience of having to wait their turn'. What was needed was stricter investigation to discourage the 'pauper habit of mind and pauper mode of life' (11 November 1927). Two years later Jowitt, the Liberal who became Attorney-General in the second Labour government, rhetorically asked, 'Are we to legislate on the lines that these people should think that they need do nothing themselves; that they should wait at home, sit down, smoke their pipes and wait until an offer comes to them?' (H. C. *Hansard* Vol. 232, Col. 2686, 5 Dec 1929). No one could seriously claim that jobs were available, yet thousands tramped the country in a vain quest, participants in 'a futile and sometimes brutal ritual' (Deacon, 1976, p. 61).

The 'genuinely seeking work' test was removed by the second Labour government in 1930. But the massive increase in unemployment as the world economic crisis deepened (an increase from 1.27 million at the election in 1929 to 2.6 million at the end of 1930) provoked a fresh burst of public indignation about abuse of the dole and malingering. In November 1930 a 42-page memorandum on abuse was prepared for the Cabinet and a couple of months later MacDonald told the TUC:

> There is a very large and growing section of my letters protesting about the way in which unemployment benefit is being used coming from our own people. I am glad to see it, the people who have been with us building up the labour movement and agitating

for unemployment insurance, the stories they write to me of neighbours or fellow-workmen abusing this are very heartening indeed. [Deacon, 1976, p. 78]

A Royal Commission on unemployment insurance provided a prominent stage for views like this, while the deepening crisis fed the anxieties and diffuse anger that filled MacDonald's post bag. The report of the May Committee, outdoing Geddes' report a decade earlier, urged massive reductions in public expenditure, including a cut in unemployment relief of 20 per cent.[61] The subsequent Cabinet split and the formation of the National Government in August 1931 were the political lava from an economic volcano whose major victims were the unemployed (benefits were cut by 10 per cent in October 1931). While the papers firmly jumped on any suggestion of a 'bankers' ramp' behind the budget decisions, they were able to establish a ready link between dole abuse and the country's difficulties.[62] Established financial opinion rested on an unshakeable pillar of moral judgement.

Perhaps worse than the cut in benefits (the cost of living was indeed falling) was the imposition of the household means test under the jurisdiction of the Public Assistance Committees, appointed bodies under local councils that had replaced the elected Boards of Guardians in 1929. The administration of the means test, with its attendant questionnaires, interviews and inspections, created an aura of indignity and control that has remained at the heart of social security ever since. The methods and values of the poor law were at once imposed on a new and more self-regarding clientele, though the result was not only outraged opposition but a reinforced contempt for the undeserving.

Opposition to both unemployment and benefit regulations erupted spasmodically throughout the inter-war years, and images of the hunger marches are the period's most enduring visual legacy. Six major marches were organised by the National Unemployed Workers Movement between 1921 and 1936 under the banner of 'work or full maintenance at union rates'.[63] From the very first, in 1922, the press was quick to label the marchers as unwitting dupes of a red plot. By 1930 the marchers were becoming more tactically sophisticated and politically significant, and in 1932 a Cabinet Committee was set up to consider the marches. Jailing the NUWM leader Wal Hannington, and even more provocatively the aging and venerated union leader Tom Mann, added to the public sympathy that no reiteration of the Communist nature of the NUWM leadership could prevent (Turnbull, 1973). Government use of the press became more insistent, more frequent and more subtle as support for the hunger marches increased, and the openly hostile propaganda against the 1934 march was the occasion for the founding of the National Council for Civil Liberties.[64]

The Unemployment Insurance Act of 1934 restored benefits to their 1931 level. It also created the centralised Unemployment Assistance Board to administer benefits and a uniform means test. Confusion over the UAB scales produced two years of further protest and parliamentary oscillation, with continuing evidence of regional variation in administration from the brutal and punitive to the lax and generous. The Board was greatly exercised by the attitudes of its clients, and both responded to and fed the rekindled suspicions of malingerers as unemployment dropped in the pre-war recovery period (Branson and Heinemann, 1973, pp. 51–4).

On 20 February 1934 *The Times* appeared in a special silver edition, announcing 1934 as 'The Year of the Silver Lining to the Dark Clouds of Depression, Bad Trade and Unstable Money'. As the world crawled out of recession Britain found itself a new country, with a managed economy, new centralised planning mechanisms, a superstructure of industrial conglomerates and a lurch to corporatism that marked a new age in political organisation and a new economic surge resting on cheap paper money and the end of Free Trade. Unemployment fell from 22.1 per cent in 1932 to 12.9 per cent in 1938, and especially after 1936 the gathering pace of armaments manufacture swept economic recovery along with it. Unemployment soon became inexcusable again even though it remained at a very substantial level. By 1938 it was not uncommon to hear calls for work camps and labour colonies once more, particularly from those impressed by the efficiency of the National Socialist 'Labour Service' in Germany or the Italian Academia Fascista (as suggested by *The Times* 29 January 1938).[65]

Five themes emerge from the complex kaleidoscope of imagery about poverty in the inter-war period. First, the divided fortunes of the working class increased the gap between the new 'prosperous' working class and the poor. Second, a new pervasive metaphor of the 'national interest' was forged by the hammering of a mass popular press on the anvil of economic recession. Recurrent unmasking of hidden enemies, frequently in 'red peril' scares, cemented political orthodoxy around an assumed and, as a result, a real consensus. One constituent usage was reference to 'common knowledge' of affairs, a shared insight into a world unknown to a suspect Establishment. Thus the *Daily Telegraph* in 1922: 'Everyone is familiar with cases in which work has been refused because the relief to be obtained by the workless is so generous as to remove the inducement to industry' (16 February). *The People* in 1925: 'It is well known that in many instances persons who do not want work take steps to ensure that employers will decline to engage them' (3 May). *Daily Telegraph* in 1927: 'Most householders know from their own experience cases of thoroughly undeserving and idle persons who abuse the "dole" ' (26 November), and the same paper in 1934: 'At a time when public assistance was never so well organised actual hunger among the workers is a pretence. That everybody knows. In this matter the general body of the public is not to be fooled' (26 February). This manufactured 'common knowledge' was crucial to the emergence of a new imposed consensus, powerful because of its grasp on the material realities and inchoate anxieties of working-class experience. In this the mass media, including the steadily spreading broadcasting system, were pivotal.[66]

The third theme is the dwarfing of poverty by unemployment. As a temporary and often voluntary state, it could be and was implicitly argued, unemployment was a definitive cause of undeserving poverty and, by extension, poverty was an insignificant and passing condition for the individual. The shift in public expenditure was massive. Whereas in 1920 £5.4 million was spent on outdoor relief and £8.7 million on unemployment insurance, by 1938, although outdoor relief had risen to £19.4 million, unemployment benefits were £51.7 million, plus another £41.3 million on non-contributory unemployment allowances (Parker, 1972, Table 12.21, p. 402). Much later social policy was rooted in the inter-war studies that related and almost equated poverty with unemployment. One result was that arguments in the clamour for policy initiatives started from the immediate needs prompted by financial calamity rather than the considered claims of justice and redistribution (cf. Runciman, 1972, pp. 82–3). Welfare policy was anchored in minimum provision for temporary distress and entirely divorced from larger ambitions or philosophies.

Fourthly, abuse of welfare schemes returned to the centre of debate, and coloured every shift in insurance or poor relief administration. More importantly, the potency of the undeserving poor as trouble-makers was successfully integrated into an expanded image of abuse. In a relatively sympathetic account of an East End dole queue in 1921 the *Daily Telegraph* noticed 'In a little by-street hard by the conditions of the times were revealed in another but not less cruel way—a way moreover which hides a dangerous undercurrent of mischief. There a small knot of youths were gathered under a red banner . . .' (8 January 1921). Fear of social disorder was a powerful spur to the laggards of reform. The NUWM never attracted mass support, and Wal Hannington wrote wistfully of 'how much more could have been done if the vast masses of the unemployed had been united in constant organisation and action!' (1973, p. 323). But its influence was ever-present and lack of mass support was in part due to the successful deployment of the new apparatus of consensus manufacture.

The fifth theme is precisely this reconstruction of popular imagery in journalistic form, a distillation of centuries of prejudice and mythology into the commonplace formulae of the daily press. News management by the state was an important part of this shift, at times a tacit collusion, less commonly but at times of crisis a deliberate and manipulative ploy.[67] More consistently, ruling definitions of the needs and presuppositions of social policy were now provided with a massively extended apparatus of cultural distribution. As Runciman has suggested, the mass media certainly conveyed images of exalted life-styles to the working class, but presented them as 'too close to a fantasy world to engender feelings of relative deprivation' (1972, p. 123). The manufactured divisions between employed and unemployed, or between prospering and distressed areas, allowed for a continuous rallying cry around the benefits of social order, a settled contract that only perverse or malign interests could refuse to join. The ground was thus well prepared for the cautious compromises of post-war welfare policy and the reconstruction of social security around some tried and familiar nostrums.

CONCLUSION: NATURALISING IMAGERY

It is only in recent years that the history of either social policy or the mass media has advanced beyond the narrative chronicle. Much work remains to be done. Our leap-frogging summary has obviously done much violence to the complex reality of this history. It has, however, illustrated the roots and potency of some of the imagery examined in the remainder of this book.

By the time that Beveridge arrived, stalking his Five Giants of Want, Disease, Ignorance, Squalor and Idleness like so many characters in a morality play, the imagery of poverty and welfare with which the new utopia was to be constructed were deeply engraved into popular expectations. Three key ideas formed the tripod on which public understanding of poverty and welfare rested. These were efficiency, morality and pathology: efficiency of the labour market and the economy; morality of the work ethic and self-sufficiency; and the pathology of individual inadequacy as the cause of poverty.

We have suggested that these ideas have lengthy pedigrees in popular consciousness. But they have been 'fixed' into the prevailing discourse in two key periods. In the 1880—1920 period of the politically democratised and thoroughly centralised ('representative—interventionist') state the ideals of Victorian social reform emerge replenished by the new vocabulary of the lower middle-class commercial press created by the retail revolution and extended communications. In the second fixing period between the wars, ruling images became 'naturalised', and the now genuinely mass circulation popular press, bound by its economics to an uncritical acceptance of the social order, provided an authorative voice for an emasculated reformism more concerned with social control than with the redress of injustice or inequality (cf. Gramsci, 1971, pp. 323—6, 419—22). In the retreat from utopian promise in the post-war period there was no difficulty in finding excuse or scapegoat. In the age of the welfare state God's poor have been less visible than the Devil's.

NOTES

1. All citations to this report refer to the 1974 Checkland edition.
2. Chambliss notes a forerunner statute in 1274.
3. On the causes of poverty in the sixteenth century see Lis and Soly (1979), Pound (1971), Hill (1969) p. 254.
4. In More's *Utopia* (1516) begging was forbidden and work was obligatory for the sturdy poor. No mercy was to be shown to 'sturdy and Valiaunte beggeers, clokinge their idle lyfe under the colours of some disease or sickness'. See also Campbell (1930).
5. Charity was itself both discriminating and socially calculating. The establishment of almshouses for the impotent poor and houses of correction for the sturdy rogues was a prudent way for munificence

to be dispensed by the merchant classes. Cf. Hill (1969) p. 258, Jordan (1959) *passim,* Pound (1971) ch. 6.

6. A literature sensationally depicting this underworld soon began to proliferate. Lis and Soly instance John Audely's *Fraternity of Vacabondes*; see also Neuburg (1977) pp. 19—55.

7. The phrase is a summary of Marx's reading of Eden (1797) from whose work he quoted the conclusion 'What divides the rich from the poor is not the ownership of land or of money, but rather the command of labour'. Marx comments 'Poverty as such begins with the tiller's freedom—the feudal fetters to the soil, or at least the locality, had until then spared the legislature the task of occupying itself with the vagrants, poor, etc' (1973, p. 735). See also Marx's quotations from Tuckett (1973, p. 785).

8. See Locke (1697) and the comments of the Webbs (1927) p. 112. Locke was keen to put idle beggars in the navy, or perhaps ship them off to the colonies (Locke was responsible for the constitution of Carolina). He was also an enthusiast for putting children to work from the age of 3 to get them used to labour at an early age and to release their mothers for useful work.

9. See also Henriques (1979) p. 17 and Marshall (1926). Distinguishing the pauper from other citizens remained important. An act of 1697 requiring paupers to wear badges was not repealed until 1810.

10. See also Coats (1960).

11. Fielding's knowledge of life among the lower orders was probably more extensive than Defoe's. His proposals for a more efficient House of Correction system were set in the context of a not unsympathetic awareness that the poor were not entirely to blame for their own misfortunes (see Fielding, 1753). But the economic theory was nonetheless stark in its assessment of society's inability to tolerate an idle and impoverished dependent stratum: 'When the price of labour is once established all those poor who shall refuse to labour at that price . . . may properly be deemed incorrigibly idle' (Fielding, 1751, p. 70). For '. . . nothing can surely be more improper than to suffer the idleness of the poor, the cause of so much evil to society, to go entirely unpunished' (p. 73).

12. Coats quotes Jonas Hanway, the influential philanthropist (and reputedly first man to use an umbrella) whose energetic researches and campaigns to save the souls and bodies of pauper children produced 'Hanway's Act' of 1767. Hanway was still shrewd enough to 'question much if we should be near so rich as we are if the common people did not live so much from hand to mouth' (Coats, 1976, p. 114).

13. The vagrancy laws did not subside until roughly 1814—16, and of course increased vagrancy after the Civil War had given them a boost. The severity with which wanderers were whipped and sent back to their place of settlement is equalled only by its frequency.

Slack's study of Salisbury finds over 600 vagrants dismissed from the town in this way between 1598 and 1638, many of them single women propelled into the town by rising prices and bad harvests (Slack, 1972). By the later eighteenth century, containment of vagrancy was still in force and enforced, but was no longer the crux of poor law administration. However, for details of later survivals of settlement procedures see Rose (1976).

14. As Nassau Senior, the intellectual force behind the *Poor Law Report*, wrote in a pseudonymous pamphlet reflecting his satisfaction with progress seven years after the Act, 'as a generation educated in pauperism grew to manhood, a new and still more alarming symptom showed itself, the demoralisation of the labouring classes'. Trade in the beer-shops had gone down since 1834, and people were less often getting married and having children to get more money from the parish. It was well-known that 'among the able bodied paupers are always found the worst characters of the parish; the men whom their indolence, or dishonesty, or intemperance, exclude from the employment of individuals' (Senior, 1841, pp. 18, 111).

15. As the authors reflect on such evidence, the pauper given easy money by the parish does not care for it in the way he might if it were earned, but wastes it 'in the intemperance to which his ample leisure invites him . . . It appears from the evidence that the great supporters of the beer-shops are the paupers' (*Poor Law Report*, pp. 167–8).

16. Thirteen years later the *Morning Post* cautioned that 'we must reform the homes of the poor. But is not every attempt to do so a mockery on the part of the legislature, so long as it indirectly demoralises the homes of the poor by encouraging the gin-palace?' (23 June 1857). Quoted in Hindle (1937) p. 221.

17. In no other country, noted the report, has provision been made 'for more than the relief of indigence . . . It has never been deemed expedient that the provision should extend to the relief of poverty' (*Poor Law Report*, p. 334).

18. *The Morning Chronicle* (18 April 1834) echoed this view: 'One great object of the new plan will be to make the labourers once more independent, by restoring the distinction between the labourer and pauper.'

19. Tawney was writing of the continuing invocation of 1834 principles in opposition to the Liberal reforms of 1906–11.

20. Frequently the workhouse test and the attendant apparatus of the new poor law were not adopted in northern areas until some years after 1834. In the West Riding, for example, by 1854 only nine of the twenty-seven unions could provide workhouse places for one per cent of their populations (Ashforth, 1976, p. 133).

21. As Digby shows, even in rural areas the workhouse contained the minority of able-bodied paupers. From the 1840s to 1890s about

three-quarters of the adult able-bodied paupers in Norfolk were on outdoor relief (Digby, 1976, p. 162).

22. Ashforth notes that 'as late as 1856 twelve of the fifty most populous parishes and unions in England and Wales were administered under local acts' (1976, p. 128).

23. As the official *History of The Times* (1935) points out, 'The year 1834 was crucial in politics and in journalism, and the relations of both to *The Times* were to undergo a vital change' (p. 288). Harriet Martineau, popularising disciple of Malthus and dedicated opponent of state intervention, wrote that 'with *The Times* on our side we felt pretty safe'. Like Martineau, *The Times* was especially vexed by any welfare provision for family support, as in the new Act's 'bastardy clauses'. 'The bill', it thundered, 'which allows the worthless self-gratifying sluggard to people every parish *ad libitum,* and which imposes the consequences of the scoundrel's self-indulgence on the industrious and honest rate-payer, which in fact gives a letter of licence without check, control, or punishment to every brutal libertine to scatter his profligate image round the land—can such a bill be considered a cure for the evils consequent on reckless debauchery? Is it not rather a premium on vice?' (*The Times,* 23 June 1834).

24. The Association for the Improvement of London Workhouses issued a booklet collating press opinion (1867). The general tenor of quotes indicates the balance between sympathy and efficiency as the guiding objectives of press indignation. After all, as the *Daily Telegraph* pointed out (20 April 1866), reformers were 'contending on behalf of a class which they themselves admit to be squalid, deplorable, untrustworthy'. Sharper classification was what was needed. 'It was necessary to make the workhouse an undesirable habitation, because a system of more spacious benevolence would have been a direct discouragement to industry'. But 'in the present instance one very important distinction has a good deal slipped out of notice. Pauperism is a condition into which a man may fall by his own choice. Old age and sickness are not . . .' (*Saturday Review* 10 March 1866). These quotes are all contained in the Association's pamphlet.

25. The Rev. S. Barnett, himself a leading reformer, and founder of the settlement movement, wrote impatiently of the 'scamps and idlers' who 'come forward with cries that get popular support' (Barnett, 1886). More sardonic still was Mr Punch: 'It is to be hoped that the poor will be enabled to live better, but there is much tall writing and sensationalism on the subject, that the sensible Public is beginning to ask How the Journalists and the Publishers and Pamphleteers live? If the answer is "By the Poor", it is not so pleasant' (*Punch,* 15 December 1883, p. 285).

26. Stead's most notorious exploit was the publication in July 1885 of his series on 'The Maiden Tribute of Modern Babylon', a sensational

The Library
Saint Francis College
Fort Wayne, Indiana 46808

exposée of child prostitution. Stead himself procured a young virgin for £5 and subsequently spent two months in prison, but after rocking the outraged sensibilities of the nation he achieved his aim with the raising of the statutory age of consent from 13 to 16.

27. Booth's motives and moral assumptions have been subjected to recurrent scrutiny in recent years, provoking an agitated debate. See Brown (1968), Lummis (1971), J. Brown (1971), Hennock (1976).

28. *The Times,* commenting on Booth's volumes, found one overriding lesson to be learnt, 'the folly and mischief of indiscriminate relief . . . It weakens and it degrades. It unfits its recipients for earning their own living and it deprives them of the wish to do so. Mr. Booth's volume tells us, among other things, how large a part of the misery of East London has been due to this cause' (15 April 1889).

29. It was a distinction much lauded among the artisan classes themselves. As Wright, 'the journeyman engineer', had written nearly twenty years earlier, 'there are many of the casually employed classes, and of the poorer kinds of regular labourers, and others who are not poor, who habitually prey upon charity, ordinary or special. To these pauper-souled cormorants the bread of charity has no bitterness, and they seek it with a shameless, lying perseverance . . . but the really decent mechanic, who in ordinary times has never dreamt of asking for or accepting charity . . . should be treated better, with comprehensive, centrally administered relief' (Wright, 1970, pp. 287—9).

30. According to Thompson (1977, p. 291) 100,000 copies were sold in England between 1881 and 1883. Wohl (1970, p. 49) gives 60,000 between 1881 and 1885. It is reasonable from all accounts to conclude it was an influential best-seller! Wohl suggests his impact 'cannot be exaggerated'.

31. cf. Lord Wemyss, who had become Chairman of the Liberty and Property Defence League, telling his fellow peers that the Royal Commission on the Housing of the Working Classes 'would cause demoralisation because it would teach large classes that they had not to look to their own exertions and that the State must come forward and lift them out of the slough of despond'. If the state built houses 'where were they to stop? If they built houses would they furnish them? Would they put fire in the grate or food in the cupboard?' (Lords *Hansard,* Vol. 284, Col. 1703, 22 February 1884).

32. These oft-quoted words had a more limited context than is sometimes implied, coming in the aftermath of the increase in the franchise by two million voters the previous year, and aimed at, among other things, the promotion of peasant proprietorships.

33. On Booth's plans for labour colonies see Brown (1968) and, for an earlier plan for emigration widely supported by the provincial press, Thompson (1971) p. 26. See also J. F. Harris (1972) ch. 3.

34. The view that social reform was the result of the extended franchise runs through Gilbert's study of social policy in this period (Gilbert,

1966a).
35. See also Smiles (1875).
36. Peek, Chairman of the Howard Association, was a passionate opponent of indiscriminate charity 'by means of which the vicious thrive . . . All these unwise schemes for the relief of destitution . . . are in reality sources of demoralisation and a direct encouragement to vagrancy and mendicancy' (1888, preface). Not enough attention was given, argued Peek, to the moral condition of the poor. Careful investigation of the poor, encouragement of self-denial, thrift and industry, these were the answers (see Peek, 1883, pp. 7—8, 181—6, 197—8).
37. For a development of this theme in the context of music hall see Stedman Jones (1974). See also Berridge (1978).
38. Party loyalty rather than party affiliation continued, of course. By 1910 the morning press was overwhelmingly Conservative in sympathy.
39. See Mason (1978) on the influence in the 1880s and 1890s of the periodical reviews, and especially on their successful equation of reform with national efficiency and the fight against socialism.
40. The livelier papers occasionally carried stories such as the *News of the World* (26 March 1905) 'Love in a Workhouse', which reveals the 'amorous conduct of certain of the male and female paupers' in the Folkestone Union workhouse.
41. See more generally Semmel (1960) on social imperialism in its twin forms: that stressed by Chamberlain and the Tariff Reform League (that imperial strength would serve the best interests of the working class) and that of the Liberal Imperialists and the Fabians (stressing the vital contribution of a fit working class to the needs of Empire). Both were intensely nationalist and aimed at 'efficiency'.
42. Where he wrote, as he put it, 'nothing to do with politics' but only on social questions. See Harris (1977) p. 62.
43. Even, for example, by radical reformers like Henry George, who warned that 'To give the suffrage to tramps, to paupers, to men to whom the chance to labour is a boon, to men who must beg, or steal, or starve, is to invoke destruction. To put political power in the hands of men embittered and degraded by poverty is to tie Firebrands to Foxes and turn them loose amid the standing corn . . .' (George, 1883, pp. 376—7). The notion that material development and social order should precede the universal franchise is a familiar one to third world politicians, who were advised in such terms by the political science of the 1950s and 1960s in very Henry Georgeian terms (see Golding, 1974).
44. So, too, he argued 'surely a sensible and benevolent man may well ask himself whether England as a whole will gain by enacting that the receipt of poor relief, in the shape of a pension shall be consistent with the pensioner's retaining the right to join in the election of a Member of Parliament' (1914, p. xxxv).

45. The majority report of the Royal Commission recommended amending the regulations so that disqualification would not apply if on relief for less than three months in the year. The minority report, very much the work of the Webbs, recommended removal of disqualification, characteristically as much in the name of efficiency and administrative simplicity as of justice.

46. See Briggs (1979) for evidence that the disqualification had, in fact, been inefficiently enforced for years. However, we are here concerned more with sentiment than administrative exactitude.

47. '. . . the tendency has always been for Guardians to allow [outdoor] relief to become permanent . . . When this is the case there grows up a nucleus of loafers, who have found the stoneyard under lax supervision an easy way of earning a scanty living and who act as a centre of corruption . . .' (Royal Commission on the Poor Law, 1909, p. 204, para 454). The report complains of 'the way in which a form of relief originated for the benefit of the genuine worker in times of distress is taken advantage of by the good-for-nothing loafer' (p. 462). The minority report masterminded by the Webbs was preoccupied with the inefficient mixing of the deserving poor and the worthless in unspecialised institutions.

48. London's friend goes on 'Oh, e sez we're no good, a lot o' blackguards an' scoundrels as won't work. Tells all the old tricks I've been 'earin' for twenty years an' w'ich I never seen a mug ever do'. Dole queue mythology has a long and continuous history. See London (1977) p. 47.

49. Beatrice wrote in a letter in 1911 that 'It is no use letting the poor come and go as they think fit . . . destitution must be prevented and where necessary penalised as a public nuisance' (quoted in Rose, 1972, p. 46).

50. W. S. Churchill, 'Notes on Malingering', 6 June 1809; document quoted in Fraser (1973) p. 259. As he wrote the same year, 'With a "stake in the country" in the form of insurance against evil days these workers will pay no attention to the vague promises of revolutionary socialism' (J. F. Harris, 1972, p. 366).

51. Debate continues over the success of social control by welfare in this period. Some have stressed the effectiveness of switching from 'bribery through the market to bribery through institutions'. Others have noted the strong counter offensive from within the labour movement. See Foster (1976), Hinton (1973), Holton (1974, 1976), and Hay (1978).

52. In a leader commenting on a demonstration against unemployment and poverty in Trafalgar Square the previous Saturday.

53. With 1930 as 100, the cost of living index was 126.8 in 1921, 111.8 in 1925, 92.4 in 1931, and 89.2 in 1934. By 1938 it had risen to 98.9 (Bain *et al.,* 1972, p. 122). The estimated average size of completed family dropped from 3.37 in 1900—1909 to 2.19 in 1925—1929 (and

from 3.94 to 2.49 for manual workers). The birth rate per 1000 population fell from 28.2 in 1901—1905 to 19.9 in 1921—1925 and to 15.0 in 1931—1935 (Rollett and Parker, 1972, pp. 51, 56).

54. However, for evidence of the relative stability of wage rates between occupational groups see Atkinson (1975) p. 23 and p. 74. The point is the masking of large and structural levels of severe earned poverty by an overriding picture of booming working-class affluence, the theme that bestrode both sociology and political cliché in the 1950—1965 period.

55. Total consumers' expenditure at constant 1958 and 1963 prices rose from £9,289 million in 1922 to £12,470 million in 1938. In the same period, expenditure on furniture, electrical and other durables rose from £356 million to £594 million, and on cars and motorcycles from £39 million to £152 million (Bacon *et al.,* 1972, pp. 89—90).

56. The quote is from an article by Harold Cox on 'The Cost of State Charity'. Cox was a former socialist, later Free Trader, and a former editor of the *Edinburgh Review,* a leading opponent of the pre-war Liberal reforms. He continued to write on the iniquities of unemployment benefit in the *Morning Post* and later in the *Daily Telegraph* with which it was incorporated in 1937.

57. More generally see MacLeod (1968) and MacNicol (1978, 1981) for evidence of the Treasury's role in sanctioning family allowances as a measure to preserve 'less eligibility' rather than to relieve family poverty.

58. A *Telegraph* editorial 'Scandal of Poor Relief' (16 February 1922) makes most of the more general points afloat in public debate at the time. 'We are in danger of creating . . . conditions in which it pays better for many a man to be idle than to work, even on full-time . . . The self-respecting and hard-working man knows very well that the flat rate of out-relief is fundamentally wrong. It is paid not only to the deserving but to the loafer . . . This system is contributing not merely to moral decadence but to national pauperism . . .', etc.

59. The full story for 1921—1931 is admirably told in Deacon (1976).

60. Not without considerable opposition, particularly to the rule that allowed benefit to foreigners. Viscount Ednam told the House: 'It is intolerable that these aliens should be allowed to come over here and be kept in idleness largely at the expense of the British taxpayer' (H. C. *Hansard,* Vol. 172, Col. 340).

61. Keynes called the report 'the most foolish document I ever had the misfortune to read'. In quoting this comment Taylor adds his own view of it as 'a report compounded of prejudice, ignorance, and panic' (Taylor, 1970, p. 363).

62. For example, 'There is only one thing which will impress the people who know in this country and abroad, and that is the sight of the axe honestly laid at the roots of the upas-tree of colossal expenditure which the nation cannot afford . . . Instructed public opinion will trust

the new Government and not be moved by the threatening invective of those who hope to find their best rallying cry in "Hands off the Dole" (*Daily Telegraph*, 21 and 25 August 1931).

63. The story is told by the NUWM leader in Hannington (1973).

64. See letter by Lascelles Abercrombie *et al., Manchester Guardian* 24 February 1934. For background on political and police responses to the hunger marches in the 1932—1936 period see Hayburn (1972). In February 1934, *The Daily Telegraph* assured its readers 'this march is organised by the Communists and does not represent a genuine working-class movement' (6 February 1934). *The Times* (19 February 1934) in a leader on the marchers thundered mildly that 'the general good sense of the country is revolted by this shameless manoeuvre to make political capital out of the individual hardships of unemployed people'. With a general strike raging in France and howitzers being used on socialists in Austria it was a timely piece of reassurance.

65. A *Times* leader (22 February 1938) 'Idle and Content' argued that 'there are hundreds and thousands of young men who do not show any disposition to bestir themselves to get out of unemployment into employment . . . In a considerable number of the chronically or constantly unemployed young men there is a slackness of moral fibre and of will as much of muscle . . . an act of justice to the honest and unfortunate workman can be abused by the malingerer and the shiftless . . . The personal welfare of the Shirkers themselves and the credit of the assistance scheme and its honest dependents alike require that a notorious abuse should be remedied'.

66. Work on the social impact of pre-war broadcasting has barely begun. However, in an invaluable article Scannell describes the BBC's tentative dabbling with social issues in the 1930s, in which he identifies the 'exclusion of the unemployed, its concealments and evasions, its transformation of the problem into an exercise in good neighbour-liness'. The BBC saw its job as remoralising the unemployed and encouraging people to befriend and assist them, and soon retreated with its fingers burned from early attempts at social documentary (Scannell, 1980). We are grateful to Paddy Scannell for use of a pre-publication version of this article.

67. This is one of the central arguments in Middlemas (1979).

II   Fourth Estate and Welfare State

Hitherto, while one-half of civilization has always been in a mess, the other half has run the papers; and so matters have been kept in decent darkness. [*George Bernard Shaw,* Pall Mall Gazette, *11 February 1886*]

In the following three chapters we discuss the ways in which the welfare and social security apparatus is routinely portrayed in the mass media. In chapter 3, after a case study to identify the issues, we apply the quantitative techniques of content analysis to calibrate the extent, nature and emphases of news about welfare. Chapter 4 enlarges on these findings by examining the themes that can be detected throughout such material. In chapter 5 we ask why news about welfare and social security should be as it is. For our evidence we turn, in the main, to those responsible for the production of news. Social security and its appendages are not major obsessions of the news media, but for many people, including the welfare state's clientele, the media remain a major source of the concepts, values and images by which they make sense of their direct or indirect experiences of the welfare state. In Part II we attempt to discover the precise form and origin of this imagery.

CHAPTER 3

Exorcising Demons: The Detection and Trial of the Sturdy Beggar

The media do not invent social concerns, nor do they deliberately organise the priorities in public debate. But in particular periods of real social change they cut through popular uncertainties with a display of the political eternal verities around which social consensus is sustained. The period we examined in particular detail, 1976, was 'the year of the cuts'—a label applied without the benefit of prevision. Major reductions in public services were announced in February, July and December, the earliest of these reducing previously planned programmes by £4,595 million. It became orthodoxy that the social services should 'share the burden' at a time of national economic misfortune.

Against this background, and the growing unemployment figures, the increasing evidence of recession needed explanation, a task for which the news media are strategically placed. The period produced a shrill and mounting antagonism to the welfare system and its clients, focused in particular on what Deacon (1978) has aptly termed 'scroungerphobia'. The period seemed to fit well into the pattern Cohen has called a 'moral panic', in which 'A condition, episode, person, or group of persons emerges to become defined as a threat to societal values or interests' (1972, p. 28; see also Popay, 1977). The notion of a moral panic suggests a sudden and novel eruption of demonology. We are arguing that, at least in the context of poverty and welfare, the process is much more the recurrent refurbishing of a series of images and beliefs that have a historical continuity and that lie very shallowly below a veneer of apparent 'welfare consensus'.

We have identified three stages by which this exhumation of ideologically functional images occurs. In the first, a precipitating event sensitises the media so that their surveillance procedures and journalistic categories are sharpened to capture similar subsequent events and give them considerable prominence. Second, the ensuing period evokes a steady stream of previously latent mythologies about the 'social problem' thus dramatically 'uncovered'. Third, the legislative, administrative and possibly judicial responses to this cultural thrust reinforce its potency and provide a real shift in the structure of state responses to the definitions provided by the moral panic. These responses in turn provide news material and confirmation of the arrival of a new matter of concern on the political agenda. In the period we examined this led an initial orchestrated indignation about welfare abuse to be broadened into a general scepticism about the purposes and extent of social security, and in turn to a strengthening of the role of the welfare apparatus itself as a mechanism for policing the poor.

The unveiling of latent belief systems is led by an initial precipitating event of sufficient dramatic power to orchestrate a number of the themes that become the leitmotivs of ensuing debate. In an examination of crime news, Chibnall locates such an event in the shooting of three policemen in Shepherd's Bush in London in August 1966. The consequent concern with the increase in criminal violence in British society, and more generally what Chibnall calls 'The Violent Society theme', gave a cultural homogeneity to news coverage of a range of subsequent events, linking the Krays with football hooliganism, student protest, teenage violence and political activism (Chibnall, 1977, pp. 84—8). Hall and his colleagues have described a similar sequence, setting the career of the label 'mugging' in its origins from transatlantic import to its precipitation as a scene-setting theme by the coverage of a lethal attack on an elderly widower in London in August 1972, and a similar violent robbery of a man walking home from a pub in Birmingham in November the same year (Hall *et al.*, 1978, pp. 3, 81—8). The precipitating event in our period was the trial of a 42-year-old unemployed Liverpudlian, Derek Peter Deevy, at Liverpool Crown Court in July 1976.

PRECIPITATION: THE CROWNING OF 'KING CON'

Deevy's was the case that launched a thousand clippings. He was charged with three specimen indictments of obtaining supplementary benefits by deception, the three charges totalling about £57. The total overpayment mentioned in the charge was £500, and it is worth remembering that this was the only figure substantiated in the trial, although Deevy's claims of £36,000 fraudently claimed, which may or may not have been extravagant exaggeration, came to exert a hypnotic effect over Judge and media alike. Deevy pleaded guilty and was sentenced to two years for each of the three indictments, to be served consecutively.

Media coverage of the case was extensive and hysterical. We obtained a copy of the transcript of the trial proceedings to compare with this coverage. What we expected to find was a systematic and selective distortion of a kind familiar to media researchers under the label of unwitting bias or 'inferential structures'. That is to say, journalists will view an event through the prism of their knowledge of previous, apparently similar events, and their expectations act as a template in producing news about the later event. This is normally explained in terms of the demands of journalistic routines, and the exigencies of production and presentation of news.[1] In fact, when we looked carefully at the trial transcript, we found the trial to be quite accurately reported. Media and court alike had shared in borrowing prevailing and dominant beliefs about the welfare state, and in so doing had amplified and relayed them through the reinforcing system of the media. Five such beliefs appeared frequently in the trial proceedings. First, like the social explorers of the last century (see Keating, 1976, pp. 11—32), the lawyers in the case showed a distaste mixed with righteous ignorance of the world of welfare institutions. Second, the social security system was repeatedly attacked for its ineptitude as a watchdog of the public purse, while Deevy was elevated into the role of a social benefactor for his boastful revelations of the soft, open-hearted and lax system he had exploited. Third, a major refrain was the notion that Deevy was, as the Judge put it, 'the tip of a national scandal', though the court had it both ways by also insisting that this was an outrageous case, the like of which had never been seen. Fourth, despite confusion about the actual sums involved, Deevy's luxurious life-style was lengthily discussed and illustrated. Finally, there was anxiety that welfare was too easy to get, expressed in concern that publicity for the trial might encourage imitation and reveal Deevy's methods. We can follow the story as it picks up these themes.

Luxurious life-styles

Every story made sure to mention cigars, suits and indolent comfort. For some time this was paramount. The *Daily Telegraph,* which had two separate stories the same day, headlined one '£10,000-a-year life-style for Dole Fiddler', opening its coverage by noting Deevy's life of splendour. The *Sun* front-page headline, '£36,000 Scrounger' was followed by an underlined sub-headline, 'Six years for Dole Cheat Who Spent £25 a week on the Best Cigars'. The *Daily Express* coined the epithet King Con, and above their front-page headline 'Incredible Reign of King Con' was a strap, '£200-a-week tycoon on social security'. The story gave great prominence to the Judge's remarks about people asking 'what's the good of working?' The *Daily Mail* front-page story 'Biggest Scrounger of the Lot' also drew attention to Deevy's Corona cigars and expensive suits. The *Daily Mirror* lead story 'King of the Dole Queue Scroungers' (a phrase clearly implying a host of like followers) began 'Nothing was too good for Derek Deevy. His weekly cigar bill came to £25 and he regularly bought expensive suits. The fact that he was out of work didn't spoil his life at the top'. There is little doubt that however little the average reader knew about the real extent of social security abuse, or about the size of unclaimed benefits, he certainly knew the cost of Derek Deevy's Corona cigars.

Cartoons are an especially effective and economical way of capturing stereotypes and injecting them firmly into popular demonology. The luxurious life of claimants like Deevy was a rich vein for the cartoonists. Giles in the *Daily Express* (15 July 1976) had an irritated but clearly well-fed elderly patron at an opulent garden party retorting to a smirking fellow-guest, 'I resent that remark, Harry! I do NOT do it all on Social Security'. Franklin in the *Sun* the same day had five dishevelled merry-makers gorging themselves on champagne and caviar in a Rolls-Royce labelled 'Social Security Beano for Fiddlers'. They are singing (a rare moment of humour) 'Oh you Beautiful Dole, You Great Big Beautiful Dole'. In case we miss the point the car is being driven between a doorstep-scrubbing housewife and two astonished, sweating, road-labourers.

The *Daily Express* editorial the next day pointed the moral: 'It is no use inviting people to work harder for the country if they feel, with justice, that the product of their effort, in part, is going to cigars and drinks and a good tax-free life for bums'. A week later in the *Express* this had been generalised. Below an editorial commenting on the latest unemployment figures (1,463,456, though 'many of these people are not unemployed in any serious sense') another editorial recalled the Deevy case and repeated the demand for a thorough investigation. But now it was a demand that went beyond investigation of illegality: '. . . there is a strong case for the view that the whole system needs to be looked at again. Even the perfectly legal largesse looks excessive.'

How many more?

Deevy was immediately enthroned as King of a teeming population of scroungers and spongers. His trial and conviction were confirmation of the suspicions voiced earlier by Conservative MP Iain Sproat. The question, how many others?, seemed always to be rhetorical, inviting the reader to nod knowingly in affirmation of the suspicion that prompted the question.

The *Daily Express* (14 July) carried a centre-page feature by Iain Sproat headed 'I believe we have seen only the tip of the iceberg', which recounted the by now familiar tales from Mr Sproat's postbag to illustrate his point that the Deevy case exploded 'the myth that abuse of the welfare system is some minimal problem'. The *Daily Mirror* began to gather in the evidence in a story (15 July) headed 'Doing the Scrounge Rounds'. This featured four cases (three in Manchester) of people 'On the Scrounge'. Given this massive evidence it was no surprise to learn in the first line of the story that 'Britain's army of dole-queue swindlers were on the run last night as a Government Minister warned he was going gunning for them'.

A variant on this theme derived from the trial is the contribution Deevy had made in shedding light on this unsavoury den of parasites and their cunning manipulations. Cartoons are again best at distilling this cultural brew. Cummings in the *Daily Express* (16 July 1976) had a queue of bowler-hatted gents from top companies waiting outside Deevy's cell. The jailor (whose colleague's newspaper is studded with Deevy's references, 'inventive', brilliant with figures', and so on) is telling them, 'You'll have to be patient! He's now being interviewed by Dennis Healey for a job at the Treasury when he leaves prison . . .' Waite in the *Mirror* had a related idea. An anxious Deevy is sitting at a desk worriedly working on piles of claim forms and files, while his tea-bearing wife warns him, '141 Social Security false names and addresses—why don't you get a job and take things easy?' The *Sun* characteristically got the domestic view of Deevy the hero, quoting his wife on 'the frustrated genius' of her husband. The *Daily Telegraph* was equally complimentary in its editorial of 15 July: '. . . the full inquiry into the Social Security system obviously carried out by DEEVY, the Fiddler of Genius, was a timely, if expensive, public service'.

Social security is a soft touch

Not only had our welfare state been shown to be distributing largesse on a mammoth scale, but was obviously doing so with a minimum of control. Staffed with naive bureaucrats who have none of the worldly cynicism of the press to protect them from the guile of men like Deevy, the social security system is an open treasure house without a doorkeeper. A *Sun* editorial gasped that 'The men from the Ministry (alias the taxpayers) didn't even seem to look up as they shelled out the cash'. The *Daily Mail* story (14 July) headed 'Biggest Scrounger of the Lot', described how Deevy 'milked' the system. The cartoon by Mac in the *Mail* the following day had a cigar-chomping claimant, dolly bird by his side, standing impatiently at the DHSS counter while his chauffeur-driven car waits outside. He is telling the counter-clerk, who is counting out piles of banknotes for him, 'Do hurry up—I've got twenty-six other labour exchanges to get to today y'know'. It is, in fact, extremely rare for cash to be handed over counters in either Employment Exchanges or Social Security offices, and has been so for many years. The image of banknotes being 'shelled-out' is a powerful one, however.

Time to clamp-down: the politicians speak

If we are dealing with 'A National Scandal', then the shift to the political arena will not be far behind. Ministers are forced to defend the existing arrangements, thereby confirming the need for control mechanisms rather than denying the extent of abuse. If the problem is defined, not as inadequate provision or complex administration, but as undue liberality, the solution automatically must lie in further policing of potential abuse.

Most media shifted their attention quickly away from the unseemly practices in the homes of the poor or the DHSS offices they plagued, to the more familiar battle-ground of party politics. In the *Daily Express* (14 July) it was 'Crack-down on Scroungers

Call by Angry M.P.s'; in the *Sun* (14 July) 'Angry M.P.s Demand a Big Probe'; in the *Telegraph,* 'Tory Storm Over £36,000 Dole Fiddle'. The demand for a public inquiry was almost universal, though there was almost no mention of the Fisher Committee, which only three years earlier had concluded its extensive report on social security abuse with the view that the problem was relatively negligible. The shift from the trial, via an unquestioned generalisation that here was an instance of a general problem, to the arena of public debate in party politics is a routine of news production. It is familiar to students of news in other areas like race relations or trade unions, or of news in general. In transferring the attention of news consumers to the terrain most central to routine news collection and production, it confirms the existence of a general phenomenon as 'a national scandal' or as a problem to be solved, and equally legitimises the solution of that problem in the actions of the state—tightening up, clamping down, and so on. The next two themes illustrate further how this appears.

The deserving must be sorted from the undeserving

As we see below, much of the post-Deevy debate involved a public reclarification of the classic distinction between the deserving and the undeserving poor. By extension this becomes a redrawing of the boundaries of citizenship, inside which reside the honest, the taxpayer and the deserving poor, while outside reside the undeserving, dishonest spongers and scroungers, as well as other deviant or suspect groups.

In coverage of the Deevy case this theme appeared mainly in editorials and the quoted speeches of politicians. The Social Services Secretary David Ennals, hard-pressed and defensive, was widely quoted in this vein: 'The ordinary tax-payer is entitled to insist that benefits go to those they are intended for, and not swindlers and criminals.' Iain Sproat's claim that half the people claiming unemployment benefits were not in fact unemployed, nailed the label firmly on this group in particular—the cigar smoking, liquor swigging good-life bums of the *Express* editorial.

Lynda Lee-Porter in the *Daily Mail,* in a column that frequently gives voice to populist cries of righteous indignation, illustrated the deserving/undeserving divide (14 July): 'The philanthropic social security have after all cushioned and accustomed out-of-work labourer Derek Deevy to a life of luxury for seven years.' Lynda's dad, it appears, used to walk three miles to collect her grandad's pit pension. As her dad is a proud man who would starve rather than take social security, '. . . I feel I've got the right to condemn the scroungers'. To show the heart beneath the stern exterior Lynda tells us she disagrees with Sir Keith Joseph—people *do* live in 'slummy slutty conditions' and there really is poverty. 'The ordinary decent kindly majority of us know there are people who need help. We want them to have it. We only get resentful and bitter when we see it going to the able-bodied, parasite, malingerers.'

Fighting the good fight: the armies line-up

Prominent and recurrent among the imagery of the post-Deevy coverage was that of armies, fighting and battles. As we shall see later, this is an important part of the rhetoric that establishes the claimant as outsider, or even enemy, of the nation. The most spectacular battle-cry was in the *Daily Express* on 15 July. Blazoned across the front page in huge capitals was the headline 'Get the Scroungers'. The report, based around Secretary of State David Ennals' promise to 'crack down as hard as we can on all forms of Social Security fraud', reports on fraud statistics and suggests 'Civil Service union leaders are angry that Social Security investigators will be hit by coming Government cuts'. (In fact the union had protested about the cut in officers available for house visits. Special Investigators have consistently been one of the few areas of expansion). A week later, in the *Express,* readers were writing to complain about 'the King Con Brigade' (20 July). As the battle-dust died down the lines of the ensuing campaign had been clearly drawn. The fight was to draw on a lot of old battle manuals and war-cries as it progressed.

Before providing more quantitative analysis of welfare and social security news, a final footnote to the Deevy case bears mentioning. On the same day as the main Deevy coverage (14 July) came the news that the general manager of the Wakefield Building Society had been suspended from his post, while police were called in to investigate a previously undiscovered loss of £600,000. The fraud, for such it was, disappeared beneath the enormity of Derek Deevy's outrages. It made page nine in the *Daily Express,* page five in the *Daily Mirror,* page fourteen in the *Daily Mail,* and page seven in the *Sun.* The case was ironically parallel to Deevy's. The fraud had given the manager an income of £10,000 per year, most of which had gone on gambling. The sentence was six years. Yet all of this information could only be found on an inside page of *The Times* at the time of sentencing, where it was one of eighteen stories on the page (17 January 1978).

We have discussed the Deevy case in considerable detail for two reasons. First it illustrates most of the themes that echoed through the ensuing scroungerphobia period. Second it reveals the mechanics by which a single event is translated by a series of institutional manipulations into a general cultural obsession. Authoritative sources, here the courts and parliament, are the original definers of popular concern and a national sense of right and proper attitudes. The media selectively relay, simplify and colour these in the light of historically derived popular mythology and demonology. Thus does a ruling ideology become popular indignation.

COUNTING THE COST: AN ANALYSIS OF WELFARE NEWS

Content analysis is an economical method for charting the major categories of news that appear over a period of time. It is not a subtle technique and makes no pretence at capturing the nuances that permeate any piece of prose. It does, however, provide a reliable statistical summary of the prominent features of news coverage. To provide such a summary we analysed a randomly chosen period to assess media coverage of welfare and social security news. The period analysed was the second half of 1976 (5 July to 24 December inclusive). All national newspapers were included other than the *Morning Star* and *Financial Times*. In addition, the sample included the local papers in the two cities in which the survey research described in part III was conducted, viz. the *Leicester Mercury* and *Sunderland Echo*. As well as newspapers, the analysis looked at local radio in the two cities (BBC Radio Leicester, BBC Radio Newcastle and Radio Metro, the Newcastle-based commercial local radio station). Finally the main evening television news bulletins of ITN and BBC1 were analysed. In all, then, fourteen media were included in the analysis.

To avoid losing running stories, every day in the sample period was included, but weekends were omitted. The sample period thus comprised 125 days, and consequently, in theory, 1,750 newspapers or broadcast bulletins. In practice this number was slightly reduced by strikes and other interruptions to production.[2]

The initial task was to decide which stories were to be included in our sample. The instruction given to coders defined the area of interest as 'all stories dealing with aspects of welfare as defined by the responsibilities of the Secretary of State for Social Services. This means local authority social services and social security. Excluded by this definition are, inter alia, education, housing, health, and all Home Office related services. However, stories in these four which are predominantly about welfare aspects within such fields, for example free school meals, school health and specific health benefits such as free prescriptions, rent and rate rebates, and so on are to be included. There will certainly be marginal cases which will have to be judged individually, the main criterion for inclusion being that the story should mainly be about the administration, use, politics, or provision of welfare.' The unit for coding was the news story. This excluded (for the purposes of the quantitative analysis) features, editorials, cartoons, letters, reports of parliamentary proceedings in daily debates columns, and formal law reports. The final sample included 1,063 items.

Our first finding was that welfare is not big news. The number of items culled in this period, despite the wide definition used, was less than the number of separate newspapers or broadcast bulletins examined. This is despite the fact that the period chosen turned out to be a comparatively heavy news period for welfare and social security. Social security abuse became a major issue following the attention given to the Deevy case in July. Consequently considerable news mileage was obtained from the publication of the Supplementary Benefits Commission annual report in September, and the uprating of benefits in November. Despite the emphasis given to these issues in this period it is nonetheless apparent that the subjects of social services and social security are not the stuff of which news is made.[3]

In the period we studied, stories about social security and welfare comprised roughly a third of all social policy stories. This proportion was generally lower in local media, which give more attention to education, housing and other matters with considerable local authority interest.

The major conclusion, however, is that social policy as a whole is not a major news subject, and social security and welfare even less so. The importance of this will become more apparent in the next two chapters. Our argument will be that welfare is news when it obtrudes into other news areas—crime, sex, political conflict. This skews attention in welfare news toward some aspects of social policy rather than others. One result of this is that social policy news is given greater prominence in the 'popular' media. Roughly twice the proportion of stories reached the front page in popular papers as in the *Times* and *Guardian.* The *Daily Express* put 31.3 per cent of welfare stories on its front page, including 13.4 per cent that were lead stories. In the *Times* and *Guardian,* however, less than 10 per cent of stories were on the front pages, despite the higher number of stories carried by the more densely packed front news pages of the 'heavies'. Here again is circumstantial evidence for the view that social security and welfare make news when they are packaged in the news values of popular journalism rather than because of their intrinsic importance.

A closer look at the type of stories given prominence shows two areas to be dominant: unemployment benefit and social security abuse. Of all stories in our sample that made the lead in their medium, 21.1 per cent involved legal proceedings about social security abuse cases. Of the various claimant groups represented in stories, either individually or collectively, the unemployed featured in 40.5 per cent of lead stories and 37.9 per cent of other front page stories (or second or third stories in broadcast bulletins). When welfare becomes big news it is more likely to be the transgressions of the unemployed that have made it so than any other subject category.

The news items were analysed to show what kinds of welfare become news stories. Not surprisingly the vast labyrinthine apparatus of the welfare state is given uneven coverage. The news media provide news, not documentation of social policy. For this reason it is news values not social values that shape coverage of welfare, leading to an emphasis on areas of contention or appeal rather than socially significant matter. To examine this hypothesis we looked at the types of welfare prominent in news coverage.

The emphasis is on the major nationally administered benefits rather than on local social services, except in the local media, although even here less attention is given to local welfare provision than might be expected. National Insurance benefits get rather more attention than supplementary benefits, and unemployment benefits accounted for 62.5 per cent of National Insurance stories. Of supplementary benefit stories, 67.8 per cent were not explicitly about any sub-group of benefits, while 31.2 per cent dealt with allowances—the benefits paid to people below retirement age—and only 1.0 per cent dealt with supplementary pensions. Very few stories dealt with family allowances (or Child Interim Benefit),[4] even though these are the most widely received welfare benefits. In 1975/76 family allowances accounted for £532 million of public expenditure compared to £1,187 million spent on supplementary benefits. Pensions, despite their relative neglect in the news, cost £1,578 million, whereas unemployment benefit cost less than a sixteenth of this figure, £214 million. Stories dealing with low pay or Family Income Supplement, the benefit intended to assist low wage earners with families, were also scarce. Thus, of contributory benefits, greatest attention is given to unemployment benefits, while among non-contributory benefits the focus is on people below pension age (although until very recently the majority of supplementary benefit recipients has consisted of pensioners). This is confirmed if we look at the range of claimant groups represented. The unemployed are given greatest coverage while the low paid are relatively invisible. The *Times* and *Guardian* were the only national media to give consistent coverage to the disabled, while devoting less frequent attention to the unemployed than the 'populars'. Overall, the distribution confirms the general observation that news attention stresses areas that are problematic or dramatic—a news value rather than a social value.

To give a more complete picture we analysed the kinds of events that made news in the area of social security and welfare. As with other categories of news, formal routine events predominate. Legislation, the publication of reports, or statements (normally from press conferences or press releases) make up the bulk of stories. A closer look at these categories makes this clearer. Of the stories dealing with legislation, more dealt with existing welfare law than with changes or with calls for or opposition to change. The statements and reports were mainly from government, or from government figures; 17.3 per cent of all stories were based on such pronouncements. Very few such statements or reports were attributable to social workers (only 2.3 per cent of all stories) or trade unions (3.0 per cent). Administration was a major component in 40.3 per cent of all stories, and of these finance (13.3 per cent) and organisation (9.9 per cent) were the major sub-categories.

The most striking figure is the proportion of stories dealing with the trial, conviction or prosecution for fraud of social security claimants. No fewer than 30.8 per cent of all stories dealt in some way or other with social security abuse, and 12.6 per cent with legal proceedings. In other words, one in eight of all stories in all media during this six-month period that were about social services, welfare or social security, dealt with the criminal proceedings consequent on social security abuse. This figure was highest in the *Daily Telegraph,* the *Sun* and *Leicester Mercury,* lowest in broadcasting and the *Guardian.* We shall look more closely at this extraordinary finding below.

A second way of assessing the type of stories in our sample was to look at who were the major figures to feature in them. Studies of news generally demonstrate a concentration on elite figures and especially on those people who seek exposure, such as leading politicians (see, for example, Golding and Elliott, 1979, pp. 159— 63). The Secretary of State for Social Services appeared in 11.3 per cent of all stories in our period (14.3 per cent of stories in national media). Other politicians were well to the fore. Ministers appeared in 10.4 per cent of all stories, the 'government' as a corporate entity in 9.9 per cent and MPs in 10.9 per cent of stories. In local media, councillors managed to feature in 12.4 per cent of stories. Surprisingly, local MPs seldom appeared, suggesting this is not a subject area in which they are notably active or vociferous locally. Pressure groups are an important news source, and made appearances in 19.5 per cent of all stories, mainly as producers of reports (29.8 per cent of stories involving pressure groups). Top of the pressure-group league table was the Child Poverty Action Group (4.9 per cent of all stories)—the *Guardian, Times* and *Daily Mirror* accounting for most of its appearances.

Other than the spectacular overspills into crime news, then, social security and welfare news is framed by the activities of government and political leaders on the one hand, and the reports and actions of the more strenuous pressure groups in the field on the other. This latter source, however, has little impact on broadcasting or the more conservative newspapers apart from the *Times.*

News stories tend both to create and reflect current themes or issues in any given subject area. For events to be recognisable as news or 'newsworthy' they must resonate with ideas of acknowledged interest. By emphasising some such themes rather than others, news concentrates attention in such a way as actually to define the perspectives from which we view social events and processes. In preparing the content analysis schedule, we located thirty-two such themes that seemed to occur most frequently in preliminary and pilot analyses. These were introduced into the coding schedule, and coders were instructed as follows: 'Story themes should be coded regardless of support for or discrediting of the theme in the story, but merely to register its appearance "on the agenda". The theme should be clearly implicit in the story but need not be referred to explicitly by the labels we are using here. However, it should be present in the text, not merely available to a reading of the "deep structure" of the item. If referred to, e.g. by one story source, but denied by another it still gets coded.' Coders were given a clear explanation of what was meant by, and could be included in, each theme label. By far the most important themes were those involving abuse of welfare and social security. Such abuse either involved actual fraud (illegal claiming, for example of supplementary benefits while working or from more than one address) or excessive, though legal, claiming—more popularly characterised as sponging. Whether the subtle distinction between scrounging on the one hand and sponging on the other is a major category in popular thought or not, it was a convenient distinction within the content analysis. Fraud (in 17.8 per cent of all stories) and sponging (16.6 per cent) were paramount in news coverage in this period. We shall look at these themes in more detail before looking more generally at the statistical summary of other themes.

Stories about 'abuse' or that involved aspects of abuse were 30.8 per cent of the total. The largest category, as we have seen, was the routine coverage of court cases, followed by stories reporting politicians' statements complaining about the extent of abuse or ritually denouncing some new manifestation of it. The period of our analysis was rich for such stories. Many now see this period, with hindsight, as the peak of a campaign against social security claimants. The 'welfare backlash' was certainly whipped up by the frequent and widely publicised, though largely groundless, statements of Iain Sproat, Conservative MP for Aberdeen South. We shall examine this more fully in the next chapter and in chapter 6. As the survey analysis of questionnaire responses will suggest (see chapter 6), although the pitch and vigour of the public antipathy to welfare may have been heightened in this period, the backlash was merely an exacerbation of more persistent values and beliefs. The content analysis period was selected before it became apparent that we were entering a spell of public flagellation of the welfare state and its clients. However, the result was probably to enlarge certain categories of anti-welfare news rather than to discover new ones. If the above argument is correct, the analysis of this period will show more clearly the categories within which unsympathetic coverage of welfare news occurs, but will not significantly distort the extent to which such news is distributed in these categories.

Court proceedings are a case in point. The routine coverage of court cases will always throw up the regular social security fraud, or marital cases that have social security aspects. This is a fact of news production routines, not of selective perception created by a welfare backlash. Such cases continued to appear with their usual regularity long after the 1976 'scroungerphobia' period, particularly in local media for which court proceedings are a staple diet.

An aspect of exaggeration of routine news is the prominence given to abuse stories. Over a third (37.8 per cent) of such stories were front-page items or in the first three stories in broadcast bulletins, including 11.3 per cent that were lead stories. This category included many of the more spectacular scroungerphobia stories, which will be examined in the next chapter.

Finally, it is important to note some of the variation between media in the presentation of abuse stories. Here, as elsewhere, it is necessary to separate the *Daily Telegraph* from the other 'quality' dailies. Conventionally it is bracketed with the *Times* and *Guardian*. Its coverage of welfare news, however, is much closer to that of the populars, particularly the *Mail, Sun* and *Express*. On subjects like this the *Telegraph* is populist rather than popular, and certainly requires separate treatment. No fewer than 43.7 per cent of *Telegraph* stories contained explicit reference to social security abuse, including nearly one in five (18.5 per cent) based on court proceedings. The *Telegraph*'s diligent and extensive reporting of crime news, whether from Press Association reports, stringers or its own correspondents, accounts for this massive total. In fact the *Telegraph* alone accounted for 18.7 per cent of court case stories and 17.9 per cent of all abuse stories in our sample. For *Telegraph* readers the world of social welfare is populated by the criminally indigent being brought to justice. The populars (*Mail, Mirror, Sun* and *Express*) have an even higher average than the *Telegraph*. Nearly half (48.2 per cent) of their welfare stories dealt to a greater or lesser extent with abuse. These four papers differed little in this proportion, ranging from 45.2 per cent in the *Mirror* to 53.4 per cent in the *Sun*. Local newspapers had a much lower figure, though this disguises the fact that the *Leicester Mercury* carried a proportion of such stories (23.7 per cent) nearly twice as high as the *Sunderland Echo* (13.6 per cent). In the broadcast media we are dealing with much smaller figures, but the evidence shows the more popular medium of television to have a higher proportion of abuse stories.

By contrast with fraud and sponging stories, other themes do not surface so frequently. Finance is the exception. Coders recorded this theme for all stories 'about the (problematic, high, rising) costs of welfare, reference to difficulty in maintaining services in a period of inflation, the need for economy or cuts, the general problem of high public expenditure, etc.' Because of debate about the cuts in expenditure on public services announced in February, July and December 1976, the theme of financial stringency predictably weaved its way through a large proportion of stories, being detected as explicit in about a quarter of all news items (24.1 per cent).

On the other hand, several important themes in general discussions of the welfare state were given very little news coverage. The low take-up of means-tested benefits was mentioned in only 3.8 per cent of stories for example. In general, those themes emphasising legal or financial aspects were more frequent than social or political themes. Once again, some interesting variations between media appear. The inefficiency of welfare services (mainly in terms of their inability to control spending or their excessive administrative costs or methods) was mentioned in 8.6 per cent of stories, a figure that rose to 14.9 per cent in the *Daily Mail.*

Some themes attach to stories about particular groups of welfare claimants. This becomes clear if we look at the three commonest themes, beginning with finance. Of all stories invoking this theme, 15.2 per cent dealt with unemployment benefit. Looked at the other way, 32.5 per cent of stories mentioning unemployment benefit were coded as having the finance theme. Unemployment benefit is also strongly related to the fraud theme, accounting for 15.9 per cent of stories in which it appears. Conversely, the theme of fraud was present in 25 per cent of all unemployment benefit stories. Supplementary benefits also attract the fraud theme, accounting for 26.5 per cent of the stories in which the theme appears (all but one of these stories related to supplementary allowances rather than pensions—in other words to benefit paid to people below pensionable age). The converse figure is even more stark here, showing that the fraud theme was present in 53.2 per cent of supplementary allowance stories. No other category of benefit attracted similar association with fraud (though 14.3 per cent of sickness benefit stories did). In sum, fraud was most likely to be mentioned in cases involving the unemployed or people under pension age claiming supplementary benefits. In the latter group, half the stories dealt in some way with fraud.[5]

The third major theme, sponging, was defined for our coders as 'stories containing reference to unjustified, though not necessarily illegal, dependency on welfare'. As we have seen, it was picked up in roughly one in six of all stories. Unemployment benefit stories accounted for 31.6 per cent of these, supplementary allowances for 24.9 per cent.

SUMMARY

Discussion of the Derek Deevy case showed how a single event can precipitate latent belief systems into public debate if given sufficient articulate prominence by institutions of cultural centrality like the courts and parliament. If sufficiently well rooted in popular mythology, these belief systems facilitate a period of orchestrated moral indignation, as economic uncertainty is explained away in stark, simple and plausible accounts of social deviance that speak to the real anxieties and experiences of a large number of people. The media serve to dramatise and serialise these accounts. Our quantitative analysis shows that welfare and social security is not a major area of news coverage. When it is reported it receives greater prominence in the popular press, particularly when satisfying journalistic demands for crime news or political conflict. The unemployed and unemployment benefits receive most widespread reporting; low pay and child benefits least. The emphasis is on routine news derived from official statements or reports, with considerable attention being given to relevant government leaders. 'Abuse' of social security, either by fraud or putative excessive claiming, is a major theme of news coverage and is given great prominence.[6] Other significant news themes stress the financial difficulty for the nation in providing welfare, rather than the problems faced by people living on social security.

The analysis shows a coherent distrust of the welfare and social security system and its clientele. In chapter 4 we examine more broadly the ideologies involved. The Deevy case, and the 1975—6 recession more generally, declared open season on the welfare state. But the ammunition used was of an old and tried calibre. Underneath the acrid 'scroungerphobia' of the late 1970s was the musty odour of the workhouse.

NOTES

1. The seminal work is Lang and Lang (1955). See also Halloran *et al.*
   (1970) and the discussion in Golding and Elliott (1979) Ch. 2. A more
   detailed account of the trial appears in the research report on which
   this chapter is based, available from the authors.
2. For reasons of space we have been unable to include tables of results;
   these are obtainable from the authors.
3. A survey for the Royal Commission on the Press found that social
   policy news was only 3 to 4 per cent of all news in their analysis period,
   despite their fairly broad definition (McQuail, 1977).
4. The period of our analysis was in the switchover period from family
   allowances to child benefits (the latter replacing family allowances and
   child tax allowances). Child Interim Benefit was paid to single parents
   in this period, preparatory to the introduction of the Child Benefit
   Increase for single parents.
5. In fact these are not necessarily the groups most involved in what fraud
   there is within supplementary benefits. One of the more common areas
   within the limited extent of 'fraud' is the inadvertent failure by
   pensioners to disclose resources that are later recovered from their
   estates after death.
6. For the view that our results do not show an undue concern with abuse
   see Lythgoe (1979), and for a reply Golding and Middleton (1979).

CHAPTER 4

Dismantling the Welfare Consensus

The Deevy story in July 1976 opened the floodgates. All the pent-up anxieties and prejudices fomented by recession, unemployment, dropping tax thresholds and growing economic uncertainty burst through in a great surge of anti-welfare cant and venom. Very quickly there was a shift of targets. Initially news was concerned with fraud—its extent and the threat it posed to tax-payers and the moral welfare of the genuine claimant. Later this changed to a concern with the welfare system more generally—its generosity, inefficiency, laxity and cost. What started as an anxiety about abuse of the welfare state by excessive or illegal exploitation of it, was turned rapidly into a more general suspicion of the entire apparatus and the philosophy on which it is constructed.

In this chapter we examine this shift by exploring the themes that dominated welfare and social security news in the second half of the 1970s. We isolated five major themes over this period.

THEME 1: THE TIP OF THE ICEBERG

1a. Widespread abuse

After Deevy the labels and prejudices created by the case began to embrace much routine reporting of criminal proceedings. This is a common observation in media analysis. An event precipitates concern about a new, usually threatening phenomenon, and subsequent quite disparate events are sought, recognised and portrayed in line with the expectations aroused by this signal event. The process has been plotted in coverage of various social episodes, from 'mugging' (see S. Hall *et al.*, 1978) to Mods and Rockers (Cohen, 1972). In examining the latter, Stan Cohen has neatly described this as a moral panic in reaction to a folk devil. He summarises the process as follows:

(i) the putative deviation had been assigned from which further stereotyping, myth-making and labelling could proceed; (ii) the expectation was created that this form of deviation would certainly recur; (iii) a wholly negative symbolization in regard to the Mods and Rockers and objects associated with them had been created; (iv) all the elements in the situation had been made clear enough to allow for full-scale demonology and hagiology to develop. [Cohen, 1973, p. 238][1]

The cycle takes a crucial move forward in the discovery of many instances of the newly uncovered devilry, a whole host of pretenders to the throne of 'King Con'. The iceberg was steadily revealed as case after case of social security fiddling was reported. As we have seen, our six-month sample in 1976 produced 134 cases of stories based on litigation about fraud. In August that year ITN embarked on a series of special reports about welfare abuse, in anticipation of the report of the enquiry being conducted within the DHSS. The first report was built round an interview with Iain Sproat, the Conservative MP for Aberdeen South who had, by now, made something of a career of knocking welfare state scroungers. Once again viewers were treated to scandalous cases from Mr Sproat's postbag. Sproat claimed that he was out to protect those people 'who really need it', and suggested that 'scroungers are taking up the money and it is literally running into, I would estimate, a minimum of 250 million a year'. The next night, following an item reporting that the unemployment figure had reached 1½ million, the special report focused on an interview with a man who was off by taxi to collect his Employment Transfer Disturbance Allowance. On Wednesday the reporter moved to Glasgow to look at the problem of rent arrears written off by the Corporation, even though many of the tenants received supplementary benefits including a rent allowance, money they apparently wasted on other things, though on what was not made clear. This exciting series was interrupted on Thursday due to 'pressure of news', but was concluded on Friday by an interview with Stanley Orme, the Minister responsible for Social Security. The extent of fraud and its potential danger were now firmly established. Orme was at great pains to point out the increase in the number of prosecutions. So the question was not 'is there widespread fraud?' but 'what can be done about it?'. The more exaggerated accounts were dismissed, but extensive abuse was acknowledged—as in this exchange:

> Interviewer: How do you react to allegations which have been made that as many as one Social Security claim in every five might be fraudulent?
>
> Orme: I say that's nonsense. We've no proof of that whatsoever and if proof was put to us or evidence we would have it examined. But, quite frankly, there is no such evidence.
>
> Interviewer: There is evidence that there is abuse on a fairly widespread scale. What can and ought to be done about it?
>
> Orme: Well, as you've probably noticed recently, somebody went to prison for six years for fraud, and we've doubled the number of prosecutions, our success rate is 98%.

It was December 1977 before the report of the Coordinating Committee on social security abuse actually emerged (DHSS, 1977b). Despite the delay and its minimal distribution there was little chance that it would disappear amongst the barrage of paper produced daily by Whitehall. The content of the new report did not matter. It was a green light from officialdom for the big stick to be wielded. Hence the double-think of such as the *Daily Express* editorial (18 December 1977).

> The scale of fraud in Social Security is alarming and there is every reason to believe that it is growing. That much is clear from the report issued yesterday by the Department of Health and Social Security. The amount lost through fraud in 1975—6 was £2,600,000. But that may only be the tip of the iceberg. It is the official figure based upon frauds which have been found out. Nobody knows how much larger the figure would be if we could take into account the undiscovered fiddlers and thieves.

If nobody knows, how do we know it is the tip of the iceberg? The *Morning Star* was the only paper to give prominence to the Minister's estimate that the amount of unclaimed benefits was about 100 times greater than the amount lost through fraud. The indeterminate statistics of this area were in part responsible for the repeated refrain that there was a vast industry of welfare abuse just beneath the unpleasant surface revealed by the routine coverage of scrounger stories throughout this period. In the face of lack of hard evidence, a slightly different approach is used, the indicative instance. This rides on the common paradox of journalism that in repeatedly reporting the unusual it sustains a view of the unusual as commonplace. A singular event becomes emblematic of a widespread practice. In 1979, for example, the *Daily Mirror* gave over its front page to a story that had discovered 'Wives on the Fiddle' (2 August 1979). This began 'Housewives all over the country are taking Social Security bosses for a ride'. In fact the story, picked up by a local stringer in the midlands, was based on a single fraud case in Coventry involving four women, one of whom had 'decided to confess to the *Daily Mirror* about this because I'd had enough. I carried this secret around with me for more than a year'. Despite the absence of any supporting evidence, the *Mirror* story confidently claimed that 'an army of cheats throughout Britain is believed to be using the same system to defraud Social Security'. Lack of hard evidence can also be masked by another approach.

1b. What everybody knows

If evidence of abuse is lacking, confirmation of its seriousness and extent could be found by tapping popular beliefs. By constant reference to common knowledge, popular journalism is able to create the very mythology it seeks to evoke. The populist slant that has become common in popular journalism in recent years is, at least in part, an aspect of a general strategy aimed at launching papers beyond the constraint of a narrow partisanship to a position straddling the central band of opinion (see Golding and Murdock, 1978).

Such strategy is found in editorials referring to ordinary people's knowledge of events and processes that others (academics, politicians, civil servants, experts, social workers) see only from afar. This commonsense insight is claimed by the press because of its intimate contact with the mundane world of back street reality, and given expression by it in its role as tribune of the people. The *Express* editorial referred to above, for example, speaks of the moral impact of social security fraud on working-class communities 'where the old fashioned work ethic is still believed'.

A good example of this sentiment was displayed at the time of the publication of the Fisher report on social security abuse in March 1973 (Committee on Abuse of Social Security Benefits, 1973). The *Daily Telegraph's* editorial then asserted that:

> It did not need all the panoply of a government appointed committee to tell us there is enough abuse of Social Security benefits to cause justified alarm. Who but that small stage army of middle-class fanatics for state welfare also believe that such benefits cannot really be abused, and who are so profligate with cash other than their own, has ever doubted it? Certainly not the great body of working-class tax payers, who have knowledge of these matters at rather closer hand since they can often identify individual malefactors . . .

The widespread reporting of abuse is, of course, a major source of such common knowledge, as we shall discuss in Part III.

THEME 2: THE BOUNDARIES OF CITIZENSHIP

2a. Tax-payers versus claimants

In a famous essay published in 1950, T. H. Marshall argued that the rights of citizenship include three elements: guarantees of liberty before the law, political enfranchisement, and a right to economic welfare and a share in the standards of living prevailing in society. Welfare was thus the right of a citizen. Much of the explicit and implicit debate about the welfare state has revolved around the implications of this view. As Parker has pointed out, such a view is

> in conflict with many of the practices of a market economy and the ideologies which are associated with and support it . . . The contradiction is clear. Independence, wealth, and the ability to buy services of all kinds are highly regarded, but a belief in the idea of citizenship would require their opposites to be similarly approved. [Parker, 1975, p. 146]

At the same time, citizenship might be claimed as a privileged status granted only to those who have paid their subscription as tax-payers, as active participants in the labour market, or as contributors to a communal insurance scheme.

This opens wide the possibility of marking out boundaries between 'us' and 'them'. Once again this is a theme that has been seen at work in other areas of journalism. Studies of the portrayal of various peripheral or deviant groups in the media have noted how such groups are demarcated from the mass of the population by a subtle labelling process. On the inside is the public, including the media as *vox populi*, while on the outside are the threatening, deviant or suspect group (see, *inter alia*, studies in Cohen and Young, 1973).

Much of the media commentary in recent years has picked up this theme—of what the public would stand for, where the decent tax-payer would draw the line, what ordinary working people wanted, or were fed up with, or demanded. A *Daily Mail* story (22 September 1976) announced an initiative in fraud investigation by reference to the 'public outrage' following the Deevy trial. Claimants, especially suspect ones, are not by definition members of the public. Such rhetoric is common at the time of the annual uprating of benefits (see theme 4c below) where the unemployed, in particular, are singled out as receiving privileged protection against inflation unavailable to ordinary working people. A *Daily Telegraph* editorial (28 July 1976) drew attention to 'the bitter resentment of all those who pay taxes to finance this spree; working-class wage earners, who know best what goes on, are probably the most resentful of all . . .' In 1979, budget proposals were greeted with twin headlines in the *Daily Telegraph*, in adjacent front-page columns (14 June 1979): one announced 'Inflation "17½ pc By The Autumn"—Ministers Gamble on Pay Restraint'; the other proclaimed 'Record Rise in Benefits'. The contrast was self-evident. Yet again the hard-working majority laboured on while social security claimants reaped the benefit.

One way of focusing this distinction is the emblematic selection of particularly heinous cases of scrounging for doses of righteous indignation. A *News of the World* front-page story (17 October 1976) was headlined simply 'PARASITES', and subheaded 'The Scrounging Kinches cost you £500-a-week'. The Kinch family were introduced to us as 'surely the most sickening bunch of super scroungers in Britain'. Having built up rent arrears, the family had seen several of their children taken into care (hence the £500 calculation, which was, in fact, nothing to do with the social security benefits received by the family but the estimated cost of the children's maintenance in care). The family had, rather unwisely as it turned out, come to the *News of the World* for advice and support. It was, however, 'tax and rate payers' who were given advice, to be wary of such as the Kinches. The Kinch family, like many such reported cases, were Irish, and had been told by one Judge to 'Go back to Ireland'. This common, and rather simple, xenophobic method of portraying claimants as an out-group did not, in fact, appear that frequently in 1976.[2]

More directly, the distinction between the law-abiding majority and the deviant claimant is confirmed by organised surveillance of the latter by the former. Many social security fraud investigations begin from anonymous tip-offs, and the suggestion in February 1980 by John Carlisle, Conservative MP for Luton West, that people should report their neighbours was willingly taken up by the press ('Shop Scroungers Neighbours Urged By Tory MP'—*Daily Telegraph,* 26 February 1980).

Popular antipathy to scroungers produces many bizarre suggestions for their corrective treatment. *The Guardian* (29 October 1976) reported the case of a local councillor who wanted people in rent arrears to be put in temporary tin huts 'Like Soviets'. Not all reaction was quite so dramatic, but much of it was part of a process of redefining the rights, and boundaries, of citizenship.

2b. Fighting the good fight

Among the most striking language used in reporting of social security is the rhetoric and vocabulary of warfare. This is part of the theme of citizenship, licensing a battle of attrition against those who threaten the ethics and values of the hard-working, tax-paying majority. Once again this is parallel to the media treatment of other issues, notably race. Hartmann and Husband, for example, have drawn attention to the way in which blacks and immigrants are portrayed as threatening outsiders 'invading' our culture (Hartmann, Husband and Clark, 1974).

In recent years this imagery has been employed at every hint of ministerial investigations or authoritative inquiries. In the *News of the World* (25 July 1976) a headline declared 'Big New War on the Dole Cheats' as a summary of Stan Orme's response to the Deevy furore. The publication of the Supplementary Benefits Commission annual report in September was the occasion for another round of sabre-rattling, the 'clamp-down' being virtually the only aspect of the 258-page report to attract attention. In the *Daily Mail* it was 'War on the Welfare Scroungers' (22 September 1976); in the *Sun* we were warned of a 'No-Mercy Drive on Welfare Cheats' in a story beginning 'A crackdown on the Social Security fiddlers who milked more than £2,000,000 out of Britain's welfare state was launched yesterday'. The *Daily Mirror* headlined 'Orme's War on Cheats', recalling its announcement two months previously that 'Britain's army of dole-queue swindlers were on the run last night as a Government Minister warned he was going gunning for them'.

The same language returned later in the year, following the uprating of benefits in November and hints that the Chancellor was considering taxing unemployment benefit. A year later, following the report of the Coordinating Committee on social security abuse (DHSS, 1977b), battle lines were drawn once again. In the *Daily Express* it was 'War on the Swindlers', assuring us that this time 'The war on Social Security swindlers has been dramatically stepped up . . .'. In the *Daily Mail* the whiff of grape-shot produced heady anticipations: 'More Detectives join the Great Scrounger Hunt' it proclaimed. In January 1979 a press conference on social security fraud, which showed that prosecutions had doubled in three years, produced the news of a 'Blitz on Welfare Fiddlers . . .' (*The Sun* 12 January 1979), while the hue and cry for scroungers at the Conservative Party conference in October that year called up a 'Spy Army to Crack Down on Fiddlers' (*Daily Mirror* 12 October 1979). This story began 'The Tories are calling up an army of snoopers. Social Services Secretary Patrick Jenkin said that they could wage war on the state benefits "scroungers".'

Of course the vocabulary of dramatic conflict is routine grist to the media mill. Terse, concise, brief, dramatic, charged with excitement and urgency—the language of warfare is employed in the reporting of many fields, from parliamentary debate to the FA Cup. It fills the lexicon of reporting in the age of the commercial press, a familiar aspect of popular journalism since its origins in the growth of a cheap, entertainment-oriented press in the later nineteenth century. The difference here is that the opposed parties are not politicians of equal stature, or football teams from rival towns. The conflict is between society and a deviant minority. The language and implicit meaning derive more from the xenophobic excesses of the war correspondent than from the amiable exaggerations of the sports columnist. Clamp-downs, crack-downs, swoops, ferreting out, battles; all are aimed at a group outside society, challenging its most hallowed values and exploiting its largesse. It is here that the welfare scrounger joins hands with the immigrant, political extremist and moral deviant beyond the pale of social approval.

THEME 3: THE NANNY STATE

The later themes outlined here deal rather more with the welfare services and social security as a system, than with the unacceptable or illegal use of this system by a marginal minority. A first sub-theme derives from the fear that the welfare umbrella has been extended over too wide a range of clients, at great social and economic cost. Secondly, the welfare state has become too large, and has spawned a needless army of incompetent bureaucrats and social workers for whom the rest of us have to pay. These two sub-themes can be described separately.

3a. The overgrown welfare jungle

In many stories, and in the consequent comment and discussion of them, the extension of welfare is related to the growing power of the state. This invites the Orwellian imagery of repressive interfering paternalism that popular, or populist, journalism often employs in discussion of government, and particularly Labour government, activities. In this context the welfare net is seen to have been spread too far. What should be a restricted emergency service for the helpless has developed uncontrollably into the nanny state. Two ideas get confused here. One is the complexity of welfare administration, which can quite reasonably be seen as a major problem for claimants or potential claimants. The other is the extent of welfare, its 'bigness', a concept seen as part of the problem of red-tape, bureaucracy and the intrusive state.

A *Sun* cartoon (29 July 1976) captured this notion very well. It followed a well-publicised case in which a family stranded on the motorway had had their bill paid by Social Security (as Popay, 1977, notes, no paper followed up the story to see if, as was very probable, the money had to be repaid by the family). The cartoon, by Tim Holder, shows a smiling couple watching as their car is showered with bank notes dropped from a helicopter labelled 'Social Security Rescue'. Back down the road is a queue of breakdown trucks and lorries labelled 'hotel transport', 'meals on wheels' and 'Town Hall handouts', driving past a guest house advertising 'vacancies': 'Don't worry about the bill', the cartoon is captioned, 'here come the cavalry!'

The extensiveness and complexity of welfare are frequently

exhibited. The Supplementary Benefits Commission annual report in September 1976 focused on this issue. In response to the report, the then Secretary of State, David Ennals, announced the setting up of a review team to look into the complexity of supplementary benefits, and there was much reporting of 'the tangled web' of social security. 'Nanny gets a dose of salts' was the headline for the *Guardian* leader (16 September 1976), or, in the *Express,* 'Baffling! Verdict on the State Hand-outs' (16 September 1976). *The Sun* pronounced on 'The Big Benefits Muddle' in a story beginning 'Britain's costly state hand-outs scheme, which helps one in eleven of the population, is bogged down in red tape' (16 September 1976). The *Daily Mirror* editorial 'Human Face, Empty Head' began 'Britain's welfare system is in chaos. It is too big. And too complicated', referring back again to the car breakdown case to clinch its point. The *Daily Mail* had the problem of reconciling its distaste for state power with its concern to crack down on spongers. This issue gave it the logical escape route. It is welfare complexities that create abuse—'the tangled and hopelessly dense and entwined system of social benefits, which now provide such splendid cover for scroungers. It is the burdensome complexity of our taxes and the well intentioned inefficiency of our welfare state that is making Britain a land fit for scroungers and spongers' (22 September 1976). The *Daily Mail* returned to this theme a year later, when, along with the rest of the media, it was quick to jump on the report of the Public Accounts Committee showing inefficiency in social security. It commented 'the welfare system, complex and cumbersome, now covers the whole body politic with a rash of benefits, payments and allowances' (30 September 1977). In the *Express,* social security was 'the giant that's gone out of control'.

Simplification became the watchword and the central rationale for the changes in the supplementary benefit scheme heralded by the review team report *Social Assistance* and brought into effect by the 1980 Social Security (No. 1) Act. The reduction in discretionary additions and the 'rough justice' that the report admitted would follow from nil-cost changes were hidden in public debate by the splendours of simplification. As 'rolling back the state' became a winning slogan for the New Conservatism, the demon of 'big welfare' began to cast a long shadow over any attempts to unmask 'simplification' as a cut in essential welfare provision. In a feature by the *Daily Mail*'s political columnist, Andrew Alexander, the demon was given a name borrowed from William Cobbett, 'The Thing':

What we might call *The Thing* today— or perhaps *The System*— is that great web of politicians and semi-politicians, single-issue pressure groups, salaried agitators, quango-place-men, and bleeding-heart journalists who fight ceaselessly to stop the government applying the simple standard of good housekeeping to the national accounts. That we should live within our means. [30 June 1980]

One way of focusing this theme is in stories showing the wrong groups of people getting benefits. Needless extensions of the welfare state (to students, the work-shy, the affluent, and eventually to everybody) thus illustrate its uncontrollable growth. A *Daily Mail* 'exclusive' splashed across its front page (19 December 1977) the news that there were to be 'Benn's Fivers For the Boys'. This picked up the £5 addition to supplementary benefits and Family Income Supplement provided in one week in January 1978 to help with winter fuel bills. The *Mail* was scandalised to discover that this would include some unemployed school leavers, and claimed that up to 100,000 of them would get the money. The story did not point out that a major part of the scheme was a 25 per cent discount to electricity consumers in the winter quarter, available only to the bill-payer and only if the bill was over £20. Nor did it point out that a similar scheme the previous year had attained a take-up rate of only 57 per cent, a major reason for switching to a universal addition to benefits.

The final elaboration of this idea is the conclusion that welfare is not merely reaching the wrong people but has totally outgrown its utility, to the point where it is weakening our whole social fabric. A *Daily Telegraph* editorial (29 July 1976) headed a 'Land Fit for Scroungers' commented:

Yet worse than the waste, worse than the bitterness, is perhaps the damage done to the national character. What a state it is which thus encourages and rewards idleness, mendacity, contumacy and fraud! We hear much of people getting the Governments they deserve. Governments may get the people they deserve.

The paper returned to the theme in September (editorial, 16 September 1976). It now argued that social security was a malignancy that

is outgrowing the ability of the host body—the rest of us—to
sustain it . . . poverty has become in some ways even more
degrading than it would have been but for the intrusions, well-
meaning but ill-judged, of the State . . . if handouts approach the
lavish, the provident are impoverished and more are encouraged
to join the ranks of the 'poor'; while if benefits are modest, they
can only be a palliative which, like other palliatives, tends to
become more of a burden than the disease. The clear lesson is
that supplementary benefit should be what it used to be known
as in a less euphemistic era: assistance. It should be a safety net,
strictly for emergencies, not a featherbed for every hard luck
case around.

This notion was graphically outlined by the *Daily Mail* as part of
the general outcry at the benefits uprating in November 1976.
Opposite an editorial complaining, once again, that 'the balance of
this country's resources continues to tilt away from private
enterprise towards public welfare', was a feature inviting the reader
to 'Put your family to this payout test'. A large circle illustrated
how one man found that in his immediate family circle twenty out
of twenty-four adults were in some way drawing money from the
state. The reader is invited to be shocked by working out his own
'octopus' (15 November 1976). The *Daily Express* had a similar
idea a year later in a feature headed 'Can anyone stop this mad
money-go-round?' (14 December 1977). A cartoon showed a circle
of happy bureaucrats taking in rates and taxes and passing on free
school meals, rebates, family income supplements and so on. The
feature began by asking us to 'Ponder the latest iniquity of the
welfare state in action', a clear enough cue as to what our general
view of welfare should be. The *Express* made its complaints more
explicit a week later in an editorial asking 'Why Should We All
Benefit?' (19 December 1977). This was a denunciation of child
benefits in particular, and of the 'universalist complex' in general.
At its simplest this was, of course, simply a failure to understand
the relationship between the introduction of child benefits and the
gradual withdrawal of child tax allowances—the implicit use of
child benefits as an embryonic tax credit system in other words.
But it was also a symptom of the strength of opposition to the
welfare state now being expressed by much of the press in the form
of sniping attacks on the extension of welfare either to undeserving
groups or to everybody in the form of universal benefits.

Underlying this idea, in turn, is the view that poverty has largely been eradicated, and thus the great bureaucracy aimed at its victims is a pointless waste. As a *Daily Express* feature (12 February 1980), in response to a Low Pay Unit report, pointed out,

> If the hollow-eyed parents and hollow-bellied kids of Charles Dickens' world were alive today they would have a good laugh at yesterday's news headlines. Statistics in a new report claimed that today's poor were more poverty stricken than in 1886, when Queen Victoria still had a few years to reign. Do you believe such nonsense? Neither do I. Ah but the statistics prove it! Statistics can prove anything . . .

and so on.[3] The feature is decorated with a woodcut of 'The harsh reality of Dickens' world' and the finger-wagging heading 'This absolute nonsense about the "struggling" families of 1980'. Keeping at bay any attempt to inject standards of relative economic position into the debate about poverty is of course central to the ideological thrust of the post-war consensus. We shall return to this in the final chapter.

3b. Nanny's helpers: the unwanted 'social shirkers'

Periodically thrown into the media stocks for public stoning are some of Britain's 23,000 social workers.[4] Inevitably caught on the horns of a dilemma that demands that they do society's dirty work yet risk instant condemnation for interfering when they fail, social workers naturally occupy a prominent place in the front line facing the barrage of criticism about the growth of bureaucratic altruism.

Such research as there is suggests that routine news stories incidentally involving social workers are not particularly hostile (see, for example, Mawby *et al.,* 1979). This routine coverage, however, is dwarfed by the occasional seismic cracking of major faultlines in the social services, usually involving children sexually or violently assaulted. The Maria Colwell case in 1973, in which a 7-year-old girl was beaten by her stepfather while under supervision by a social service department, has been a bench mark for such cases. One such case led to a complaint to the Press Council by the British Association of Social Workers that made little headway.[5]

In January 1980 the parents of a 14-month-old boy were jailed for neglect that led to his death. The *Daily Mirror* headline was

'Malcolm Died as he Lived. Freezing cold, starving, and surrounded by social workers' (16 January 1980). That such children suffer from ineffectual intervention by incompetent social workers is a common theme in these cases. In the following month a *Daily Mail* leader headed 'Social Shirkers' began, 'Yet another baby has died because of the stupidity and neglect of professional social workers' (21 February 1980). The reference was to a 13-month-old girl who had died at the hands of her drug addict mother, who received a five-year sentence for manslaughter. The theme of the extensive coverage was, as in the *Daily Mail* headline, 'Carly, victim of do-nothing welfare team', over a story that began 'Less talk and more action might have saved baby Carly Taylor from a cruel death'. In the *Daily Express* it was 'The Case of the Social Workers who did nothing but talk'—'Little Carly Taylor was battered to death by her drug-addict mother because welfare workers talked too much and did too little' (21 February 1980). Social workers represent in human form the excessive intervention of the state in people's lives, and also the naivety of the bureaucratic mind. As the *Daily Mail* put it (21 February 1980), 'What is so awful is the frequency with which these so-called experts make errors of judgement which to the most ordinary folk would be unthinkable'.

Public outrage at the wretched death of a young child is readily whipped up and requires expiation. Hence such headlines as 'Welfare woman in row over a dead baby' (*Daily Mail,* 4 November 1980) dominate what coverage social work does receive. The *Daily Telegraph* drew the inevitable conclusion in commenting on a strike by social workers in London ('Unnoticed Absence', 7 June 1979). The leader observed that social workers are 'inexperienced in general, never having worked for a living in anything else' and concluded on a familiar note: 'Many of the tasks they perform ought to be done by the individual concerned, or by his neighbours and relatives, or by voluntary agencies, or sometimes by no one at all'.

Thus social workers are too numerous, do not act when they should, and are largely unnecessary. As Melanie Phillips, social services correspondent of *The Guardian,* points out

> Unless Grub Street can clearly see, because of the absence of social workers, that so many babies are being beaten to death or that so many old people are dying of hypothermia, it follows that social workers are superfluous. Superfluous that is until the next child is killed. Then the moral indignation of the press knows no

bounds . . . Suddenly the social worker's role becomes defined as the policeman of domestic disasters, whose job it is to ensure that the tender scruples of the press are not offended by such evidence of human bestiality. [Phillips, 1979][6]

The cross-cutting axes of fake expertise/everyday common-sense, and overbearing state interference/self-help and sufficiency, frame this particular corner of welfare journalism in a peculiarly stark form, but are pivotal throughout the themes we are describing.[7]

THEME 4: THE UNDESERVING POOR: THE MANY FACES OF 'SUPERSCROUNGER'

Our fourth theme is the notion that we no longer adequately sustain the distinction between, on the one hand, those groups whose poverty is due either to membership of a deprived group (the old or sick) or to blameless individual inadequacy (physical or mental handicap, for example), and on the other hand those whose poverty is the result of individual anti-social behaviour—laziness, profligacy, irresponsible family planning and so on. Many stories in this vein focus on the fecklessness of individual claimants or families, and in particular their indulgent leisure spending, laziness or reckless fertility.

The *Daily Telegraph*, still smarting with outrage in the post-Deevy period, decided that many of the unemployed were actually going to great trouble to avoid work (the decline in the labour market apart, which it did not consider worth discussing). Reflecting on one of its own earlier reports, an editorial headed 'Land Fit for Scroungers' explained this deduction:

'How To Be a Failure And Get Paid For Doing Nothing'—this was a headline in Tuesday's *Daily Telegraph*. The story underneath described how various scroungers contrive to make themselves unemployable in order to go on drawing the dole. Scruffy dress, surly rudeness, loudly proclaimed 'militancy', feigned infirmities, dissatisfaction with the working conditions offered, even threats ('You'd better mark me unsuitable, because if you do employ me . . . I bloody well will be unsuitable'): these are now the passports to fortune and success, as a 20th Century Samuel Smiles would have to concede. [29 July 1976]

We shall see in later themes how this theory leads naturally to demands for stricter control.

Many such stories draw attention to the size of the accused's family. Even sympathetic stories can have an unintended effect because of presuppositions about the causes of poverty. Journalists anxious to find a deserving hardship case will expect, and thus find, such a case among families with several children to support. The *Daily Mirror* (16 November 1976) for example, in the midst of the hysteria over the annual benefits uprating, carried a feature with a title designed to tap the wellsprings of sympathy in its older, traditional working-class readers—'Love on the Dole'. The story featured a 43-year-old unemployed building labourer and his family, and was a sentimental picture of the cruel blow to his pride exacted by his failure to find a job. But, the family had seven children. In fact, most children in poverty are not in large families: 74 per cent of families receiving supplementary benefit have one or two children, while only 10 per cent have four or more children (H. C. *Hansard,* Vol. 986, 11 June 1980, Col. 217).[8]

A more spectacular case was that of the Knight family. John Knight, an unemployed 42-year old, lived in Cornwall with his legal and common-law wives and the twenty children these two had borne him. Already featured on BBC's *Nationwide,* a *Daily Mirror* story about baby number 21 was able to refer to him as 'Britain's most controversial father' (17 May 1978). A front-page teaser asked 'Superdad or Scrounger?' The centre-fold feature was headed 'Another Day, Another Knight', and was not unsympathetic. Not for the first time the family's evident artlessness, and John Knight's candid, unrepentant and gentle demeanour, seemed to triumph over the scandal of his £130 weekly social security. The story was quite romanticised, beginning 'In a tumbledown cottage on a hillside with buzzards wheeling overhead the amazing Knights have produced with gentle glee and a complete indifference to public criticism, the 21st addition to the Family'. Others seemed less tolerant. It appeared that the Knights received threatening letters from all over the world, including one labelling him 'The Bed-Hopping Madman of Bodmin Moor'. The *Mirror* invited more letters and, when they came, predictably they were two to one against the Knights (letters, 25 May 1978).[9]

Many other offenders get nominated to the title of 'super-scrounger'. The inevitable presentation of individual cases as typical instances is thus confirmed by a label that leaves little doubt about the widespread abuse each of these virtuoso deviants represents. The sub-plot is one of ever-increasing impudence as scroungers up the stakes in a game of nose-thumbing contempt for the decent values and tax-induced deprivations of the ordinary citizen. Each individual case is special, but the cumulative message is clear. As the recession tightened its grip toward the end of the decade, this story was so routine the language became almost stylised. In the *Daily Mail* (9 February 1978) an unemployed Londoner sentenced for six months for 'failing to maintain' was 'Sponger Supreme'. In May 1979 an Australian mother became one of the few white immigrants to be nominated for the title; in the *Sun* (9 May 1979) 'Scrounger Cynthia jets in to new home'. A day later in the *Daily Express* it was 'Now, Free Furniture! That's the latest demand from superscroungers'. The title was reaffirmed a month later when the *Sun* (21 May 1979) followed up with 'The Super Scrounger's Husband to Find A Job'.

The deviant superscrounger, as we have noted earlier, is quite often an immigrant shrewdly exploiting the guileless generosity of British welfare. The most spectacular cases have tended to involve airport arrivals housed at public expense, most notoriously the Malawi Asians placed in a Heathrow hotel in 1976 (see Troyna, 1980, Ch. 2; Evans, 1976, pp. 14—18). More commonly, scrounger stories involving ethnic minorities are couched in 'adjectival racism'—the gratuitous use of ethnic labels when irrelevant to a story—in the routine of local fraud and abuse stories. One notable exception in the superscrounger stakes was Neimat Zafar, who became 'The Super Scrounger' (headline *Daily Star,* 5 April 1979). Zafar had lived in England for twenty-one years, but his crime was to have invented nearly fifty fictitious children whose fake medical cards he used in claims for child benefit and child addition to National Insurance benefits. The case thus neatly tapped a familiar prejudice about immigrant fecundity. The story occupied acres of newsprint for two or three days, and quickly became generalised. In the *Daily Mail* (6 April 1979) a centre-page feature began 'Britain emerges today as a nation of phantom children, fictitious dole-collectors and fraudulent form-fillers . . .' The judge in the case suggested identity cards for claimants. Features appeared on 'the detective who cracked the case' and, as a *Daily Express* editorial in self-fulfilling justification put it ('Fiddlers on the State', 16 April 1979),

The case of Mr. Neimat Zafar . . . is bound to raise again the

whole issue of scroungers on the welfare state . . . Hard working
people, often on modest wages, can and do feel a burning sense
of grievance against the minority of scroungers who batten on
the welfare state which they pay for. Should there be identity
cards for welfare claimants? This is not a pleasant idea. But
something needs to be done to protect the public from abuse . . .

The end for the 'Pakistani accountant' (*Daily Telegraph,* 6 April
1979) was given massive coverage, summarised in the *Daily Mirror*
headline (6 April 1979) 'Jail Ends Reign of The King Scrounger'.
The case, it should be remembered, immediately preceded the
general election and helped to re-establish scroungerphobia on the
hustings. It brought to a head what had been a consistent political
theme, well summarised in a *Leicester Mercury* editorial (26 May
1977) reacting to the announcement of the forthcoming 1977
benefit upratings. The editorial, headed 'Scroungers Supplement',
argued as follows:

When the average man or woman have the misfortune to lose
their jobs they scurry around busily looking for a new one.
Happily there is still dignity in labour for most, a pride in earning
a wage. But there is a growing element living off our society who
cheerfully grab all the handouts that are going and find no
indignity in money for idleness. They choose to be on the dole
rather than working for a few pounds more than their regular
handout. Social Services Secretary David Ennal's decision to
raise the dole payment by the same percentage as those for the
sick, disabled, and retired just does not make sense. Not because
the genuine, out-of-luck man does not deserve support, but
because it will make the scroungers harder to detect and more
difficult to winkle out of their comfortable bolt holes. The need
and the willingness to work should be positively proved before
these parasites get an extra penny in handouts that are totally
financed by the efforts of the hard-working masses.

The *Mercury* appears not to have heard of Unemployment Review
Officers, nor does it look closely at the amounts of money it refers
to as 'comfortable bolt holes'. Not least it fails to mention the
roughly 10 to 1 ratio of unemployed to vacancies that prevailed in
the Leicestershire area at the time. It is, however, a concise

statement of the deserving/undeserving distinction that, as we
have seen, is soon brought to the surface in any period of extended
media coverage of the welfare state.

THEME 5: 'KIND HEARTS AND CON TRICKS' (*Daily Mirror,*
21 SEPTEMBER 1976)

In the general run of social security news the most explicit theme
has been that dealing with generosity and inefficiency in the
welfare apparatus. As the concern has shifted from individual
abuse to the system itself, more and more of the reportage was in
this area. Three sub-themes could be detected. First, the social
security system is failing adequately to control its clientele.
Secondly, social security had become too easy to get. Thirdly,
welfare benefits have become excessively generous, encouraging
indolence and insulting the honest worker.

5a. Inefficient control: the cunning claimant

We have seen how, in the Deevy trial, social security was subtly
transformed from an agency for the preservation of living standards
into a policing mechanism to control the scrounger and sponger.
This symbolic transformation was continually reinforced after
1976 by extensive coverage of official investigations into supplementary benefits. Typical of reports in the post-Deevy period
was a *Daily Telegraph* story that found many examples of apparent
slackness in the control of job-dodgers of which the 'Authorities'
are 'blissfully unaware' (27 July 1976). The story goes on 'but the
majority of the hardline dodgers, say experts, are invariably men in
the 18 to 36 age group who are "idle to the backbone and twice as
devious". Such people smirk at the stupidity of the Social Security
authorities'!

This idea is not unrelated to theme 1a—what we all know as
journalists-of-the-world or neighbours of the idle dodgers being
hidden from the unseeing gaze of the enfeebled Social Security
clerk. It is related, too, to the popular stereotype of the unworldly
civil servant, blinded by form-filling and tea breaks from seeing the
harsh reality outside his office.

The September 1977 Public Accounts Commitee report was
rich material for this kind of reporting. The *Sun* (30 September
1977) announced 'Red-Tape Blunder Cost £5m—Handouts Over-

paid by Clerks'. The *Daily Express* full-page spread was headed 'Double Bungle', being a joint story about 'Social Security—the giant that's gone out of control' and the underestimate in the costs of the Liverpool Teaching Hospital. Most of the stories, somewhere deeply buried in their later paragraphs, mentioned the Committee's calculation that the inaccuracies amounted to only 1p in every £8 correctly paid. Nonetheless the predominant impression conveyed was that of the *Daily Mirror* headline, 'The Bonanza Paid in Error' (30 September 1977).

Three months later the report of the Co-ordinating Committee on social security abuse focused attention once again on this particular area of overspending (DHSS, 1977b). As we have seen (theme 2b), it provoked a declaration of war on scroungers. The reporting was almost entirely about the new measures being taken to clamp down on fraud, very rarely about its comparative rarity. The report had shown, however, that the amount lost through fraud was equivalent to only 1½p in every £50 paid out, roughly 100 times smaller than the amount of benefits unclaimed by those entitled to them.

The emphasis on policing had begun a year earlier, at the time of the Supplementary Benefits Commission annual report. BBC news (21 September 1976) was couched in terms of 'spot checks and unexpected interviews', and reported that a 'team of nearly 500 special investigators' are 'looking into the increased amounts of fraud. The Ministry says their men ferret out as many as 1,000 new cases of swindling every week', which figure might usefully have been compared to a prosecution figure only about a third as high. The *Daily Mirror* (17 September 1976) was not alone in claiming that welfare was 'so complicated that the system can no longer be properly policed'.

By 1979 the steady trickle of reports and the corollary increase in fraud investigation staff had moved to midstream in social security reporting. In January the second Co-ordinating Committee on Abuse report (DHSS, 1979), despite the emphasis given by its authors to the difficulty of calculating precise figures, attracted large-scale coverage, confidently reporting on the '£20m Dole Diddlers' (*Daily Mirror,* 12 January 1979). The *Daily Star*'s stoic headline was 'The Idlers Are Here To Stay' (12 January 1979), a gloss on Social Services Secretary Stan Orme's remark that 'In a free society we have to learn to live with some of these small problems'.

The selective perception (or inferential structures) now operating in social security reporting meant that, one month later, when the report of a survey of claimants was published (Ritchie and Wilson, 1979), its major findings were displaced by the interest in control.[10] In the *Daily Mail* (15 February 1979), under a headline 'Scroungers Out', the story picked up one obscure curiosity in the report, with opening paragraphs that read:

> Ex-jailbirds should be recruited as Social Security staff to help cut down abuses of the system. They would know all the dodges that some like-minded people get up to and therefore be able to forestall them. It might help, too, if some members of staff were given courses in psychology so that they knew what they were up against.

The story is accompanied by a Jon cartoon showing a cigar-smoking scruff, in a comfy armchair in a Social Security office, being served by a wine-bearing waiter saying, 'while you're waiting, sir, perhaps a drink?' In April, following the Zafar case, the *Daily Mail* drew the conclusion in a feature headed 'Yes it *is* easy to fiddle' (6 April 1979). A highlighted quote suggested 'Never has the tempting fruit of the social security tree been plucked by so many so falsely'.

The notion of social security as a policing mechanism creates the complementary image of the claimant as criminal, to be policed, checked, investigated, suspected and controlled. No clearer mechanism for the dissolving of any distinction between economic and moral inadequacy can be found than in the creation of a system whose most publicised purpose is the discovery of cunning, deception and fraud among its clients. The assumption rarely needs explicit statement, so obvious is it in the coverage of the policing mechanism itself. Such is the view captured in Franklin's cartoon in *The Sun* (23 September 1976) showing a Social Security office outside which are two warning notices: 'New Crackdown on Cheats', 'Spot Checks to Catch Fiddlers'. The horde of scruffy claimants pedalling or walking to the office, including a Chinaman and several Asians in turbans, is going past a traffic warden remarking to his colleague, 'Hello, not so many arriving in Daimlers and Alfa Romeos today!'

The extension of the need for policing the unscrupulous is found in the view that social security abuse is becoming an organised crime, committed by professionalised and highly organised gangs. Deevy's evidently systematic and diligent fraud was a key for this.

BBC news (21 September 1976) announced that 'The battle to outstrip the ingenuity of the professional cheats' was being waged more successfully. The *Daily Mail* (22 September 1976) referred to the Minister's aim to get the 'organised criminal gangs who have set out to swindle the public'. The 'professional cheats' had been a major target of Iain Sproat's parliamentary campaign. On ITN news (23 August 1976) he told his interviewer that he was out 'to bust what I consider to be the biggest racket probably in this country today'. In fact, about seventy people were convicted in 1976 for major social security crimes involving organised groups. But the 'professional cheat' was an image by now largely inseparable from social security fraud as a whole. In a period when suspicion of social security is so intense it is, with little difficulty, extended to any claimant whose needs are not entirely obvious.

By firmly setting the policing of claimants on the agenda in this way, even sympathetic reporting tends to reaffirm the existence of the problem. A *World in Action* (ITV) report 'Claimant, Scrounger, Snooper, Spy' (3 March 1980) focused on the energy being invested in fraud control, and its interviews with people convicted of fraud sympathetically stressed their difficult circumstances. But this rare interruption in the flow of scroungermania is contextualised by programmes in the general stream like an ATV programme two weeks earlier (*Format Five,* 21 February 1980) that opened with the extraordinary claim that a recent, unnamed, study had shown 90 per cent of claims to be fraudulent. Using the by now ubiquitous Robin Page,[11] the programme showed 'how easy' it was to defraud the DHSS and emphasised the criminal underworld ambience of social security fraud by interviewing an acknowledged fraudulent claimant in the disguised silhouette style normally reserved for terrorists or sexual deviants.

By default, an important distinction being outlined by this theme is between the morally repugnant offence of social security abuse and the acceptable, even laudable, practice of tax evasion. That music-hall figure of fun the income tax inspector is fair game, and tax evasion is, nudge nudge, wink wink, no more serious than parking on a yellow line. It is an offence committed not by 'outsiders' against 'us', but by the more successful of 'us' against 'them' the bureaucrats. And good luck to you if you can get away with it.

In fact, tax evasion only rarely makes news. The contrast between the two crimes was highlighted in 1979 when Lord Denning condemned the raids made on a banker's home by Inland Revenue officials investigating tax fraud. Lead stories voiced the indignation of free-born Englishmen everywhere. In the *Daily Express* (17 August 1979) it was 'Tax Men Blasted'. In the *Daily Mail* 'Taming of the Tax Man', accompanied by a picture of Lord Denning, 'The Judge Who Fights for Freedom'. The *Mail* leader hit out at KGB-style raids 'swooping at dawn'. Such concern for the tender susceptibilities and civil liberties of tax evaders has rarely been extended to people under investigation for the usually rather smaller sums involved in social security fraud.

But the tax evader is not merely a victim but a hero. This was made clear by the case of the Vestey family, owners of the Dewhurst butchers shop chain. Using a trust based in Uruguay the Vesteys had exploited section 412 of the 1952 Income Tax Act to minimise their tax commitment. In 1978, on profits of £4.1 million they paid tax of £10. When the story eventually surfaced it received low-key treatment—'Our Tax Loophole', a justification by Edmund Vestey (*Daily Express,* 6 October 1980), being one of the few stories in the populars. The story only got going when Peter Thorneycroft, Conservative Party Chairman, issued a statement saying he 'would not criticise the Vestey family who have, of course, contributed greatly to this country in employment and wealth. Good luck to anyone who can make a success of business'. This candid and refreshing support for entrepreneurial initiative was soon taken up: 'Tory Chief Defends Tax Leak' (*Daily Express,* 7 October). Quickly the attack was turned onto the tax man. An *Express* feature ('In For a Penny—in for a £. Is the Tax Man Really Fair Game?') homed in on Denis Moorcroft, the Director of the Inland Revenue division concerned with tax evasion. 'One prominent tax accountant told me "Denis Moorcroft and his staff behave like men with a mission. They say they are dedicated to their job, but I say they pursue the benefactors of quite reasonable, though ingenious, tax avoidance schemes with unbelievable hostility".' The *Daily Telegraph* (8 October 1980), in a leader 'A Matter of Conscience', felt the massive wealth of the Vesteys did make this particular case slightly embarrassing, but 'If there is resentment against the Vesteys might it not, *en base*, be envy for their polo-ponies and their almost numberless acres, for their brilliance in avoiding what we wish to avoid but cannot?'

The double standards at work here were thoroughly revealed when later in the same month the Public Accounts Committee reported on the 'Black Economy' of moonlighting and tax-dodging. The language was indeed very familiar: 'Great £3,500m cash swindle', 'A massive crackdown on tax-dodgers was demanded yesterday' (*Daily Mail,* 30 October 1980); 'Hunt Down Tax Dodgers!' (*Daily Mirror,* 30 October 1980), and so on. But, as the *Daily Express* argued in its leader (30 October 1980),

> Less taxation and a simpler tax system is the right answer. What would be utterly wrong would be for the Inland Revenue to follow the advice of Mr. Joel Barnett, Chairman of the Public Accounts Committee. He wants the taxmen to act on anonymous letters about people who allegedly live above their income. This is a thoroughly nasty idea. It would give legitimacy to nosey parkers and all the mean-spirited and envious people in every street . . .

Swooping down, ferreting out, clamping down and tightening up should, it would seem, only be used with judicious selectivity in saving the British taxpayer from the enemy within.

5b. It's there for the taking

In harmony with the theme that controls are inadequate is the idea that social security has been made too easy to obtain. This is at odds with the complaint that our welfare system is too cumbersome and complex, but this is not an area of popular mythology in which logical consistency is paramount. The publication in November 1976 of the Child Poverty Action Group's welfare benefits handbook (it is in fact published annually) was greeted with widespread dismay. Conservative MPs were quick to label it a 'scrounger's charter', a theme immediately taken up by the press. The handbook came out in the midst of the row over the benefit increases and it was seen as a treacherous arming of a fifth column in the war against the scrounger. A number of similar explosions followed as the media discovered the welfare rights lobby, fellow-travellers in the same battle. A *Daily Express* story, for example, tacked on to its report on the Public Accounts Committee findings (30 September 1977), is headed 'Here's the pay-off', and reports an evening class in Derbyshire run by a social worker to explain supplementary benefits to other social workers. The fact that they are not themselves claimants (but 'students', in inverted commas), and the very existence of the class, are offered as telling symptoms of the mess into which we have strayed.

One way of elaborating this theme is to compare our apparently easy-going system with the sterner practices in other countries. Possibly a part of the 'grass is greener' refrain that sometimes seems to have replaced jingoism in contemporary British culture, this idea was illustrated in a *Sun* news feature (17 March 1978). Headed 'Eurodole', and with a 'strap' saying '*The Sun* asks: Can skivers cash in on the Common Market', the *Sun*'s reporter is shown 'finding it's not so easy to cadge from our Euro-pals'. The general message in big letters was 'Jamais de la vie (which is French for not on your life)'. Our unemployed would get short-shrift from the hardheaded Europeans, but 'Back in Britain, we're more big-hearted with the taxpayers money—or barmy, depending on how you look at it'. A *Daily Telegraph* story, on its Home News page, pointed the same moral (19 November 1976). Headed 'Crackdown on State Welfare Cheating in US', it had no apparent story peg, but cited various recent cases of abuse. Its main purpose seemed to be to record that 'the opportunities for abuse are even wider than in Britain'. Salutory tales from abroad of this kind have become common, as in a *Daily Mirror* story (15 January 1979) announcing 'A big crack-down on social security cheats is underway in France'. These provide a useful counterpoint to the continuing generosity with which we apparently treat visitors to Britain.[12] Apparently it is still easy, as a *Daily Star* story suggested (14 December 1979), to be 'Broke—But Great To Be Here! Immigrant dad flies family to luxury'.

If something harmful is made too easily available and is liable to be abused, over-indulgence and, ultimately, dependence are the inevitable result. The comparison with drugs and alcohol is obvious. The parallel was made dramatically explicit in a *Daily Mail* news feature (26 September 1977) headed 'The Welfare Junkies'. It begins: 'One in ten of Britain's once-proud people now depend on a last-ditch semi-charitable handout from the State.' It points out that 'there is a dangerously addictive influence at work in the welfare system. As in the world of drugs, it seems that young people are particularly susceptible'. The article's heading proclaims that 'Among the young, there's no shame in squeezing cash out of the system'. Continuing the medical metaphor, the article is pleased to note that 'a dose of realism has recently been injected by the need for public spending restraints'. The article is clearly worried by deeply ingrained attitudes in many people that 'allow them to accept charity'. It concludes, 'as red tape continues to proliferate and the borders between "official poverty" and "official comfort" become blurred, many thousands more of us may become ensnared'.

The medical analogy is an important one. We have already seen the 'rash' of benefits and the malignant growth of welfare. The notion of the welfare cure being worse than the poverty disease is common to many of the themes we have illustrated. It is important because it defines, by default, the natural, healthy state of the social organism as one without social security. By implication, any application of welfare is a risk or harmful, not merely excessive provision.

5c. The good life

The dangerous generosity of our welfare provision is always most visible when benefits are increased. This was especially clear at the time of the November 1976 upratings during our content analysis period, when the routine, annual adjustments became front-page headlines. In the *Sunday Express* (14 November 1976) it was 'An £8 Rise—If You are On The Dole'; in the *Daily Telegraph* 'Tory Outcry at £100 on the Dole: Pay Code breached by welfare rises'. The *Times* (15 November 1976) had 'Conservatives attack State "scroungers" ', while in the *Daily Mail* it was 'Don't Rock the Dole Boat'.

The upratings inevitably produced the bizarre numbers game that is annually revived by such debates. The initial headlines were about the absolute amount of the increase. The 'huge cash bonanzas for people on the dole' mentioned in the *Sunday Express* took a little finding on closer inspection. The '£5,000 a year men' featured in the *Daily Telegraph* would have needed at least eight children to approach this figure, not a common situation as we have seen. Nonetheless the cartoonists were predictably out in force. In the *Daily Mail* (16 November 1976) Mac had two drinkers at a bar, one asking the other, 'I heard you're on the dole, Harry—I wonder if you could lend me a quid or two until I lose my job?'.

However, the news about the amount of the increase rapidly merged into the question of the relative advantages of working or not working. Again, Mac in the *Daily Mail* captured the mood. A queue at the Social Security office (sign: 'Get Your Dole Here, New Rates! Better Than Working') stretches far down the street. In the queue one man is looking over his shoulder at a lone, tool-carrying, overalled worker, and remarks 'There goes that dreadful Entwhistle fellow—he's in trade you know'. Many stories took their cue from Ralph Howell, the Conservative MP for Norfolk North, who has asked a battery of parliamentary questions designed to illustrate his argument that 'it pays a man not to work'. In fact his calculations were based on including tax rebates in the income of the unemployed. The dole for a single man had only risen in November 1976 to £12.90 a week. But this led to several features like the *Daily Mail*'s City Page article (17 November 1976) 'How the £75 a week man is better off on the dole', while the *Daily Express* (15 November 1976) claimed confidently that 'millions of men might find it financially more worthwhile to be on the dole than at work'. In fact, in informed circles, it was considered that Howell and his name-sake David Howell, Tory MP for Guildford, had spoiled their case by exaggeration. David Howell's talk of people failing to 'keep up with the stay-at-home Joneses' (*Sunday Mirror,* 14 November 1976) was based on the national £8 a week rise headlined in the *News of the World* (14 November 1976) and elsewhere. But since benefits had gone up by just £2.90 for a married couple and by 55p for each child, the arithmetic was a little puzzling. Howell's figures would apply to very low wage earners with several children, and his calculations assumed total take-up on means-tested benefits. By 1979, however, the 'better off out of work' rumblings had grown to a roar, and were heard clearly in the election period. After the election it became a political priority, and Ralph Howell was yet again the source for regular features such as, in the *Daily Express* (10 August 1979), 'When A Man Won't Work—We must change the crazy system that makes it profitable not to take a job'. Jeremy Gates' article, topped by a picture of the iconic John Knight and his 'wives' argued that 'The incentive not to work—resulting from the generosity of the benefits scale—is one cause for the present puzzle in which we have 1.3 million unemployed—and 800,000 vacancies'. That unemployment had been soaring while benefits remained static was part of the puzzle left uninvestigated.

In fact, the numbers game was merely the stray flak away from the central battle over the rising level of unemployment. As *The Times* social services correspondent noted in an inside page article (15 November 1976, 'Why Some People are Better Off On the Dole'), 'All the examples are hypothetical and in reality are not likely to affect many families'. However, across the page in the leader column, we could read that 'Mr. Howell's detailed statistics may be open to challenge, and they could apply with precision only to relatively few, but the broad conclusion is evident'. Never mind the facts, feel the indignation. And indeed this was an accurate reading of the reporting of the debate, since the outrage at the putative advantages of being on the dole was rarely cooled by close inspection of the income that would ensue.

Hints about plans to tax unemployment benefit began to emerge from Chancellor Healey, though they did not become firm policy until 1980, when it was announced that National Insurance benefits would be taxed from 1982.

The whole debate about incentives and the debilitating effect of welfare was given a newsworthy lift by the intervention of the ever-quotable Prince Philip. In the issue of *The Engineer* current at the time of the 1976 benefit increases he had written on article in praise of innovation and enterprise—the usual mixture of individualistic philosophy and a view of industrial progress as the product of garden-shed invention. In it the author had written that 'the welfare state is a protection against failure and exploitation, but a national recovery can take place only if innovators and men of enterprise and hard work can prosper'. It was music to the headline writers' ears: 'Duke's criticism of the welfare state' (*Times,* 15 November 1976); 'Philip's Right' (*Daily Express* editorial, 15 November 1976); and several other headlines indicating the political nature of opposition to his views: 'Left-Wingers hit back at Prince's welfare warning' (*Daily Telegraph*) 15 November 1976; 'Philip on "State Aid" rumpus' (*People,* 14 November 1976) and so on, made the most of the article. It provided the right philosophical context to the row over upratings. Benefits were too high; benefits were too high relative to wages; benefits were too high for the good of the country. The three steps in the argument were complete. All subsequent coverage of any one would, by evocation, imply the others. Thus before the April 1978 budget the statisticians were in dispute once more. A *Daily Express* front-page headline, based again on Ralph Howell's parliamentary questions, declared unequivocally 'It Pays Not To Work' (13 March 1978).

The relative advantages of unemployment, however, are seen to be more than merely marginal. An important part of news coverage, ever since Derek Deevy's Corona cigars, has been the comfortable, even luxurious, life-style supported by social security benefits—providing a 'featherbed for every hard-luck case around' as the *Daily Telegraph* had put it. The *Daily Express* (20 September 1976), commenting on a Gallup Poll finding that the British seemed more contented than in other countries, decided this was because 'we worry less about money because there is always Social Security to make life pleasanter than actually working'.

The life-style provided by benefits is frequently a target of cartoonists. Heath in the *Sunday Times* (2 October 1977) had a cigar-smoking tycoon standing by a news-stand announcing 'Social Security Paid Out £10m Too Much'. A bystander is observing, 'He started with nothing, now he's on Social Security'. Equally subtle was a cartoon by RAP in the *Leicester Mercury* (7 December 1976) set in a Social Security office in which a claimant is reading a newspaper with the headline 'Wealth Tax Moves'. Another claimant is saying to the clerk 'I just hope we're not going to get any corny cracks . . .'. As such cartoons suggest, this mythology lends itself to television treatment, and has proved a rich source of material, especially for situation comedy. '*Mr. Big*' (by Peter Jones and Christopher Bond) is a small-time operator constantly in search of a quick profit. One episode (4 February 1977, BBC1) portrayed his cousin Sydney who, when he arrives with his dolly-bird partner in a Rolls, explains how a quick trip to the Social Security office will ensure that 'the cash will come rolling in by giro cheques'. The central characters trip round to various offices giving false names, and eventually end up in a Fraud Investigation Office. Two sterotypical civil service 'twits' are in conversation: 'You mustn't accuse people of being feckless layabouts on social security.' 'But they are.' 'Yes, I know that but we mustn't say so Miss Twining.' In *Mind Your Language* (London Weekend Television), a comedy series about an English as a second language class, the following exchange took place. 'Teacher: What do you do for a job? Pakistani: I work at the Labour Exchange. Teacher: What do you do there? P: I collect my unemployment benefit. T: Yes but that's not a proper job. P: Yes, but I get more than I would working' (December 1977). *Shelley* (by Peter Tilbury, Thames Television) is about the adventures of an unemployed graduate. In one episode (19 July 1979) Shelley sits in a pub, buys a drink with a note peeled off the wad in his pocket, and mentions it's his signing-on day. In the deserted Social Security office he is called for interview, says he can manage on the money and admits 'I'm a layabout'. After his girlfriend announces she's pregnant he goes back to ask for a job, and she signs on as well. As in many such portrayals this is a world devoid of prosecution, benefit suspension, cohabitation rules, Unemployment Review Officers, or any of the panoply of control that for many real claimants is the core of their experience with social security.

The most spectacular coverage of the good life enjoyed by

claimants was in August 1976, when it was claimed that the unemployed were taking Spanish holidays on the dole. This derived from Britain's signature of an agreement with twenty-eight countries about pension rights when out of the country or origin. A circular from the National Insurance Commissioner confirmed that this applied to Spain, and that absence there on holiday would not of itself disqualify anyone for unemployment benefit, though the claimant would have to be available for work. In fact no case was ever confirmed, but the story was written firmly into popular history. As was to be expected it was a field day for the cartoonists. In the *Sun* (5 August 1976) Franklin had a theatre queue ('Scroungers and Layabouts queue here') outside 'The Whitehall Theatre's New and Greatest Farce: "Fringe Benefits: Hilarious Joke of Holidays in Spain on the Dole" Taxpayers' Trousers Continually Taken Down'. In the *Daily Express* (5 August 1976) a long-haired layabout is sitting outside a Spanish hotel ('Dole Cheques Accepted') with a senorita and a bottle of wine. He is writing a letter: 'I am writing to you as my MP to demand that you raise in the House that the present dole is totally inadequate for a year's holiday in Spain.' In the *Daily Mail* (5 August 1976), unabashed by the failure of his news-page colleagues to furnish any evidence, Mac has a returning holidaymaker visiting his Labour Exchange. He is in the 'Dole Stockpile Room' wearing a sombrero, accompanied by two senoritas and pushing a banknote-laden wheelbarrow. He is remarking to the astonished claimants' queue, 'I'm heartbroken—a whole year in Spain and they still haven't found a vacancy for a sewage sluice stopcock scraper operator . . .'

Despite the lack of evidence, the *Daily Mail* remained unrepentent and the following summer, true to form, its columnist Lynda Lee-Potter contributed a piece headed 'Scroungers by the Sea' (13 July 1977).

Our bronzed, healthy, young hedonistic army of self-unemployed are holidaying by the sea at our expense this year and yes, I do resent it. I resent working to support the idle loafers who have a laugh at our expansively generous system which allows them to get away with legalised plunder. The seaside Social Security Offices are thick with subsidised cigarette smoke, the smell of alcohol paid for by the state, and the smuggly tanned faces of the leeches feeding off the hard-working, ordinary, silent majority.

As usual, Miss Lee-Potter expresses the populist view in its most elemental, graphic, and ill-informed version. But a year after the Spain-on-the-dole rumpus it was interesting to see a myth kept alive. In June 1979 it was resurrected when the Supplementary Benefits Commission issued its response to *Social Assistance* (DHSS, 1978), the report on the official review of the scheme. In fact the response was an attack on the nil-cost proposals of the review. The *Sun* headline (20 June 1979), however, was 'Have a Holiday On the State!' A leader comment, addressed to the Commission's Chairman, Professor David Donnison ('Dotty Prof.'), was outraged that he had 'dreamed up a new way of spending your money . . . It's just another dotty idea from the man who once described the millions of pounds fiddled by scroungers as "a drop in the ocean" '.[13] In fact the *Sun* had misquoted Donnison on both counts as a brief apology a few days later acknowledged (25 June 1979).

The focusing of moral outrage is an important part of such coverage, creating as well as drawing on the division between those who apparently reap the comfortable benefits of welfare dependency and those whose inadequately rewarded labours finance them. To express general concern is to create it. A *Daily Express* front-page story about the row over civil servants who claim unemployment benefit as well as their pension at 60—'Fight for Dole Bonus' (15 November 1976)—remarked 'Ironically the Government's bid to cut dole payment comes as a wave of anger greets today's big rise in Social Security benefits'. The 'wave of anger' can only exist among opposition MP's and the press until it is whipped up by stories suggesting it already exists. It is in this sense that 'public opinion' is simply that version of it given voice by popular journalism.

SEX, CRIME AND POLITICS: WELFARE NEWS BY THE
BACKDOOR

The map of events and processes in the world of the news is shaped in part by its own gathering and production processes and by the visibility of different public institutions and figures (see Golding and Elliott, 1979). Social welfare is not one of these continuously surveyed arenas, whereas party political conflict, sex and crime all are. These are commonly, therefore, contexts in which welfare news appears (see chapter 3).

Many of the examples we have described in this chapter resulted from, or in, political debate—by which is meant the gladiatorial displays of parliamentary gamesmanship. The upratings row, for example, became a party political altercation ('Labour Taunt in Dole Storm'—*Daily Mirror,* 15 November 1976). During the £5 fuel bonus story ('Last night the situation boiled up into a political storm'—*Daily Mail,* 19 December 1977) the treatment was the same. The parliamentary battlefield is the major arena in which welfare will appear. It is thus bound recurrently to be a sounding board for political slogans and war-cries, in which, given the complexion of the British press, the dominant voice will not be that of welfare claimants or their representatives.

The other major context is crime. As we have seen, routine coverage of social security is above all else found in the mundane reporting of court cases involving fraud. The statistics of this are set out in chapter 3. With such reporting social security is bound to appear a system too open to abuse and thus fundamentally inappropriate or excessive.

Finally a news category into which welfare news occasionally strays is that of sex. Often this surfaces in the recurrent pillorying of social workers, as in 'Sex Client was Social Worker' (*Daily Telegraph,* 7 September 1976), or the same story in the *Sun* ('Welfare Man Paid for Sex with Schoolgirl'), or 'Scandal of the Social Work Sex Beast' (*Daily Star,* 2 October 1980). Even agony columns can join this game, as in 'How Do I Change a Workshy Lover's Lazy Ways?' (*Sun,* 3 September 1979). The Supplementary Benefits Special Investigators' concern with cohabitation allows a rare opportunity for stories that richly combine sex, crime and welfare abuse into a sub-editor's dream, with such winners as 'Mr Quick's Top-Speed Sex Snoop on Doreen' (*Sun,* 10 August 1976), or the *Daily Star*'s special double-page spread (29 October 1979) on 'The Sex Snooper in the Long Grass', which revealed the 'Amazing Secrets of Social Security Investigators'.

All three contexts are important as outlets through which welfare and social security news can escape its accustomed invisibility. In so doing, however, it takes on the form and substance of these categories, with the results we have described in the earlier themes.

CONCLUSION: THE WELFARE CONSENSUS DISMANTLED

By the 1979 election the thin veneer of the post-war welfare consensus had been stripped down to a barely visible remnant. As the dole queues lengthened, the focus on the iniquities of the unemployed began to soften a little. During 1980 unemployment rose by 888,000 to 2¼ million, the largest annual increase since 1930. A new theme with an ancient lineage began to emerge—the need to remoralise the workless millions to ensure the continued vitality of the work ethic and the preservation of law and order. This was entwined in a curious mix with repeated attempts to show that unemployment was not really so extensive, that the *real* level of unemployment was lower than it appeared to be.

This shift of focus completed the transition set in train by the great scroungerphobia of 1976—77. The refrain was now a popular and insistent opposition to the welfare system based on the twin themes that it was both unnecessary and an excessively costly burden. The new culture hero was the shopkeeper/entrepreneur, the inventive and energetic archetype of Samuel Smiles' mythologies for whom welfare was an insulting and expensive irrelevance. Throughout this transition the mass media had played a crucial role in providing a ready interpretation of the obvious failings of the welfare state. As we shall discuss in the concluding chapter, the scroungerphobia episode had provided a switchpoint, diverting attention towards one set of explanations rather than another, towards the laxness, excessive generosity, inefficiency and vulnerability to exploitation of the welfare system rather than towards its failings as a service to its clientele or to the process of redistribution. That this could be achieved so readily required a pre-existing and powerful set of beliefs about welfare and poverty that could be tapped at a moment of economic crisis or political uncertainty. The strength and importance of these beliefs are set out in Part III.

NOTES

1. For an interesting analysis of welfare news in these terms see Popay (1977).
2. Interestingly the *Daily Express* (18 August 1977), at the foot of page

seven, reported a Press Council adjudication that it should have carried a follow-up denial story following its reporting of Irishmen involved in social security abuse by 'criminals, Irishmen, and foreign students'. The story claimed that a secret DHSS report revealed that many Irishmen, many of them IRA sympathisers, came to Liverpool and immediately got social security benefits for bogus families. In fact no such report existed according to the Minister responsible. The complaint, brought by the Federation of Irish Societies, was upheld by the Press Council.

3. The report referred to is Pond (1979), which showed that in 1979 nearly 4½ million adult full-time workers earned less than £60 per week, and that the poorest tenth of male workers were earning only 68.3 per cent of the median in 1979, compared with 68.6 per cent in 1886. This is clearly described in the report as an observation on the *relative* position of the poorest earners. The demand that poverty should be described in absolute terms, and be demonstrated by Dickensian squalor and snotty-nosed urchins, appeared in press reviews of Townsend's important (1979) study of poverty in Britain. On this see Golding (1980a).

4. The number of social workers in the country is in fact a little uncertain. In 1978 the figure for England alone was 20,567 plus 3,000 part-time.

5. For details of the case see Mawby *et al.* (1979) and for the Press Council adjudication the *Sun,* 15 August 1979.

6. For other comment on this issue see Hills (1980), Walker (1976), Roberts (1980), Young (1979). Not surprisingly a limited survey of public perceptions of social workers found that people thought them too young, trendy, inexperienced, and probably female (Wilton, 1980). In fact, unpublished figures show that of full-time social workers in England in 1978 37 per cent were male, and only 33 per cent were under 30. We are grateful to the DHSS Statistics and Research Division for this information.

7. Much work remains to be done on the image of social work. Comparisons with other 'interfering' professions where mistakes are rife, e.g. police or doctors, would be useful. The contradictory images—middle-aged, middle-class, distanced vs. young, trendy, politicised—also need examining. The emphasis on dramatic child abuse contrasts starkly with the fact that only 1.5 per cent of the case-load of the National Society for the Prevention of Cruelty to Children relates to violence or abuse. Most is just plain poverty. We are grateful for discussion of these and related points to Tim Brown, press officer of the British Association of Social Workers.

8. Figures refer to November 1979. See also Royal Commission on the Distribution of Income and Wealth, Background Paper No. 5: *The Causes of Poverty* HMSO, 1978, Tables 7.2 and 7.3.

9. The Knight family continued to fascinate the press. Each new birth

has made the headlines. In February 1980 the *Daily Mail* reported 'Superdad takes a day off' when John Knight left his job in a Bodmin factory to seek his fortune in London by publishing a book about his love-life. In December 1980 stories appeared about Bodmin council's estimate that it would take a £50,000 house to contain the Knight family. One birth in 1979 ('Superdad Does it Again'—*Daily Star*, 6 August 1979) produced the observation by Tory MP John Farr that 'they're breeding like rats. Social Security should refuse him benefits until he has a vasectomy'.

10. Findings from this report are discussed in Part III.

11. Page, a former DHSS Special Investigator, had been a long-time campaigner on social security abuse. Using a nom-de-plume, he contributed articles on the subject to *The Spectator* in 1969 while still employed by the Department (*Spectator*, 6 September 1969), which led to his dismissal (see *Spectator*, 10 January 1970) and to a book (Page, 1971).

12. See chapter 5 note 12, for details of a particularly interesting treatment of a story about Italian visitors to Britain.

13. The *Sun*'s stablemate, *The News of the World*, had for long made a habit of knocking Donnison. When criticised he was always 'The Professor' (Donnison had been an academic and when the SBC was wound up in December 1980 he went to a Chair at Glasgow University), neatly drawing on the sterotypical dottiness/naivety attributed to academics by the strain of anti-intellectualism in British culture.

CHAPTER 5

Reporting the Welfare State

Sociologists, including those interested in the mass media, spend much of their time running away from a crude but tempting fable called conspiracy theory. In its many varieties this elegantly simple dictum proclaims the cause of a multitude of objectionable social processes to be no more nor less than the considered intentions of their central figures. Jiggery-pokery by a coterie of cunning bankers, administrative sleight-of-hand in a few smoke-filled rooms, urgent whispers amid the oak-lined splendour of the top people's reading rooms; of such beguiling stuff is conspiracy theory made.

When it comes to the media the spotlight falls immediately on men who very often seem to have been born to make conspiracy theory credible. Newspaper proprietors like Beaverbrook and Northcliffe undoubtedly played an active, and frequently dictatorial role in shaping the content of the organs they controlled. That their day has passed does not mean that a conspiracy theory of the media can safely be buried with them, but it must cause us to pause and look over the shoulders of such figures if we are to discover how and why the media produce what they do.[1]

In rejecting conspiracy theory we should never forget that news production, like all other social activities, involves real people doing real jobs about which they are able to reflect and over whose content they often have considerable autonomy. Our task is to discover the limits of such autonomy and how it is used. In discussing the different perspectives employed by sociologists and journalists themselves in explaining news production it has been pointed out elsewhere that:

> Journalists are very often concerned about the comprehensibility of news, wondering if the assumptions that are made about audience knowledge and intelligence are valid . . . Journalists, in other words, are concerned with the short-term and deliberate

manipulation of news, and with its immediate and direct effect on viewers. The sociologist has a different perspective, being concerned rather more with the long-term, routine, and non-deliberate manufacture of news, and by corollary, with the long-term and cumulative influence on viewers. [Golding and Elliott, 1979, pp. 8—9]

In this chapter we shall be trying to answer the question: 'what are the routine processes that make news about social security the way it is?'

As with other areas of journalism that have provoked critical public concern, answers to this question have been of three kinds. The first is biographical. It sees journalists as malevolent or ignorant, the articulate representatives of an unholy mass of prejudice and cant. In this view social security news is the biased and jaundiced product of well-heeled scribes who lack the sympathy or understanding to go beyond the vindictive populism for which they are such ready mouthpieces. A second explanation, which we might term organisational, takes a more generous view of the serious intent and responsibility of journalists, but sees them as the objects of a variety of constraints erected by the routines of work, of news gathering and of production, and by the deliberate and regular interventions, conspiratorial or otherwise, of those with axes to grind and the muscle to do so effectively. The third view we can label ideological, an imprecise shorthand for a variety of more complex explanations, in part incorporating the first two, which sees the personal and organisational as but two aspects of the complicated machinery by which the dominant values of British society are given form and authority by the news media. In this chapter we explore the reality of these three broad views.

Although our research was not primarily about news production, we conducted a continuing series of informal discussions with relevant journalists throughout our research period. More importantly, we interviewed at length all the social services correspondents (the title varies) in the national daily press.[2] The first task in discovering how social security news is made is to see where it comes from.

POLITICS, PRESSURE GROUPS AND PRESS RELEASES —
THE SOURCES OF SOCIAL SECURITY NEWS

Like all news about social policy, social security and welfare news
is above all news about politics. By politics is meant Westminster,
and particularly the visible clash of party politics in the House of
Commons and its attendant doings. As John Whale has written,
'Government in all its branches is a principal theme of news
journalism, and its greatest single source of information . . .' (1977,
p. 117). As we have shown in our analysis of social security news,
the political dimension is paramount, and very often comes to
displace the substantive policy issues from the centre of the stage.
Politicians have become increasingly aware of the importance of
this journalistic voyeurism, and it has become commonplace to
observe how great a part of the energies of both individual
politicians and the party and Whitehall machinery is devoted to
their public presentation via the media. Journalists frequently
disparage this as news management. Penetrating the greasepaint
and the rhetoric is seen as a key skill for the accomplished
journalist. It is striking how often this is seen to apply most
particularly to the political arena rather than to, say, industry or
commerce. Charles Wintour, for example, editor of the London
Evening Standard, has written that 'the area most susceptible to
news management is of course politics'. He notes, in a typical
comment, that 'Indeed politicians have become so careful about
the timing and presentation of news that Harold Wilson's Cabinet
was sometimes accused of spending more time on presentation
than on the actual formulation of policy' (1972, pp. 44—5).

One result of this focus on government is that the rhythm of
social security news tends to follow the Westminster beat. As the
parliamentary timetable proceeds, so news coverage replicates the
peaks and troughs of activity. Alongside this, however, is a longer
wave cycle in which journalists generally sense that certain issues
are in the foreground. In the early and middle 1970s health was felt
to be 'on the agenda' in this way. This is often symbolised by a
major continuing event, for example a Royal Commission. The
Royal Commission on the Health Service was set up in May 1976
and reported in July 1979, and throughout this period health was
perceived as having come to the fore as a political issue, and thus
as a running news story.

The colossus which bestrides this section of the political arena is the Department of Health and Social Security. The department is certainly the major reference point, if not the major source, for a great proportion of stories in this area. The DHSS press office has three press officers concerned with social security and five who concentrate on health. There are in addition twelve regional information officers (who tend to specialise in particular areas; one, for example, being a specialist on benefits for the disabled). Much of their work is the preparation of bread and butter press releases on changes in benefit rates and administration. As a consequence their output is large—up to three or four press releases a day. The officers are civil servants rather than journalists, by inclination if not by professional origin, and they have ready and frequent access to ministers and senior civil servants. Their rhythm, too, is therefore dictated by the Commons.

Relations between press officers and journalists are not without friction. Press officers tend to see many correspondents as inexpert and lazy, too inclined to use the press office as a research service for information they ought to be able to uncover themselves from standard reference sources. For the journalists it is a cliché of the trade to refer to 'suppress departments'. One insisted that

> The DHSS is not a good news source. You only get helped if your paper's politics coincide with the government's. They've never helped me much. Even when they invite you in there's rarely a story. Press officers don't help you much. You never get tips—it's you going to them. They just give you the official line. I can't rely on them for stories.

This particular journalist was described in the press office as not knowing 'his arse from his elbow'. One correspondent described DHSS press releases as 'getting between you and the officials'.

In part this view arises from the natural protectiveness of the press department, which sees itself not only as the voice of the department, but as a first line of defence against frequent, unwarranted, ill-informed or politically motivated attacks. Contrary to all the evidence from content analysis, news about social security was perceived by the press office as unduly reflecting claimants' grievances about inefficiency or official misanthropy. The issue of fraud has sharpened this defensiveness. After all, 'the buggers never point out that we've caught them'. The emphasis therefore is on the efficiency of the department in containing fraud. This attitude had been sensitised by the furore surrounding the Deevy case in 1976. 'We should have seen it coming. Deevy was a cock-up for the department. That started the whole thing going. Now we have an early warning system for such cases. The regional information officers keep a look out and we alert the ministers. If I can stop a story where there's knocking, that's good.'

Part of the job of press officers is setting up press conferences. Press conferences are infrequent, and journalists use them primarily to provide a spicy quote to perk up a dull story. They are also gatherings of other specialists who might just know something useful, especially if they have particular interests, contacts or knowledge. For example, a general social policy writer would expect education specialists to be particularly well briefed. In this way the flow of information is downward from those closest to authoritative sources. Press conferences also provide a quick way of getting responses to policy initiatives from relevant pressure and interest groups, who will often be represented. But generally there is no great appreciation or use of press conferences.

From the close-up perspective of specialist correspondents the political world is inhabited not by ideologies and pressures, but by personalities locked in a constant struggle for power and influence. This accords with the general perspective on politics created by daily journalism, obsessively close up and rarely able to see the wood for the trees, a problem most journalists readily admit. Senior MPs and ministers naturally attract, and indeed frequently cultivate, press attention, fostering an image that policies and personalities are indistinguishable. Social security is not an area that attracts a great deal of attention among backbenchers, so the available round of lunches and quotes is smaller here than in other policy areas. David Loshak, for example, thought he had met thirty or so MPs, none regularly, over five years as social services correspondent on the *Daily Telegraph.* Ministerial tête-à-têtes are much less frequent. Most correspondents spoke of lunching their minister once a year or so; junior ministers rather more frequently.

Malcolm Dean, social policy leader writer for the *Guardian,* explained the logic for these meetings:

There's a lot of contact with junior ministers. They are often denied influence and like discussion. Civil servants like these lunches—they see it as a way for their ministers to deflect criticism from the department. Sometimes there's a fair bit of kite-flying. People give so much and think, maybe, for a £32 lunch something should be given. Departmental leaks allow them to see how it runs. It won't do any harm, and it keeps the reporter in debt, and it may just raise an issue.

Inevitably, particular ministerial personalities loom large in such accounts. Very often policy seems a matter of personal style, a shift within a consensus this way or that as one particular set of personal whims replaces another. David Ennals, Labour Social Services Secretary from 1976 to 1979, was widely described as 'very much the Minister': correct, pleasant, loyal to the party leadership, inclined to get into avoidable messes that a sympathetic press would on occasion generously ignore. Barbara Castle, by contrast, was generally perceived as good for the press: flamboyant, gregarious, provocative, good copy. She was Secretary of State from 1974 to 1976, a period including the contentious Resource Allocation Working Party proposals as well as the immediate aftermath of the NHS reorganisation in 1973-74.[3] Such prominent figures thus add character to what is anyway a highly personalised view of politics. Ideology and interests seem remote and irrelevant in this close-up world of personal conflict and proclivity in which policy merely leans this way or that as the leading players come and go.

Backbenchers get neatly slotted into the journalistic require- ments of such an account. The populars, particularly, develop a set of rent-a-quote MPs on given topics—horses for courses who readily provide 'reactions', those balancing quotes that are such a vital need in the construction of a routine story within the normal canons of daily journalism.

Even before looking at other sources of material we can see how central are the activities of Whitehall, and particularly of Westminster. In the reporting of any area of social policy this might seem not merely inevitable, but proper and necessary. It does, however, have two important consequences. The first is to accept and relay an agenda of issues and interpretations manufactured within these arenas. This 'agenda-setting' presents a limited range of policy options as inevitable, probable or impracticable, very much according to the current wisdom in the higher corridors of state.[4] The second result of the close-up on government is to privilege the supply side of policy rather than its impact. The results of policy decisions are seen in the political reactions to them rather than in their social consequences. This is not unrecognised by correspondents in the field, who often express a lingering, if mild regret at this seemingly inevitable state of affairs. Some even saw it as the root of the paucity of social security news. As Pat Healy of *The Times* put it, 'social security is a main topic perhaps once a year, and generally it's not because of something that's happening out there, but because of something that's happening at Westminster'. Clare Dover, of the *Daily Express,* saw the arrival of an issue at Westminster as confirmation that it was 'real', not just the special pleading of an interest group. 'When it comes to general axe-grinding I read, I note, and I write nothing. When something is happening, like the parliamentary debate, well we have to report this and give it good coverage then'. Neville Hodgkinson, of the *Daily Mail,* put this in more long-term perspective, suggesting that social security simply had no news value 'until it became political two or three years ago'. Malcolm Dean, of the *Guardian,* spelt out the problem in all this:

> The main pegs for us are political. Newspapers are always more interested in politics than policies. Will the vote be lost tomorrow on some meaningless issue is more interesting than serious issues. We are too Whitehall orientated. It's good for the reporter to get out more, but we're generally too Westminster orientated.

Journalists have often been the first to comment on this orientation, seldom approvingly. Most commonly, disapproval is of the cosy intimacy of the lobby system, as described by John Whale:

> Politicians could get the exposure they needed for their views without the embarrassment of being held to every word of them. They could promise action without needing to be specific about detail . . . Busy journalists, for their part, had the freedom either to dignify their sources—to transmute a press officer or a Parliamentary Private Secretary into 'senior ministers'—or to mention none at all . . . The interests of politician and journalist were not identical; yet both were served by a system of frequent and unpublicised contacts. [1977, p. 124][5]

Descriptions of the lobby system of this kind are often hedged around with reservations about the mechanisms of parliamentary reporting, not their domination of other sources and accounts of policy issues and options. Such reservations occasionally erupt into more serious contention about the lobby system. In the scornful words of Joe Haines, Harold Wilson's press secretary from

1969 to 1976, 'the reliance which Fleet Street places on the twin crutches of "Whitehall sources" and "well-informed circles" is deeply etched on the platen of almost every journalist's typewriter' (1977, p. 231). Far less common is any reservation about the consequences of such a narrow political focus for the full reporting of policy issues. In this area the reporting of social policy is the 'art of the possible' in popular form.

A second major source of material for social security journalists is the array of pressure groups and interest groups that has grown up in this field. The proliferation of such groups is itself evidence of the 'politicisation' of the subject, and thus, in a sense, confirmation of the centrality of the parliamentary arena. By and large the more successful, articulate and aggressively publicity-oriented groups have been those for whom Fleet Street and Westminster are primary targets, and whose objectives seem acceptably reformist in content however radically expressed and promulgated. For the journalists, pressure groups are used less often as a source of primary material than as a source of expert comment on policy initiatives from government. They thus serve a twin function. On the one hand they act as research agencies, able to point out the inconsistencies or evasions in official versions of policy. On the other hand they provide hand-wringing reactions to the iniquities of government policy that can be used to 'balance' a story. The success of some pressure groups lies in their ability to exploit these functions and shrewdly to produce what journalists need. They also provide a short-cut for getting at the consumption side of policy, and thus further insulate journalists from the effects 'on the ground' of the various welfare institutions.

Journalists typically categorise such groups as reliable or unreliable. This is a double-edged judgement, referring as much to the newsworthiness of the groups as to the accuracy of their material. For this reason their perfectly reasonable special pleading is disliked, as though it were in some way an improper abnegation of their first duty—to provide news. Thus Melanie Phillips, of the *Guardian,* suggested that some groups 'provide very little in the way of fact and very much more in the way of subjective interpretation and analysis which can't be used'. Clare Dover, of the *Daily Express,* expanded on this point:

Some grind their axes, which I don't agree with. It can be counter-productive, I'll go on the other side. If I feel they've got a genuine story, yes, we'll give them plenty of space. I must get good straight human interest stories in. It's good to get comment and I always look at what the pressure groups send. Even if its unreliable there may be a story behind the story. But I'm not, on the whole, here to grind people's axes. If they sit there pushing out little reports, I won't give them coverage.

The more politically sophisticated groups that grew in the 1960s out of the 'rediscovery of poverty', the politicisation of patches of community and social work and the pressures of urban deprivation, tend to get labelled as more reliable in these terms. Such groups as the Child Poverty Action Group, Shelter, Mind, and so on, were most frequently mentioned by correspondents though their images had gone through inevitable cycles of credibility and suspicion. As Banting notes, writing of CPAG's initial activities after it was set up in late 1965,

> The CPAG campaign was first and foremost a media campaign. With the British media so highly concentrated in London, even a small group based there can aspire to a national role through effective public relations. CPAG assiduously cultivated the media, writing major articles themselves and helping in the preparation of newspaper features and television programmes on poverty. [Banting, 1979, p. 73]

These groups should be distinguished from interest groups as such, that is those groups explicitly advocating the cause of their members rather than presumptuously making claims for others. The unions and professional associations come into this category. The professionals do very much better than the unions in establishing credibility, and many journalists pointed to the weak and ineffective public relations work of unions in this part of the public sector.[6] The industrial relations aspects of health and social security are often, though not in all cases, covered by industrial relations specialists, leaving the 'softer' end of the subject to the welfare correspondents. As industrial relations news has expanded in the last ten or fifteen years, this has inevitably generated more extensive reporting of this aspect of health and social security, without a commensurate increase in its overall coverage.

A third source of material for correspondents is the plethora of specialist magazines and journals, particularly in the health field but also in other areas of social policy. Many of these arrive as complimentary copies and pile up in unread towers on or around correspondents' desks. They provide both a general background on what is happening in various fields as well as a source of specific stories that can be followed up or refashioned for a less specialised readership. Anything from *The Lancet* or the *Royal College of Nursing Magazine* to such exotica as the *British Journal of Sexual Medicine* can provide material for stories in unlikely reinterpretations. The paramedical journals, in particular, are valued in this way. There is far less of this kind on the social security side, where *New Society,* the general social work/social science weekly, is the only regularly read magazine.

Because of its uneven distribution, attractiveness and readability, this material provides for a fairly random search procedure. Journalism as an exercise in surveillance is, in this area at least, a fairly passive response to the publication and dissemination of primary sources. What is created, in effect, is a 'three-step flow', from specialist journal, through national press, to popular audience. This tends to convergence of content because journalists in a specialised field also read each other. One or two correspondents on 'quality' dailies even spoke rather patronisingly of a sense of responsibility to the 'populars' for this reason: 'they need us so we should tackle the issues they worry about.'

Three points emerge from this review of the sources of social security news. The first is the monumental importance of the apparatus of the state, and particularly of government and senior civil servants, in defining the amount, timing and overall direction of social policy news. In recognising this, many journalists explain the more obvious deficiencies or emphases in news coverage by reference to this prime defining source. Pat Healy of *The Times* considered that press attitudes to social security could not change because 'in the end it's up to people in positions of power to say things which will change attitudes. For example, the press is anti-Labour but Labour in power is still treated better because they have the respect of office attached to them.' Reflecting on the effective, though ill-informed 'anti-scrounger' campaign sustained by Iain Sproat MP in 1976—77, she suggested that 'If Sproat had been treated in parliament, not in the press, in a different way, I don't think the papers would have given him the coverage that they did. It's up to the leadership in the political parties to stamp on people like that.'

The government information machine has become bigger and better. It would be rare these days to get a new bill or a White Paper without a ministerial briefing the same day. The Whitehall—

Fleet Street connection has received considerable comment, and the wider constitutional implications of Whitehall's control over policy and administration are beyond the range of this book.[7] One financial journalist has observed how, in his field,

> the economic commentator starts by being parasitical, dependent on others to give him some idea of the way the internal debate is going, and the way policy is likely to change . . . his life-blood is his contact with the economic policy machine . . . The system demands close contact between the official machine and Fleet Street. [Keegan and Pennant-Rea, 1979, p. 138]

Of course this is not a closed circuit. In the world of economic policy one major partner in his formative debate is the City. Through the medium of stockbrokers circulars and personal contact, as the same writer notes, 'The City has a very direct way of communicating, and its views, via widespread coverage in the financial press, can be on ministers' breakfast tables at almost the same time as the Governor of the Bank of England hears them' (p. 133). Nonetheless, the major achievement of news coverage of economic and social policy is to mask this latter contribution, and refer back to the central parliamentary apparatus as the apparent primary source of policy and domain of policy debate. In this way such journalism achieves what one writer refers to as the 'ideological innovation' of presenting the state (and not private capital) as both the source of and the major impersonal, neutral and authoritative influence on the policy agenda (see de Brunhoff, 1978, pp. 62 *et seq.*)[8] The point here is simply to stress the primacy of the political apparatus as a source both of material and interpretation in social policy news.

The second point, a corollary of the first, is the relative obscurity of its clientele in news about social security. Coverage of social security is almost entirely defined by its ministerial and parliamentary supervision, and is rarely concerned with the impact of policy on those whose lives are largely or partly determined by the benefits and services of the welfare apparatus. This observation could equally well be made of most news topics. One cynical dictum on sociology has suggested that sociologists have 'their eyes turned down onto the down people but their hands held out to the up people'. In many ways journalism is the reverse. Firmly focused on machinations in policy-creating locales, the readership remains a source of revenue rather than news. There are two important exceptions to this general rule. First, the interest in the higher echelons is skewed towards the more visible and accessible institutions, primarily Parliament. Second, one group of consumers does indeed appear, namely the deviant and troublesome out-groups (the scroungers, loafers and spongers) who, as our content analysis showed, command such a central role in the portrayal of social security. Such people appear as individuals, not as consumer groups, and mostly arrive through the crime news delivery system. This is particularly true of the local and provincial press, where courtroom surveillance is a major source of material (see, *inter alia,* Jackson, 1971; Murphy, 1976).

The third point to note about sources is the overall importance they collectively play in the production of social security and policy news. News production becomes increasingly passive as it grows in scope and technical complexity.[9] Journalists in the field often feel besieged by paper aimed at them by primary sources, and speak regretfully of the limited opportunities for more active reporting instead of passive deskwork. This is a ubiquitous refrain in contemporary journalism, harking back to a golden age of foot-in-the-door investigation, which, if it ever existed, has certainly long since passed. 'Look at it; hand-outs, magazines, journals, press releases', said one correspondent despairingly from behind a precarious heap of unread or unopened mail. Clare Dover sifted through a typical day's mail: 'a press release from the back pain association, a load of rubbish from the Canadian High Commission, some stuff from the Neighbourhood Trust, *The Lancet,* the *British Medical Journal* (I read the last two carefully), *New Society, Nature,* some DHSS releases on some incomprehensible benefits . . .'

The passivity that is both cause and effect of this routinised processing of regular source material is accentuated by the perceived reliability of such important sources as the Press Association. As David Loshak, health and social services correspondent on the *Daily Telegraph* from 1974 to 1979, commented, work becomes very much a routine:

In the early days I went to everything, later not. Press briefings are largely a waste of time, ministers rarely said anything new. If there was a major white paper you could write the story the day before and just go along if you also need a quote for the front page. You've always got the back up of the P.A. Much of the

Telegraph is agency stories. Most days you just stick at your desk and phone.

The significance of this routine passivity is that it reinforces that dependence on the more authoritative, powerful and prominent sources on which we have already remarked. In turn this means a largely unquestioning acceptance of the prevailing definitions of what social policy is about. Most journalists recognise this and see it as an inevitable and practical problem. As one writer suggested, 'Few people are prepared to sit down and work out the nuts and bolts; they're very prepared to take on board the platitudes or sweeping generalisations put out by government spokesmen, and one can't altogether blame them because it's a difficult subject and they're very pressed for time.'

The collection of material from news sources is, then, one reason for the limited, rather passive and certainly routine nature of social policy and social security news. The skew of sources is to the state (and particularly to government), to the relevant professional establishment and, for reaction, to the more active pressure and interest groups. We turn next to the processing of this material in news production.

'CORNERING THE MARKET IN BLEEDING-HEART STUFF': THE PRODUCTION OF SOCIAL SECURITY NEWS

Social security news is news not documentation. It involves the creation of news stories with all that implies about the application of news values. The policy process grinds slowly, steadily and constantly, unlike the daily staccato emission of news bulletins or newspapers. To be news, social security has to generate events and be up to date. As one correspondent noted, 'I need a hard news event, either a complaint or a statement of some sort'. Another noted that it was 'easy to get in a big scandal about a mental hospital shock-horror report, or baby-battering cases. Any deeper studies into whys and wherefores, it's not so easy to get in. They go straight onto the spike'.

This concentration on events, not issues or processes, has become a commonplace finding of research into journalism. The implications are that social processes are fragmented and only intermittently visible. Or, as Walter Lippmann put it over fifty years ago, 'news is not a mirror of social conditions, but the report of an aspect that has obtruded itself' (1922, p. 216).[10] This is clearly true of social security news. It is accentuated by the demand for up-to-dateness in news coverage. What is needed is not just an event, but today's event. Pat Healy, of *The Times,* noted how this posed a problem with the publication of policy-related statistics;

> You need a report to get facts across, you can't use background stuff in news stories. For example, when social security statistics come out they relate to the situation two years ago. I wrote a piece but there was great opposition, I had a most extraordinary battle. It didn't matter terribly much to the people out there [indicating the news desk] that it had only·just been published, the point was that they were old figures. The fact that they hadn't been used before was neither here nor there.

Most correspondents just stoically saw this as the price of working on a daily paper. Nearly all spoke wistfully of wanting to do more considered features, taking a deeper and broader view of the issues with which they were concerned. If such opportunities had arisen occasionally, the resulting articles were readily remembered and proudly displayed. But daily journalism is not like that by definition and convention.

It was generally agreed that in recent years the haste and immediacy of daily journalism have increased. Technical and commercial changes, for example, have led to earlier copy deadlines. 'Who's got the luxury of waiting? We have our conference at 3.30 and if stuff doesn't get through to the conference it is likely not to get used' as a correspondent on one of the popular dailies pointed out.

The length of time that can be spent on any one story is often severely curtailed. Most correspondents (not in broadcasting) wrote up to four or even six stories a day, though not all or even most of these would be used. Some disappear into oblivion; others are deep-frozen in a 'flong-file', set ready in type to be used as space-fillers as required. These tend to be, naturally, the less topical, less hard-news stories. Added to this mix of speed, up-to-dateness and event-orientation is the high regard for brevity. This is particularly true in television. Robert Hargreaves, until 1979 home affairs correspondent for ITN, pointed out how rarely, as a matter of policy, ITN (and BBC) would run an item even for as long as two minutes. As he suggested, 'TV is a restricting medium, it can't go into depth'.

None of this is uniquely true of social security or welfare news. It could perhaps be argued, however, that these are subject areas requiring, more than many other topics, a concern with issues, processes and the broad discursive consideration that daily journalism cannot provide. The surface eruptions of political dispute, criminal excess or ministerial declamation are unlikely fully to represent the world of welfare and social security to those millions who daily live within its uncertain embrace.

A second group of news values crucial to understanding how social security news is made derives from the need for news to be watched or read. News as entertainment is a notion underpinning many other news values and, as we argued in chapter 2, it is in those historical periods in which popular journalism is first created and later acquires a mass audience that the guiding idioms, clichés and images about welfare have become fixed. Journalists see two barriers in getting news to its audience. First they have to get material into print (broadcast journalists produce far fewer stories and nearly all get broadcast). 'My job's to get stuff into the paper, I'm not here to serve anybody', as a correspondent on a popular daily put it. The proportion of stories written but not used is generally higher on popular papers. Traditionally, quality papers are thought of as journalists' papers though this severely under-estimates the importance of sub-editors in quality papers, and indeed exaggerates the differences between the two sorts of organ. We checked the output of the relevant correspondents on the *Sun* and the *Daily Mirror* over a six-month period, and found that, although each was writing, it was claimed, up to three or four stories a day, their average 'success rate' of stories in print was only three or four a week. Thus competition for space and a very real rejection rate means there is a clear and constant pressure to 'get stuff in the paper'.

The second barrier is of course attracting an audience. 'The first rule of journalism is still "you've got to be read" ', as one correspondent reminded us. On a popular paper the priorities are fairly clear, and what sells a paper has become relatively easy to identify. Leslie Toulson of the *Sun* counted the attractions off on his fingers: 'sex, television, children, cats, dogs, sport.' None of these looks too promising for social security news, but in practice the equally attractive genres of political conflict and crime provide access for such material.

There is some distinction, of course, between papers, though analysis suggests it is less sharp than journalists wish to believe.

Writers on the populars feel they give adequate coverage to social security, but are forced to be more crisp and concise than their more loosely disciplined peers on the heavies. One correspondent who regularly read the quality papers remarked that 'when I look at the stories I often think, well, there's no way I could have got that particular story into our paper'. The popular dailies require social policy stories in general to meet the demands of entertainment news value. As Toulson went on to explain:

> The journalist has a duty to inform, he also has a duty to entertain if possible . . . try to look for an angle that provides the most entertaining or arresting angle. If you concentrate on the aspect that might be the most important to the people concerned you often find it just wouldn't be read by the majority.

This is illustrated by analysis of the stories produced over a period of months by the relevant specialists on two leading popular dailies, with titles ranging from 'Runaway girls sell sex to keep from starving' to 'Shame of Britain's don't care mothers'.[11] All reduce to their most appealing, titillating, dramatic or humorous elements the great stream of research papers, official reports and press releases from which they are distilled.

Broadcasting has a particular problem in securing attention and comprehension. Though it is not true that the visual appeal of a story dictates its appearance or prominence in a news bulletin, it certainly influences selection and presentation. As Robert Hargreaves explained, the trouble with most social security news is that

> you can't film it you see, can you? It's a straightforward interview situation. You interview the Minister, then you interview a member of the opposition or one of the pressure groups. That's in the nature of the medium. Television is, by definition, a medium that simplifies and journalists are, by definition, popularisers. A dramatic picture stays in the mind more than a worthy sentiment.

Most journalists agree that social security is intrinsically a boring subject, just not designed to set the pulse racing. For the less involved correspondents it's simply too complex: 'I mean, who can understand it for a start? If I had enough brain to keep it all in I'd go mad.' Even the *Guardian*'s Melanie Phillips, writing for a readership widely assumed to comprise large proportions of the liberal professionals employed in the public and social services, agreed that the topic was 'dry and boring'.

> It's to do with money. It's not picturesque, unlike health— patients, wards, that sort of thing. Cuts in social security are complex, and difficult to portray, there are no picturesque images. It conjures up images of people with colour televisions not working. Even on *The Guardian* we're not quite sure that it's acceptable to most of its readers.

Journalism has insidiously acquired the language of show business in a way that cogently illustrates these concerns. A good, prominently presented story is spoken of as having had 'a good show'. Stories or topics are catalogued as being 'sexy' or 'not sexy', meaning much more than straightforward glamour—rather a general air of compelling attractiveness or fascination. Social security is decidedly not sexy. The options, therefore, are either to make it more 'sexy' or interesting, or to relegate it down the ladder of stories jostling for space.

One indirect method to increase the interest of social security material is the well-established journalistic technique of personalisation. As in other news areas, social policy, it is argued, can best be explained by focusing on the individual circumstances of implicitly typical cases, clients or victims. As Clare Dover explained,

> people do buy newspapers to have a good read, don't they? How can you make it interesting? You can personalise it by finding one of the old dears who hasn't claimed who is typical of what the story's about, in which case you're on to something much better because you can put her picture in, her story, and then you can put all the rest of it in about the booklet or report at the end of it. The only way you're going to find such people is if they happen to have written in, or have come on your telephone.

One problem that thereby arises is the classic journalism paradox. In repeatedly presenting unusual cases they implicitly appear typical or common, whereas by scorning the commonplace as dull and unnewsworthy, the routine of life's pattern is rendered invisible.

Clare Dover thought this explained the excessive concern with welfare abuse:

> We print exceptional stories. People don't read what they see in the papers as typical. Most people's lives tend to be fairly colourless. They read us to get an entertaining read about the bizarre things that are going on in other people's lives. When it comes to things like social security fiddlers, people just read it wide-eyed as a read. Can you honestly see our paper, or any other paper, running a story saying thirty claimants collected their dole this morning at such and such an office honestly, and all that?

Thus the innocent urge to entertain, now so central to the logistics of journalism, becomes both an explanation and a rationale for the skewed attention of the news media towards the exceptional. The problem, of course, is the extent to which this skew is towards certain marginal areas (say social security abuse), and not others (say tax fiddles).

To what extent do the news media actively run premeditated campaigns on such issues? It would be as foolish to suggest such campaigns are a major feature in the production of news about social policy as to pretend they never occur. Rather more significant, though, is the policy adopted by a news organisation, representing a continuing range of views rather than a short-term eruption of opinion (see the discussion in Golding and Elliott, 1979, pp. 8–9, 208–11). Most journalists recognise those more often in the work of others. For social policy specialists the prejudices and biases appear in the work of less informed reporters (for example social security fraud is 'covered by the crime reporters, or straight from the PA, not by me'), in the misguided dictates of the news desk, or in the inferior columns of other papers.

These days few journalists would explain policy by direct reference to a paper's ownership, though, as one pointed out, 'the press is owned by proprietors who are conservative, anti-welfare state. However much a proprietor may say he doesn't interfere, the fact that he is who he is is known, and that affects how the paper covers an issue'. Broadly this is usually defined in party political terms. 'I don't know why so many journalists who work for Tory papers are Labour supporters. Journalists are idiosyncratic, but owners do have an impact.' As we have argued elsewhere, the ownership of the news media acts as an indirect constraint on the structure, market strategies and ideological climate within which they produce news, rather more than as a source of direct intervention (though in recent years there have been signs of a return to an earlier model of proprietorial intrusion) (see, *inter alia,* Golding and Murdock, 1978; Murdock and Golding, 1977; see also Murdock and Golding, 1978).

Some papers are clearly identified as having a consistent and news-shaping view of social policies. Neville Hodgkinson of the *Daily Mail,* for example, conceded that the paper had given quite a lot of space to social security abuse. He argued that

> it is a characteristic of the right-inclined, Tory inclined papers that their readers are more sympathetic to stories which illuminate our industrial problems than to stories which illuminate how the part of our national wealth which is set aside to social security spending is distributed. The *Daily Mail* is interested in public expenditure when it thinks there is waste.

The *Daily Telegraph* is another paper with candid and explicit news-shaping policies, as explained by David Loshak:

> The joke used to be that the *Telegraph* didn't have a social services correspondent, it had an anti-social services correspondent. The line was 'we don't need all this'. Less space was given to the more constructive aspects of social services. Things would get elided; for example issues like homelessness. Shelter reports were not ignored, but only got a couple of paras for what was quite a searching analysis of failures in policy. It is the ethos of the paper, you find out certain things don't get in. It's the flavour of the paper. There's always the safety valve of a feature on the women's page. The paper had a thing about social workers. I can think of two or three occasions when reporters were assigned to examining the role of social workers; were they a waste of money and time, what sort of people were they? [Q: And they weren't expected to come back saying what a good thing they were, the country needs more?] No. They were deliberately angled stories, but you don't need to angle your stories if you pick your topic.

These policies, prejudices and elisions are explicit viewpoints, and their intrusion into news selection is deeper than the more pious defenders of journalistic objectivity would admit. Journalists are often more certain of the deliberate slant in other papers than in their own. Of the two undeniably right-leaning papers just described, one was characterised as 'an iniquitous institution' by a correspondent on a popular paper. Another writer, describing one of those papers, suggested that its journalists

> felt restricted by the impression they had that they were required to write about social security only in derogatory terms. Basically what they were required to do when writing about social security was to emphasise how much it was costing and how many people were getting benefits they weren't entitled to, rather than an objective, dispassionate view.

Journalists very often regard themselves collectively as a body of liberal-minded moderates, safeguarding a commonsense view of political reality from which others (some politicians, trade union activists, intellectuals, lobby groups) frequently and dangerously depart. They thus see 'distortions' in policy journalism as the result of pressures, on the one hand from proprietors or sensation-seeking news desks, and on the other hand from prejudice-laden and intolerant readers. One correspondent, for example, suggested that

> If journalists are working on papers which take a certain line they know they will be catering to the prejudices of their readership. Readers like to see their prejudices confirmed. I know reporters on, for example, the *Mail,* who are liberal, but I am sure they doctor their writing for the readership. The reporter knows what goes down well, and they are actively encouraged in this by newspaper management.

Many journalists describe the difference in approach discernible in different papers as more to do with the popular quality divide than with politics. One writer on a quality (up-market, advertising-revenue-dominated) paper suggested that on social policy generally 'we have a lousy popular press', a view frequently expressed by writers on the non-popular papers. But beneath all these differences are the underlying concepts of news and how to create it embodied in the demands and dictates of news desks. For some correspondents this was a major problem. One thought his news desk 'overdoes conventional Fleet Street news values in terms of shock and sensation'. Another, on a popular daily, agreed his news desk 'would say can we do something on this or that. They will come up and say there's been a report out today on social security fiddling or whatever.' A certain tension is created, as Jeremy Tunstall has noted in his study of specialist correspondents (1971, p. 53, Ch. 4), between the source-orientation of correspondents and the readership/revenue/market-orientation of news desks. Most correspondents felt themselves ultimately the master in any conflict. One claimed,

> I would resist instructions. It's 85 per cent up to the man who writes it. On social services I would do my own news editing. Sometimes I would get requests, like "let's put the boot into the health service bureaucrats, how much money they're wasting, how stupid they are". Or "let's show up these social workers", this sort of approach. But it wasn't brought up that often. A story is a story no matter what the implications.

Generally, journalism in this area means news-hunts more often than witch-hunts. But campaigns do occur, and, though infrequent, they demonstrate to readers and correspondents alike where the sympathies and policies of the paper lie.[12] In the interludes between campaigns there is not so much a return to neutrality as a steady retrenchment behind the boundaries constructed by campaigns. News desks, and beyond them management and proprietors, merely need to keep the props of these ideological fences in good repair to confirm the consistent tenor of coverage, which in the contemporary British media clearly means a suspicion of, or hostility to, welfare and social services as the dominant theme of coverage.

The increase in specialist correspondents is sometimes seen as a solution to the problem of ill-informed journalism. David Donnison, Chairman of the Supplementary Benefits Commission from 1975 until its demise in 1980, expressed this view in a lecture given in early 1976, at a peak period of 'scrounger-bashing' by the press. In it he argued that

> Nearly every significant newspaper has its specialist correspondents working in the fields of education, the health services and defence who have read all the reports, followed the debate over many years, and know the people who play leading parts in their field. The field of social security, which plays an equally important part in the lives of ordinary people, in public

expenditure and in the management of the economy, deserves an equally well-informed public opinion underpinned by an equally effective community of scholars and scientists. [Donnison, 1976b, p. 343]

In the development of specialisation, foreign and political correspondents came first, and in recent years there has been a proliferation of specialist journalists in most news media. The welfare apparatus has only recently attracted its own specialists following the boom in social services in the early 1970s after the Seebohm report, and in the more general climate in which, as one correspondent suggested about this period, 'social policy was just emerging—the growth of super-departments, pressure groups, *Social Trends,* and so on.'

In fact, specialisation within social policy is not very advanced. Popular national newspapers tend to have 'home affairs' correspondents covering the full range of domestic policy issues from the Home Office, through DHSS, environment and education. The main areas of welfare are health, social security and social services, and it is unusual for a correspondent to cover less than all of these. *The Times* is the most specialised, with a specialist in each of local government, environment, home affairs, legal affairs, medicine and health. The paper's social services correspondent covers local authority social services and social security. On the *Guardian* and *Daily Telegraph* the relevant specialist covers health as well as social services. Correspondents on the populars tend to be less specialised, though there are not necessarily fewer of them. The *Daily Mirror,* for example, has two correspondents covering medicine and science. Broadcasting tends to have the fewest specialists. As Robert Hargreaves explained, 'television can't afford specialists, they would die of frustration. I was ITN's first Home Affairs correspondent, covering the political side of social services, health, social security, and Home Office, environment, and local government.'

Specialisation tends to be defined in terms of Whitehall departments, and the proliferation and changing responsibilities of correspondents reflect the growth of comprehensive departments of state in such corporate fields as the environment or social services. There is considerable kudos in becoming a 'correspondent' with all that it implies in terms of by-lines, expertise and authority. It confirms elevation from the routine of bread and butter journalism or, as one correspondent put it, 'I no longer wanted to chase fire engines and write about straight bananas'.

Where correspondents cover both health and social security, as most do, it is health that dominates their time. Social security has its occasional flourishes but has to battle against a preoccupation with health that, if anything, has increased in recent years. Several journalists pointed out that social security became more visible in election years, but health was a constant concern, particularly since the NHS reorganisation in 1974. As one writer commented, 'health then became a really hot potato politically. Then you had the private beds issue, a Royal Commission, and so on.'

The major justification for this emphasis is the political fascination of health issues, and only secondarily the argument that health is of interest to everyone, social security only to a minority. It is a supply-generated demand, to do with the political news machine rather than the public news appetite. Most papers have either a medical correspondent or a freelance specialist they can call on to write on the clinical and scientific side of the subject. Frequently nowadays a science correspondent will include this area in his or her brief. This adds to the pre-eminence of health news: 'medical science is fascinating, it's a lively area full of new discoveries'. Indeed, this fantasy world of laboratory break-throughs, technological marvels and heart-rending case dramas could have been created for popular journalism. As one correspondent on a popular daily summed up the field, with no hint of intentional parody or humour, 'one tends to get material every day on some aspect of medicine, whether it's sex or heart transplants.'[13]

Not all specialists are necessarily in favour of specialisation as a solution to the deficiencies they readily concede exist in social services news. There is still in journalism widespread regard for the traditional skills of the general reporter, who it is believed undertakes a more active and mobile role in a more earthy environment than the somewhat suspect world of cosy expense-account dinners and confidential cocktails that the specialist is sometimes thought to inhabit. Specialists and reporters alike (and commonly the former preferred to be thought of as reporters— journalism contains a strong occupational inverted snobbery) pointed the finger at poor news editing rather than poorly informed reporting. Few regarded more specialisation as desirable.

This is particularly true for social security for three reasons. First, the subject is seen as intrinsically uninteresting. David Loshak enlarged on this theme:

social security is less momentous than industry and politics. Just because it's a large area of public expenditure it's not therefore important. The editor of *New Society* suggested we should have a social services page. Rubbish. There's not much to be said about social security. It's largely about the technical minutiae of benefit entitlements. It's humdrum, boring. What is there to be said?

Many agreed that you could get too close to the subject. There was considerable admiration for Pat Healy's informed and detailed social security news in *The Times*. But this was often described as an indulgence, too detailed for the ordinary reader and inappropriate in a daily newspaper, however elite its readership. Similarly, most correspondents thought the *Guardian* best for social services and welfare generally: 'it's what the *Guardian*'s all about.' But this was more often a comment on that paper's readership than an expression of envy or aspiration. Melanie Phillips, herself the *Guardian*'s social services correspondent, felt it was a mistake 'to specialise too much. You end up writing the same story over and over again. The advantages get outweighed by a growing boredom and blindness to things.'

The second doubt about specialisation is that it takes the writer too close to the sources, creating an unhealthy symbiosis that rapidly chokes journalistic independence. As one writer candidly and uncompromisingly suggested, 'specialist writers on the serious paper don't write very critical stories because they need their contacts'. There is a circularity in this in that it is the fairly narrow definition of what social security news is that creates the equally narrow dependence on a limited circle of authoritative sources. Nonetheless, the haunting spectre of utter dependence on a press relations office in Whitehall has spread distaste for extended specialisation as fast as it has in fact become reality.

The third reason for hostility to more specialisation is specific to social services and social security. Many journalists would welcome increased specialisation in some subjects, but see welfare as well down the list of likely contenders. Neville Hodgkinson on the *Daily Mail* put this in both political and journalistic terms:

The *Mail* has tended to be more interested in the Tory idea that industrial matters matter most, rather than the way the fruits of that industrial activity have been distributed. Even if we had another six correspondents social security would be low down the list, after, for example, energy or environment.

This rather begs the question of how industrial matters are reported and to what extent industrial news is produced in ways that leave vast areas of activity under-exposed. Nonetheless, it is a popular view. Social security is not important, therefore it doesn't generate much news, therefore it does not need a specialist, therefore it does not generate much news, and so on. The practicalities were spelt out by Leslie Toulson:

> It's a financial problem. There are claims for other areas but the paper has to make choices. The heavies have fine arts correspondents and all sorts. But Fleet Street's struggling. You can end up with a low productivity individual, who is being paid, in effect, for doing one day's work.

Thus antipathy to specialisation arises from the concern of journalists to avoid source-dependence and passivity, from the needs of the news organisation to maximise productivity, and from the perceived dullness and unimportance of social security.

To some extent this leaves journalists reporting social security and social services very often ill-informed about the specifics of their subject, particularly where they also report health. One writer interviewed in 1979, when average industrial weekly wages for manual workers were £98.80, spoke glibly of people 'only earning £6,000 a year', a figure in fact higher than the earnings of over three-quarters of the adult male work force.[14] Another, asked to expand on their view that there was too much red tape in social security, cheerfully rebuffed the question with 'I'm sorry, I'm not entering that one. I've got one of those minds, I can understand parliament, but I cannot understand social security payments.' Yet another thought 'if you've got a certain amount of savings you can't claim unemployment benefit, can you?', making the common confusion between a contributory National Insurance benefit and the non-contributory means-tested supplementary benefits. These illustrations are not intended to suggest the economic illiteracy or welfare rights ignorance of correspondents in the field. On the contrary, most are committed to their areas and impressively well-informed. But inevitably this expertise is spread thinly and is thus more easily penetrated by mythologies sharpened by authority or popular credibility.

To some extent this was acknowledged, but felt to be inevitable if unfortunate. Newspaper journalists are given to arguing that it did not matter anyway since television is much more important, and all the press can do is to reinforce the impressions so potently transmitted by broadcasters. This mixture of pragmatism and fatalism was just occasionally spiced with a more optimistic enthusiasm for the field as a positive area of journalistic achievement. As Roger Todd, home affairs correspondent for the *Daily Mirror* put it, cheerfully summing up his own niche on the paper, 'the science editor and correspondent do the heavy medicine and space, things like that. I've cornered the market in the bleeding hearts industry.'

TRUSTEES FOR THE LIBERAL CONSENSUS: VALUES IN WELFARE STATE JOURNALISM

Journalists are not political eunuchs, and it would be preposterous to expect their work to be untainted by the prejudices, convictions and sympathies that are as much part of their social make-up as of anybody else's. Recognising this, critics of journalism often cite these personal values as the source of such biases in news coverage as content analysis frequently reveals. Unfortunately, the professional response to such criticisms is frequently as shallow as the accusation, and tends to lean on rather weary claims to integrity and professional competence though they were, in fact, never in question. In the social policy field this is particularly fraught. The crime specialist can clearly declare an unobjectionable commitment against crime, just as the health specialist is against disease. The political journalist and the industrial correspondent have well-defined blocs of partisanship between which they can identify and occupy a clear zone of impartiality. Of course, all such claims beg enormous questions that have been provocatively explored by research in recent years.[15] But they are current in journalistic discussion. Who, to draw the parallel, are social welfare and services correspondents against? Who, indeed, are they for?

Neutrality tends to be fleshed out by a firm commitment to those decent liberal values that are loosely associated with the principles of the welfare state. These are rarely questioned in any radical way, and are largely perceived as the sober and rational view of any reasonable and humane citizen. It is a supremely apolitical view. Several journalists commented on how surprised they were in their earlier years by the very limited political interests and commitments of their colleagues (cf. Tunstall, 1971, pp. 121—5; Epstein, 1973, pp. 206—15).

What correspondents *are* against is extremism, whether in political ideology or action. As one journalist put it, 'I would see myself as a laissez-faire liberal. I don't trust people who say they have a coherent ideology or political philosophy. You should judge issue by issue.' A common reference point was the long 'winter of discontent' that presaged the fall of the Labour government in 1979, and the militant action of the public sector unions. No correspondent had any sympathy for the health service unions, and although willing to admit some of the reporting had been wilfully sensational, even hysterical, all shared a distaste for the methods employed by these unions in pursuing wage claims. 'What happened that winter was totally unacceptable', said one, adding 'they should have recognised they couldn't have more pay without staff cuts', an analysis few journalists would think contentious. Alan Fisher, General-Secretary of the National Union of Public Employees, attracted particular odium, both for his prominent part in the winter activities and his later angry accusations about press coverage of the period. One correspondent remarked, 'I shed no tears for Alan Fisher. The hospital workers had a case but they did cause a lot of misery.'

In any case, correspondents firmly believe that any distortion present in their own material, or more plausibly in other people's, will have little effect and thus no serious political or social implications. This contrasts slightly with the view, more common in the upmarket papers, that there is a small, politically significant readership, who can be addressed directly in the columns of the daily press. But as far as the mass readership is concerned, all is ephemeral, nothing seriously responsible for popular beliefs or perspectives. On the one hand television is seen as the more potent medium, and television news hardly ever deals with social security or social services. 'Most people get most of the information from TV don't they, and TV news isn't biassed except in the New Left sense', said one. 'The press doesn't have a very positive role, TV is more important. Their news values are totally distorted by an obsession with pictures, the press merely reinforces impressions,' said another. In fact, neither of these explanations is supported by research evidence.[16] On the other hand, however, correspondents also argue that any impact they might have is not their business. Their job is to set the facts before the jury, not to advocate or to agonise over the judgement. This is not an amoral view, but a pragmatic, professional one. As Melanie Phillips explained,

> Yes, the lingering impression does worry me, for example on things like abortion, the allegations and refutations. I take the view there's nothing I can do about this. It's my job not to decide, not to be judge and jury. Not to be the arbiter of whether they're saying the truth or not. But if they are making allegations, then they are entitled to have those allegations put forward. [Q: regardless of the consequences?] Yes, though the story must be balanced . . . I think it would be quite wrong for me to censor the material I write because I'm aware of the social consequences of what I write.

The guide, of course, is news values—'is it interesting, does it impinge on people's lives?' But, as we have seen, news values are not born immaculate, but derive from the news production process itself, with its heavy reliance on dominant modes of defining social priorities and preferred explanations and solutions.

Central in the liberal consensus shared by most writers is sympathy for the deserving poor. This can even extend to the unemployed; after all, 'being out of work is not a mortal sin'. More usually, this sympathy was expressed by regret that journalism could not do more to expose the plight of worthy but unnewsworthy groups. Roger Todd, of the *Daily Mirror,* suggested he would 'like more space for things that don't fit the cliches, for example kids in care being controlled by psychotropic drugs'. Les Toulson felt more coverage could be given to the disabled.[17] These nominations usually represent latent urges to conduct investigative exposés buried beneath a realistic sense of what can and cannot be done by the creaking machinery of conventional journalism. Robert Hargreaves cited a rare instance where television news had stretched the boundary of normal neutrality.

> We did a series about the rights of Mongol kids to get mobility allowance. We started it after an M.P. had brought it to our attention. The DHSS argued they had a mental not a physical handicap and were therefore ineligible. We had quite an impact. It was the nearest ITN ever came to a campaign. The Television Act obliges us to be impartial, but the message was clear.

Who could be against Mongol kids?

But in recent harsher days, when all social welfare spending is seen as fair game for the Treasury axe, it is unlikely such liberties would be taken, even for such uncontentiously deserving groups. The apparent space left for such incidental advocacy is small. This is more obvious on the 'liberal' side of the equation than on the conservative, where calls for control over public expenditure, efficiency, checks on excessive generosity and the like are not so much campaigns as part of the conceptual furniture. There is no need to defend the language and assumptions on this side of the equation when they are not viewed as beyond the consensus on which the impartiality demanded by broadcasting legislation is constructed.

If some groups are regrettably left out of the news, so are some areas and institutions. Most journalists recognise the inadequacy of coverage of local government in general, and local authority social services in particular. Many argue, however, that this is a reasonable reflection of priorities. National news is precisely that; local personal social service stories should only be covered if they have national significance. Correspondents certainly feel London based. The metropolitan dominance in British journalism is almost unique in Europe, and many journalists concede they would like to get out into the grubby industrial centres of the north and midlands, or into the vast rural hinterland of the shires, rather more than they do. This is countered, however, by the pragmatic view that 'there's not much point in running around. I need copy. My telephone reaches everywhere and we have contacts all over the country. If we really need to get out and about we do so. You can always get the papers from a conference.' David Loshak was less sanguine about this sedentary and metropolitan approach.

> The *Telegraph,* like all the other papers, is really a provincial paper for London and the south-east. If it's within a taxi-ride of Fleet Street it will get covered. That's more true now than ever. All the main organisations and government departments are in London. It's very misleading in some ways.

In identifying gaps in coverage of worthy and important issues, journalists frequently come back to an implicit statement of their social role. Despite all proclamations about the disinterested provision of information, deep down every journalist is a campaigner. Nothing brings a rosier glow than the retelling of tales about ministers embarrassed into action, bumptious pressure groups discredited, or worthy objects of sympathy aided in distress. The further upmarket the paper, the more, by and large, such tales focus on the political arena. A story might alert a minister's advisers to potential support or opposition, or 'blow the whistle' on impending but unpopular initiatives. This is a game played by insiders, to rules rarely articulated but finely balanced on a knife-edge of subtle understandings and delicate vocabulary. One correspondent related the now notorious instance of the Callaghan Cabinet's reneging on child benefit in 1976.

> In April I got wind of the proposed failure to implement Child Benefit. I delayed writing about it because I simply couldn't believe it was happening. If I hadn't started blowing the whistle at that stage which meant that other people realised that something was going on . . . the government would have abandoned it.

As Ruth Lister recalls, 'The reaction both inside and outside parliament, was overwhelmingly hostile and was further fuelled by the leaking of Cabinet minutes which revealed the political manoeuvring that had led to the reversal of the government's child benefit policy' (1980, p. 191; see also Field, 1976, 1978). Eventually a compromise, if far from satisfactory, scheme emerged.

Correspondents generally feel that if they are to have an impact it will be on the political process in this way, rather than in influencing popular attitudes or beliefs—a role they strongly deny. As Pat Healy said of her readers,

> I know perfectly well that I am not going to change the minds of the *Times* readership about social security. I would have thought that the majority of *Times* readers have one of two broad positions. One is that 'Ah yes, we must look after those less well off than ourselves'. The other is 'well, we're spending far too much'. I don't think there's any way I could change that . . . I hope I get through to a few MPs who will take action.

It is difficult and probably pointless to seek the root of such attitudes to welfare as correspondents do have in their individual biographies. There are, however, themes in the occupational ideology of journalism that do resonate with the collective view of the welfare state we are characterising as a liberal consensus. Most journalists stress their humble origins; they are quintessentially self-made and frequently claim the kind of diverse and colourful careers that used to be fashionable on the dustjackets of first novels. Of the relevant correspondents in the national press and broadcasting in our study period, more than half had been to university (three to Oxbridge). But nearly all had come from lower-middle-class or working-class homes with a very strong leaning to small businesses and independent traders (a family bakers, a plumber, a commercial traveller, and so on). Most had come up through the provincial press, and on average were a little under 40. Among broadcast journalists there has probably been a slightly more elevated pattern of recruitment. John Clare, BBC community relations correspondent, suggested that 'we're like clones, all with very similar backgrounds, the majority Oxbridge graduates . . . The reason the BBC doesn't cover the social services is because on the whole people here have no experience of it.'[18]

This strong measure of self-advance leaves a residue of faith in the work ethic and in individualism. Tales of early hardship are commonplace. One writer recalled that 'for a time I worked from a sleeping bag on a friend's floor and using public phone boxes'. Another remembered that 'when I first became a journalist I was paid £2-9-6 and I was paying three quid for digs. I used to bash a piano in a pub under age in the evenings to make up the difference.' Not surprisingly, then, few would turn readily to the social security system for help in adversity. Few indeed ever had, and few thought this anything but a sign of weakness in those who did. 'I would, on principle, rather not claim, one likes to think of oneself as resourceful and self-reliant', said one. 'I've never been a claimant, wouldn't know how to' was another proud boast. Several pointed out how a journalist with the kind of expertise a specialist correspondent could offer ought always to be able to get freelance work. This was a symbol of the flexibility and initiative many journalists feel is lacking in worlds other than their own.

This commitment to the work ethic is buttressed, therefore, by a rooted and consistent individualism. As a general comment Malcolm Dean observed that 'journalism attracts people who are least likely to be sympathetic to people who haven't got initiative and the other traits they themselves are presumed to have'. Les Toulson expressed this both as a personal and as an institutional philosophy: 'we're anti the big-mother society. Ideally those who can't help themselves should be helped. At the same time we don't want to see those who could help themselves not helping themselves because it is available. That's the concern of our paper. Not anti-welfare but anti over-welfare.'

How far these beliefs become an ideological force in shaping welfare journalism is difficult to determine. These are values prevalent in journalism generally, not merely in the esoteric corner with which we are here concerned. Melanie Phillips put several of these beliefs together:

> I have never been a claimant. I would regard it as a terrible mark of failure to claim unemployment benefit. Journalists can always find work. It would mean I had no initiative to find a job. I would feel it wrong not to work, even clerical or something. I don't see that as a virtue, it's just the way I was brought up. Perhaps I do unconsciously look on people who are unemployed in a more critical way than I think I do . . . Journalists do think other people can get work. Most are middle-class, it is beyond their experience to face structural unemployment, the whole issue of social services is alien to them. If they have problems they have middle-class solutions. The welfare state is outside the experience of most journalists.

If all of this is true, and clearly subjectively it is true even if some particulars do not apply to all journalists, much welfare journalism could be explained. Unfortunately it is never that simple. Biography is a necessary but hardly a sufficient explanation of cultural production. Nevertheless the self-made journalist, committed to the work ethic and individualistic self-reliance, will find in the occupation a well-formed occupational ideology to support these values, and much to lend weight to the equally well-nourished scepticism in British culture about the concerns of the welfare services and the motivations of their clients.

These values lead to mixed views about reporting of social security fraud and abuse. Most journalists accept that this issue has been given undue prominence, but either accept philosophically that that's the way news values work or explain it as a necessary reflection of their readers' prejudices. First, they point out, fraud is a good story and, particularly once transplanted to the political arena, it is an essential news item. 'Once it became a parliamentary issue we had to look into it.' Roger Todd pointed out that 'if there's a good story in it I do it regardless of my sympathies.' Clare Dover expanded on this: 'It's a job to make social security stories interesting. Abuse, yes, you've got a good yarn. It's a system that is working. It's like X number of airplanes took off from Heathrow this morning. You don't write it, you only write when one crashes.' Why not write about other things that go wrong, like low take-up of benefits, then? 'We do cover that, but it won't get us much space. The proud old granny who won't pick up her money, yes, we do cover that . . . but such pieces are unlikely to get into the first edition. Not terribly gripping yarns are they?'

Correspondents are mostly well aware of the standard arguments against undue concern with abuse—its relatively trivial cost; the far larger sums involved in under-claiming; and so on. Many abuse stories, particularly the routine court cases and individual spongers, are covered by general reporters, with the correspondents picking it up when it permeates through to the political level. Specialists stress this distinction. David Loshak felt that the concern with abuse on the *Daily Telegraph* had been 'wildly exaggerated. Not by me but by general reporters. My stories on this always emphasised the other side, perhaps I even went too far. If ever a story came up which highlighted scrounging it would stand a much better chance of getting in than a story which didn't.'

The problem of providing balance, then, is partly organisational—news desk values and general reporters doing as they were bid—and partly journalistic—other aspects of social security simply are not as interesting as abuse. Roger Todd had 'done stories on non take-up. But it gets a smaller and smaller show. You can't keep on at it and expect it to get the same kind of show. Once you've said it that's it, it's a one-off story.' Robert Hargreaves has described what he sees as a successful attempt to balance coverage in television news:

> . . . after long discussion ITN recently went on the air with a series about abuse, taking the view that no area should be regarded as off-limits to television. We tried to take care, though, that the series was balanced. First we presented the case against; then we gave a number of specific examples of abuse, and finally the case in favour—we would say these were all legitimate items of news, fairly covered. [Hargreaves, 1979, p. 14]

This orthodox, indeed classic statement of balanced news production ignores that vital element of the implicit message of news that researchers call 'agenda-setting'. This concept suggests that no matter how a topic is treated, no matter how carefully the pros and cons are balanced, the significant message for the audience is that the topic is itself a matter of social concern. Thus ten stories suggesting abuse is a serious problem complemented by ten stories implying abuse is of only minor importance do not in fact achieve balance so much as reinforce twenty times that social security abuse is 'on the agenda'. News, whether in print or broadcast, is not 'read' as a record or chronicle. Claims to comprehensive coverage that point to one story about low take-up of benefits in the midst of recurrent abuse items, assume greater aptitudes for rationality, recall and attentiveness among news consumers than either common-sense or psychology might expect. In practice, this does not cause journalists too great a concern for two reasons. First, journalists do in fact generally accept the need to give attention to social security abuse, and secondly they doubt the effect of undue news coverage of abuse on attitudes or behaviour. On the first point many journalists point out that, though the relative level of social security abuse may be low, it is still a lot of money. Or at least that's how the reader sees it. 'People have a right to get upset about abuse. It's the distinction between paying for something and being given something. It's a common moral precept that if you're being given something you shouldn't try and get any more', said one journalist. Others are less ambiguous about their own view. Clare Dover felt that

> unless you've got somebody who's actually skiving they'd rather not be on it anyway. I do think the situation is pretty bad at the moment where you do have these odd situations where people can earn more by not working than they can by working, and I do think the incentive to work has to be restored. I think that whilst we take cracks at those who've been swinging the lead and abusing the system, what we really ought to be doing is perhaps taking a crack at the system itself that allows this to happen.

Actually suppressing stories would be bad journalism: 'my attitude is not to be protective just because it would give the wrong impression. My attitude is kick anybody if they're doing wrong', as one of the more sympathetic correspondents put it. Many journalists accepted that their view of unemployment and the 'incentives problem' was possibly coloured by life in Fleet Street. Melanie Phillips suggested that 'Journalists believe by and large that there is no such thing as low pay. Leader writers believe that overtime and moonlighting provide good incomes. Low pay is appreciated intellectually, but when the hospital workers took action moral indignation here knew no bounds.'

The view that, in any case, people are not influenced by an excessive concern with abuse was held about claimants as well as about general readers, rejecting any suggestion that consistently hostile reporting that scroungers might inhibit legitimate claimants fearful of unpleasant labelling or contemptuous treatment. Sometimes this was based on mis-informed though widely believed generalisations:

> I don't think it inhibits people claiming benefits at all, because I think the people who don't claim tend to be the proud elderly ones, who because of the way they were brought up all those years ago believe that to accept any handouts is to accept charity. Your non-claimers tend to come from an older, much prouder generation. I don't think they tend to come from young people other than those put temporarily out of work.[19]

Views such as these—practical, liberal but not soft—resonate readily with the hard-headed individualism of journalism's occupational ideology. 'Abuse stories have been overdone, yes, but it is a real problem and our readers are concerned about it and well, we've a sneaking feeling there is rather a lot of comfortable loafing about going on. I'd never be caught sitting back waiting for state handouts.' This is to some extent a crude parody, but it does express the consonance between the journalistic view of the world and the more populist elements in anti-welfare ideologies. Another form in which this appears is in hostility to bureaucracy and the state.

One journalist even defined his job as 'putting into ordinary words the most interesting things that arise from what officialdom does to people'. It is a view of the world that oscillates between, on the one hand, a pluralist conception of pressure and interest groups jostling round more or less attentive authorities, with power being rooted in influence and status, and, on the other hand, a populism defined by sympathy for the little people against the big battalions of state bureaucracy. In part journalists arrive at this position by extrapolation from their own work. In the daily hunt for stories nothing is more frustrating than running the gauntlet of the information machine in Whitehall or Westminster. Journalism deals in simple information processed swiftly. The state deals in complex information remorselessly chewed over and jealously guarded. Journalists hate nothing so much as bureaucracy or red tape, which are contrasted in their minds with the commonsense simplicity with which affairs ought to be conducted. This feeling is exacerbated by the irritation journalists feel at their dependence on the political machine as a source of stories, while the 'watchdog of democracy' function demands that they be biting the hand that feeds them. Many correspondents are aware of the problems in this view. David Loshak put his finger on one central confusion that derives from it: 'All these attacks on bureaucrats; it confuses bureaucracy with administration. It's easy to put the boot in, not so easy when you actually try and get rid of Quangos'.

All the values we have been describing are seen by correspondents as widespread, no more nor less than the sensible mainstream of popular beliefs. They believe their work is thus reflecting rather than forming public opinion. Journalists felt they had detected a shift in public mood over the last few years (they are great believers in a *zeitgeist*). Pat Healy suggested that 'in a recession people look for scapegoats. People are no longer proud of the welfare state.' David Loshak shrewdly summed up this mood more generally: 'since the oil crisis of 1973—74 there has been a national awareness that our prosperity is not limitless. Therefore public expenditure had to be contained. The British economy and the actions of unions all led to an atmosphere of more strictness on strikes etc.'

This sense of mood or atmosphere is not backed up by one particular form of evidence, namely letters to journalists. Most correspondents receive surprisingly few letters from readers. Where they cover health as well as social services the majority of letters are medical enquiries. Television correspondents receive even fewer letters—Robert Hargreaves suggested two or three a week, mostly personal problems—and one correspondent spoke of having received an 'avalanche' of letters after one story that turned out to be about a dozen. At the other extreme, one leader on fluoridisation of water had provoked 200 letters, mostly from professionals in the field. Neville Hodgkinson expected to receive 'stacks' of letters on medical matters ('maybe thirty a week') but only a couple a week on social security matters. By default, a sense of readers' views comes more indirectly. David Loshak summed it up thus: 'There's a fair feedback from readers. Sometimes scores of letters a day on minor subjects. For example, a small piece on cystitis led to hundreds of letters. You get a lot of cranky letters. But the feeling you get for the readership is really a gut feeling.'

Despite this, letters are still used as evidence of popular feeling, and occasionally as sources of material. Les Toulson, though accepting letter writers were unlikely to be representative, felt they had their uses: 'You get letters after stories, especially from people asking you to stop them giving money to idlers, on average about six for a story like that . . . Race also gets people hot under the collar. They don't influence me unless I get a big block of opinion in one direction. Then I can say "indications are that . . .".' He felt the letters he received confirmed that

> The public feels that if someone doesn't take advantage of a welfare benefit—it's a simplistic attitude of course—the public feels that's their fault. But fiddlers are costing them money. It's a general attitude in this country, people resent anybody getting anything for nothing. I share this attitude over people fiddling the state.

Abuse stories were particularly effective in provoking letters from readers, which might in turn produce a similar follow-up. This is distinct from other issues. As Clare Dover suggested, 'I get a lot of letters on attendance allowances and other genuine grievances. I just write back and say I'm sorry.' Neville Hodgkinson noted a parallel distinction: 'We don't cover tax evasion much because if you asked people 95 per cent would say social security fraud is more important.'

What correspondents suggest they are doing, then, is to pick up the flavour of public concern and use it to season their own writing and perceptions. Neville Hodgkinson described it thus:

> Even our readers who are social security recipients are worried about fraud. There's no sort of guideline. We just judge from night to night what are the most interesting stories. Yes, we do give a lot of space to social security abuse because that is perceived as being a major problem. But it's not unbalanced. There is concern that the social security system has advanced beyond the ability of the country to sustain it . . . the concern comes from individuals not the papers. The papers latch on to areas of concern and write about them . . . it's what Mr. Average is going to think . . . it's a question of judging what the average reader thinks. The only way you can judge that is through your own instincts, isn't it? I agree Fleet Street can get out of touch. Journalists are fairly comfortable.

This candid assessment contrasts with occasional less credible claims to be constantly sampling and expressing the popular mood, by virtue of the journalists' extensive exposure to a widespread range of opinion and experience. Such letters as journalists do receive are likely to counter their more liberal instincts.[20] But, by and large, feedback from the readership is limited and recognisably atypical. When correspondents speak of discussing the issues with readers the reference is more likely upward to sources and contacts rather than down to ordinary consumers. One journalist suggested, 'I do talk to readers, that is my friends, MPs I meet, people I interview. I get a certain amount of sob-mail but mostly from professional letter-writers.' By contrast another suggested,

> I don't have a lot of contact with claimants. The trouble with contact with claimants is that I have the kind of voice that puts them off. They automatically assume that I come from a middle-class family and have a quite different background to them. I don't think it's very possible for me to spend a great deal of time with claimants.

The point we are making is that, necessarily, journalists' sense of what issues are in play and to what extent their own values are popular and typical is formed in the absence of any serious contact with or feedback from either clients of the welfare state or the public more generally. It is necessarily more likely to derive from those authoritative sources within the arenas of professional and public politics that are their major concerns.

The most direct and explicit statement of news is of course found in editorials. By and large correspondents are not much involved in leader writing. In modern journalism this has become a specialised role, and even some editors prepare leaders only infrequently (this pattern varies of course). The leader writer (or more often writers) occupies a place near the top of the professional pyramid, and even the specialist correspondent has only limited impact on what he (the gender is deliberate) writes. This is particularly true in the welfare field. Several correspondents pointed out that they were the lowest paid or lowest in status of the correspondents on their paper. The pattern was common: 'I'm not involved, I have no control over their opinions, they consult me over facts sometimes'; 'The leader writer has his own ideas, he doesn't come to me'; were typical comments.

Leader writers are not primarily subject specialists, though on some papers there is a rough division of labour by broad subject areas. But the real expertise of leader writers is in politics, the inside world of 'realpolitik' in Westminster and Whitehall. This is why such men as Joe Haines, formerly Harold Wilson's press secretary, are valued as leader writers (in his case for the *Daily Mirror*). Political connections are often close. For example, one of the leader writers at the *Daily Telegraph* was Alfred Sherman, a close associate of Sir Keith Joseph at the latter's right-wing think-tank, the Centre for Policy Studies.

Correspondents do occasionally get involved in leader writing (and it is more common for senior specialists like foreign editors or political correspondents). This can sometimes lead to odd bifurcations in their output. One correspondent recalled an occasion 'when I did a very sympathetic story on the Supplementary Benefits Commission annual report, and the same day wrote a leader knocking it because that was the paper's line'.

How policy evolves on a topic like social security is hard to determine.[21] We have been mainly concerned with the implicit formation of policy, the assumptions that never become articulated or queried and that thus frame rather than comprise editorial debate. By and large, policy evolves at two levels. At its broadest it is a set of common understandings of where the paper stands in relation to the political spectrum, though this need not be expressed in party terms. At a more explicit level it is a regular series of responses to particular events, and it is this level that is more likely to be openly discussed. The former level naturally sets the limit for the latter. It is this distinction correspondents have in mind when they refer, as one put it, to policy-making as 'a weird, osmotic process. The leader line evolves in editorial conferences, but I never felt I would have much influence, apart from the occasional corrective on fact.'

Malcolm Dean, social policy leader writer for the *Guardian,* described the process on that paper.

I write about four leaders a week, sometimes less. We meet in the morning and everybody puts a bid in for choice of subject, but the editor decides. The line on something is how we remember it. In theory the deputy editor is in charge of leaders. We talk it out at the 10.45 meeting on rough lines. These days the leader conference is earlier than the general news conference. There are certain basic things, though probably a lot of illogicality. Our policy is what the editor remembers about our position.

Most correspondents believe leaders do have an influence. Leaders are surprisingly widely read, though this is almost certainly overstated in surveys, in which readers are likely to assume that claims to read the leader demonstrate political sophistication and knowledge.[22] The more obvious influence of leaders is on a small select readership at whom they are sometimes cryptically addressed. One leader writer described this as 'occasionally having games when you know only a few will be able to follow what you've written. But I only know of three occasions on which something I've written has had a direct effect. There are specific audiences for specific leaders.' More generally, as one writer pointed out, 'leaders are only read by a few, but they may be people who matter. Over a period of time it has a subtle effect.' This subtle effect is perhaps most important internally, in signalling for correspondents and reporters the direction of editorial thinking, and more broadly the spirit or mood of opinion which is such a significant reference in journalists' evaluations of the world. Colin Seymour-Ure has summed this up as follows.

The leading article seems generally more important to the newspaper than to its readers: it is composed for the satisfaction of the former more than the latter . . . It can be seen still to some extent as a contribution to political discourse: to the small groups of readers actively involved in politics and administration, the leading article is an informed yet detached view that can serve as a touchstone . . . But also the leader, like the search for 'exclusive' news, has a professional function. As the platform for a newspaper's views it must be a spur to editors to articulate the principles which ultimately govern the selection and treatment of news as well as views'. [Seymour-Ure, 1969, pp. 522-3]

The values expressed by journalists will thus be seen in their most distilled form in editorials. The editorial is the meeting point of two dominant themes in social security news. From one direction it draws the consistent reference to the central institutions of political life, while from another it draws the values of individualism and self-sufficiency that buttress both the occupational ideology of journalism and the social values of British culture more generally.

SUMMARY

We have been examining in this chapter the making of news about social security largely through the eyes of those whose job it is. Three general observations emerge from this review. First, social security news, like other species of journalism, is highly dependent on its sources. Despite the common distrust of ministerial or administrative public relations, it is the machinery and deliberations of the central political apparatus that dictate the agenda of social security news. The routine of court reporting by non-specialists provides much of the day-to-day coverage of fraud cases and social security abuse; but the issues are framed, the disputes lined up, by the discourse and concerns of Westminster and Whitehall. It is the production of policy and not its impact on claimants or others that dominates news about the social security system. This emphasises views of social security as an expensive administrative problem, a burden borne by 'us' (the public—the readers), imposed by 'them' (the spenders of our taxes) to support other people, whose problems receive little exposure in relation to the measures employed to contain or solve those problems.

The second point to emerge is the importance of conventional news values, or pragmatically news desk values, to the shaping of social security news. Like any other portion of social life, social security has to be seasoned with the drama, language and values of the entertainment media that the modern news service has become. The subject is itself perceived to be intrinsically boring, and thus only surfaces in its more flamboyant or 'grabby' form. The social policy behind social security and the social·conditions to which it is intended to respond are invisible behind the welter of political and criminal events that actually command the energies of those who produce social security news. Specialisation, though increasing the expertise of those concerned, takes them closer to their sources and to an authoritative and orthodox view of the subject, and away from the general readership and the mundane routine of minor news events.

Thirdly, while it is clear that witch-hunts and campaigns do occur, they are only part of the explanation of the general hostility to social security and its claimants that journalists concede is the norm in British journalism. Examining the values of those who work in the area, we have identified a populist—pluralist mix of strong commitments to self-help, individualism, anti-bureaucracy and the work ethic that reinforce the absorption of these values from the dominant culture, and that filter the more liberal and compassionate perceptions of the welfare state that are common among journalists in the field.

None of these explanations is reducible to the conspiracy, or even to the biographical or organisational explanations that we posed hypothetically at the beginning of this chapter. In the following section we shall explore how the great news-consuming public construes welfare and social security, before considering in conclusion how far the processes we have described in this chapter are responsible for public images of welfare.

NOTES

1. For a fuller discussion of the shift away from the interventionist style of press barons see Murdock and Golding (1978).
2. The main interviews were conducted in 1979. With such a small group of by-lined writers there seemed little point in quoting anonymously, which might have provoked an invidious guessing game. The interviews were therefore largely 'on the record' and most quotes have been attributed. We also interviewed at the DHSS press office and other relevant sources.
3. Some of the flavour of this relationship with the press can be sensed in Mrs Castle's diaries of the period. See, for example, pp. 651—3 for a sample of the constant interaction with the press (as a significant sounding board for policy) and with journalists (as lunch companions for the 'great interpretative effort' Mrs Castle saw herself engaged in). In December 1975 Harold Wilson snaps at his colleague 'You pay too much attention to the press'. 'That from *him*' is Mrs Castle's sour comment (Castle, 1980, p. 574).
4. This is the argument advanced about the reporting of general economic policy in Glasgow University Media Group (1980). We return to the implications of this 'agenda-setting' in the concluding chapter.
5. See also Schlesinger (1978) p. 154 on the symbiotic relationship of BBC political news staff and Westminster.
6. The general failings of trades union public relations are illustrated by the interviews in Glasgow University Media Group (1976) Ch. 6.
7. See for more general comment Sedgemore's remarks on leaks and briefings: 'what is known as 'Downing Street guidance' which is a form of manipulative leaking pours out of the Press Offices of all Prime Ministers. When journalists phone up Members of Parliament

and ask for comments on certain "facts" the facts have come to them in the form of 'Downing Street guidance' (Sedgemore, 1980, p. 51). Sedgemore's book is, however, an elaboration of his thesis that it is the Civil Service that filters information going out to the public via the media, and also up to ministers. On this see Tony Benn's remarks that 'The power of the Civil Service to arrange for its view of policy to be transmitted discreetly to the media is every bit as great as is the power of ministers, and in the case of the Cabinet Office, the Treasury, the Foreign Office, and the Home Office, this delicate briefing of top opinion formers goes on on a regular basis' (Benn, 1980a). See also Benn (1980b) pp. 123—36, and Kellner and Crowther Hunt (1980) on 'the biggest pressure group', esp Ch. 11.

8. We return to this complex issue in the final chapter.
9. On this point as it relates to broadcasting see Golding and Elliott (1979) pp. 97—102.
10. See also Golding and Elliott (1979) pp. 147—51, 209.
11. Leslie Toulson in the *Sun* (stories since 1978) and Roger Todd in the *Daily Mirror* (stories between September 1978 and February 1979). Tabulation omitted here for reasons of space.
12. Occasionally great effort is put into such demonstrative stories. A curious example was provided in 1979 by the *News of the World,* which has frequently campaigned on social security abuse. A front-page picture (22 July 1979) headlined 'It's a Free Country/No wonder the scroungers are invading us', signalled a 'special investigation' on page five of 'the spaghetti scroungers'—'Latin layabouts' coming to England to get free hospital treatment and holidays on British social security. The picture showed seventeen happy young Italians behind a table laden with wine and other drink. A suspicious Lord Avebury wrote to *News of The World* editor Bernard Shrimsley to ask who paid for the drink. His suspicions were confirmed when Shrimsley replied that 'since we had no doubt that it was in the public interest that these scroungers should be dramatically spotlighted, we needed to get them all together for a special picture. As they were, by definition, happy to take anything from Britain so long as it was free, we thought it apt to get them all together by offering them some free Chianti. I am glad that this was successful, and that moves are now afoot to put a stop to activities such as theirs' (copies of Avebury/ Shrimsley correspondence supplied to us by Mr Shrimsley).
13. For a more extended discussion of news coverage of medicine, particularly the glorification of high technology treatment and the invisibility of preventive or environmental health issues, see Best *et al.* (1977)
14. In April 1979 only 23.2 per cent of all men over 21 earned in excess of £6,000 p.a. Of male manual workers only 15.5 per cent earned above figure (*New Earnings Survey,* Department of Employment, 1979).
15. Exploring, for example, the idea that neutrality is defined by the

choice of competing voices, and is always socially and culturally determined. On crime news see Chibnall (1977). For the more general issues see, *inter alia,* Golding and Elliott (1979), Glasgow University Media Group (1980), Golding and Murdock (1978), and Murdock and Golding (1977).

16. On the limited importance of pictures in the selection of TV news items, see the circumstantial evidence in Glasgow University Media Group (1980) Ch. 13. On the more difficult issue of where people get their information, press or TV, see Webb (1980) or Royal Commission on the Press (1977a) Part I, Ch. 2.

17. By extension, newspapers see themselves as 'caring corporations', a legacy of readership drives in the earliest days of the commercial press. The *Daily Mirror,* for example, still maintains a Readers Services Department. The many letters, including welfare rights inquiries and the like, that turn up on correspondents' desks get referred here.

18. In an interview with our colleague Barry Troyna. This view should, however, be contrasted with Robert Hargreaves' description of his colleagues at ITN: 'The journalists at ITN come from all walks of life—old Etonians and the sons of miners; women who went to Oxford and men who covered crime in Gateshead; Tribunites and High Tories; Scotsmen and Yorkshiremen; black people and white; women as well as men. In terms of background and social assumptions what is remarkable is how little they have in common . . .' (Hargreaves, 1979, p. 13).

19. In fact in 1977 unclaimed supplementary benefits included £85 million for families with children and £100 million for pensioners. The average amount of unclaimed benefit was very much higher for non-pensioners (£11.00 per week) than for pensioners (£3.10 per week). 420,000 families where the head of household was below pension age were not receiving supplementary benefit to which they were entitled (Supplementary Benefits Commission, annual report, Cmnd. 7725, HMSO, 1979, pp. 103—4).

20. An extreme example being a letter received by Pat Healy after appearing on LBC radio in London to discuss the *Sun* story about the family who had been rescued from a motorway breakdown at DHSS expense. Her attempts to point out that this was unusual and that the recipients were not likely to escape repayment led to a letter saying 'the interviewer on LBC today wiped the floor with you. You did not make one cogent reply. It's easy for you to propagate your marxist views in *The Times,* but as soon as you are challenged you are exposed for the fake that you are.'

21. However, see Wintour (1972) pp. 23—7, and especially Seymour-Ure (1969) for more detailed discussion of editorial policy-making.

22. A survey for the Royal Commission on the Press found 'comment about local issues' to be ranked highly among readers' interests in regional newspapers, though it is not clear if this refers to leaders, and

there is no comparable result given for the national press (Royal Commission on the Press, 1977a, p. 46). A survey by the *Guardian* suggested as many as 90 per cent of that paper's readers read its first leader.

III Poverty, What Poverty?

Pity would be no more
If we did not make somebody Poor;
And Mercy no more could be
If all were as happy as we.
[*William Blake,* The Human Abstract, *1794*]

In Part III we examine popular knowledge of and opinions about the welfare state. These chapters are largely based on a social survey we conducted in two cities in 1977, after the violent upsurge in anti-welfare feelings of 1976, but in a period of income restraint, rising inflation and much effort to 'stabilise' public expenditure.* This was the prelude to the 'winter of discontent'. Attitudes to welfare were no longer in the centre of debate, and it was a good time to examine how they settled in a broader array of social and economic beliefs. Chapter 6 reviews attitudes to the welfare state; chapter 7 discusses broader understandings of poverty and inequality.

* For reasons of space, methodological details have not been included in this book. A summary is available from the authors. 650 people (a response rate of 72.2 per cent) were interviewed in a stratified random probability sample in Leicester and Sunderland.

Sorting out the Needy:
Welfare Benefits and Claimants

Surveys provide no more than an ill-defined snapshot of people's attitudes and beliefs. Their validity is frequently the object of considerable criticism within social science and, though often confused and naive, this criticism has bequeathed a healthy scepticism about some of the more pretentious claims of some survey researchers. In this chapter we take a broad look at the more accessible beliefs held by the British population about the welfare services and their clients. We do not claim that this discussion exhausts such an investigation, or that it is valid for all times. We do claim, however, that the design and administration of the research allowed for a reasonably accurate description of views that are not only superficial or ephemeral, but part of the ideological legacy of the values we discussed in parts I and II. We examine five areas of public perceptions: knowledge of welfare benefits; attitudes to benefits; attitudes to the cost of welfare; attitudes to the social effects of welfare; and opinions about claimants.

KNOWLEDGE OF SOCIAL SECURITY BENEFITS

The survey was not intended as a test of take-up rates, and did not include enough data on household finance to provide accurate assessment of eligibility for means-tested benefits. We did, however, ask about knowledge of two major benefits: Family Income Supplement, which is for families on low wages with at least one child, and supplementary benefits, the major form of income maintenance for those not in work and with insufficient income from other sources (National Insurance benefits or pensions for example).

Family Income Supplement (FIS) was introduced in 1971. It has had a relatively poor take-up rate, rising only slowly to between 60 and 70 per cent of those believed eligible, and was received by only 81,000 families by 1979. Of our respondents 77.2 per cent had heard of FIS. Of these, however, only 45.2 per cent realised that it was for people in work, 31.0 per cent that it was for households with children, 29.6 per cent that it was means-tested, and only 1.7 per cent mentioned that the benefit equalled half the difference between earnings and the prescribed level. These extra points emerged in response to an open-ended question not a closed-ended quiz, and may underestimate knowledge. It is worrying to note, however, that knowledge of FIS was lowest among those groups more likely to need it and highest among high income groups:[1] of wage earners receiving below £40 a week, 28.0 per cent had not heard of FIS, whereas this was true of only 2.7 per cent of the wage earners receiving over £70 per week. Looked at another way, whereas 40.0 per cent of high income earners and 30.7 per cent of medium income earners named the low paid as a group they thought received benefits, only 10.6 per cent of low earners themselves thought of the low paid in this context. Similarly, when asked what kinds of people, other than the unemployed, could get help from social security, those in the higher occupational groups were far more likely to suggest the low paid than those in unskilled manual jobs. While 41.4 per cent of respondents in higher professional occupations mentioned the low paid as likely candidates for assistance, this proportion steadily dropped to 23.7 per cent among unskilled manual workers.

Supplementary benefits was a far more familiar term, and indeed is often confused in popular terminology with the more generic term social security. Supplementary benefits replaced National Assistance in 1966, and is the major income maintenance scheme in British social security. By November 1979 there were 2.85 million claimants and a total of 4.3 million people dependent on this benefit (Supplementary Benefits Commission, 1980, p. 62). Despite this, take-up continues to be a problem, rarely exceeding three-quarters of those eligible, of whom about 930,000 were failing to claim in 1975 (Supplementary Benefits Commission, 1978).[2] Only 3.8 per cent of our respondents had not heard of supplementary benefits. However, when asked to explain the benefit, only 25.6 per cent mentioned that it was means-tested, 49.3 per cent that it was for people not in work, 21.2 per cent that it was based on a calculation of needs, and 38.6 per cent that it supplemented other sources of income. In response to open-ended questions, the commonest descriptions of supplementary benefits were in terms of the groups believed to receive them: 'extra money for the pensioners', 'money for the unemployed', and 'money for poor people'.

Clearly, ignorance of the very existence of Family Income Supplement may be an important reason for its failure to reach many of those for whom it is intended. This is less likely to be true of supplementary benefits where, although knowledge is vague and very often inaccurate, the existence of the scheme is familiar. The problem of take-up here is far more likely to derive from the more complex issues of fear, stigma, pride and bureaucracy. This is the general conclusion of most research on take-up. The scale of the problem, though imprecisely known, is clearly massive. By 1974 there were probably 1.4 million people with incomes below supplementary benefit level (Lister, 1976, p. 4). By 1977 this had risen to over 2 million. In 1976 the National Consumer Council estimated that the value of unclaimed benefits for five major schemes totalled £645 million (p. 35). The Supplementary Benefits Commission, though requested by the Conservative government to reduce its efforts to measure low take-up levels, estimated on the basis of earlier figures that in 1979 £400 million of supplementary benefits alone were unclaimed (1980, p. 113). Publicity and information campaigns have made little difference, leading to considerable doubt about their relevance to the real basis of non-claiming. As Lister suggests,

> it might be the factor of stigma which prevents potential claimants from absorbing the information which is presented to them about means-tested benefits. Certainly, people seem to be far less ignorant about those benefits which do not involve a means-test, even though they tend to be less publicised [Lister, 1976, p. 7]

As Michael Young succinctly puts it: 'Improved publicity, however excellent, cannot over any length of time sell a poor product; and so it is with means-tested benefits' (National Consumer Council, 1976, p. 7).

The relative importance of stigma and of ignorance in the low take-up of means-tested benefits remains uncertain. Ignorance is the easier problem to tackle and has therefore attracted greater efforts. While our research was not primarily addressed to this issue, we return to it after a review of attitudes to social security benefits.

ATTITUDES TO SOCIAL SECURITY BENEFITS

People generally feel that benefits are too high and too easy to get. As we shall see in chapter 7 this may well be because they also tend to overestimate the level of social security benefits. Six out of ten people agreed that benefits are too generous, and an even higher proportion of older people and of non-manual workers accepted this view. The same proportion of people felt that 'people living on social security can manage quite well nowadays'. Of those with experience of receiving benefits, 54.6 per cent agreed with this view. When asked to nominate groups doing better than themselves, some respondents even suggested claimants. As a retired housekeeper living only on her pension put it, 'Well I think them on social are better off, they seem to get all they want'.

Six out of ten respondents (59.5 per cent) agreed with the view that 'The trouble with welfare benefits is it's too easy to get them'. Among low wage earners this proportion was even higher (64.4 per cent). The actual process of claiming benefits gets judged variably. Over half (52.9 per cent) felt 'it's embarrassing to have to claim welfare benefits'. This figure was much higher in the working-class district of Sunderland included in our sample (Southwick). This suggests our initial hypothesis in constructing the sample was disproved. That is, we believed that in an area like Southwick, with long experience of chronic unemployment, more tolerant and positive attitudes to welfare dependency would be exhibited. In fact the opposite appears to be true. This may indicate that the wearying business of claiming benefits, seeking work and enduring the diffuse hostility of prevalent cultural norms may well erode such lingering resistance.

Whether this is true or not, a belief in the stigma associated with benefit claiming was thus most prevalent in the locality with the greatest need for benefits, though this need was created by the least sympathetic cause—unemployment. It was noticeable that the same locality had a markedly high belief in the need to limit help to 'only the really deserving cases', which may well explain the perceived stigma associated with claiming. One important result to note here is that the notion that it is embarrassing to have to claim benefits is at least as widespread among the young as among elderly groups. Indeed, agreement with the statement 'having to ask for social security makes people feel ashamed' increased steadily from older to younger people. These two results together shed some doubt on the wild assertions common in the press during the recent period that young people have become, in the *Daily Mail*'s thoughtful phrase, 'welfare junkies' (see chapter 4). The dominant association of welfare dependency with guilt, shame or embarrassment is at least as common among the under-25s as any other age group, and is only denied by those groups least likely to have to experience the consequences of such beliefs.

This generalisation can be supported in two ways. First, is the objective evidence of under-claiming by younger groups. Of the 930,000 people not claiming supplementary benefits to which they were entitled in 1975, over a third (330,000) were under pension age (Supplementary Benefits Commission 1978, p. 26). In money terms this group accounted for £175 million of the £240 million believed to be unclaimed. Secondly, the evidence from other research confirms that stigma is not necessarily associated most closely with pensioners. Ritchie and Wilson, for example, found that about a quarter of claimants they interviewed felt 'ashamed at getting charity', and that this kind of negative view was far more prevalent among those below pension age (1979, pp. 23—4; see also Townsend, 1979, p. 846). The major factor would appear to be the type of benefit rather than the type of claimant. For example, Blaxter's study (1974) in Scotland of claims for prescription charge exemption suggested that stigma attaches to benefits not clearly associated with unavoidable need (sickness for example, or 'life-stage' benefits like maternity grants or pensions[3]). Benefits to meet need were only stigma-free where that need had an unambiguous, recognisable and socially acceptable cause. Taylor-Gooby confirms this in a study of rent benefits. Despite several waves of publicity, the eventual take-up of rent rebates and allowances following the 1972 Housing Finance Act was disappointingly low. By May 1974 take-up was 75 per cent among council tenants and only 25 per cent among tenants of unfurnished premises, and as low as 10 per cent among tenants of furnished premises. Taylor-Gooby's study charts the relative ineffectiveness of publicity campaigns, which were unable to push take-up levels higher than in nearby, publicity-free 'control' towns. He suggests that ignorance of benefits, though offered as a reason by most respondents, was less important than fear of rebuff in the claiming process and the diffuse anxieties we label stigma. He generalises his results to conclude that market relations link command over resources with an equivalent payment. Entitlement to means-tested benefits is emphatically dependent on proof of need. The recipient must show that he has failed to support himself in the economic market. Stigmatisation is the sanction for deviancy from market norms. [Taylor-Gooby, 1976, p. 47]

We cannot here review all the studies of stigma and low take-up of benefits. The evidence suggests a sharp move away from the individualised notion of stigma, which after all had its origins in clinical psychology, to a broader view of the social obloquy surrounding institutions, the practices they employ and the people who use them. We should turn our attention, in other words, away from simply getting information to individuals, useful though such exercises may be symbolically or catalytically, to the nature of the services they are being advised to use, and the wider cultural values associated with them.

PAYING THE PRICE: ATTITUDES TO SOCIAL SECURITY
EXPENDITURE

There is very widespread concern about expenditure on social services, and at the time of our survey this had been given considerable legitimacy by the massive cuts imposed on public expenditure during the previous year. As Alt (1979) has shown, in re-analysis of polling data, there was a growing awareness of and antipathy to public expenditure right through the 1970s, coupled with a hardening of attitudes to social security in particular as a sense of national and personal economic decline took root. Nearly half of our sample (46.8 per cent) thought too much was spent on welfare and social security, over twice the proportion of people who thought too little was spent. Of the minority who did think more should be spent, two-thirds (67.5 per cent) were willing to see the added expenditure financed by higher rates or taxes. This should be compared with the finding that 41.3 per cent thought 'it would be better to pay low rates and taxes and let people pay for services as they want them'. This classic statement against state welfare provision was agreed with most often by the young and those in middle-class neighbourhoods, which one might explain by the lack of experience of a non-welfare state among the former and the traditional rate-payer lobby among the latter. There does not seem to be widespread eagerness to escape the economic implications of publicly financed welfare.

As with so many subjects, people have contradictory views. It has become commonplace to observe that there are popular demands both for better social services and for lower rates and taxation. The prevailing motif in public debate in the 1970s was the equation of 'better' with leaner, more efficient, less bureaucratic, more selective, discriminating and conditional social services, thus resolving the contradiction ideologically while facilitating support for cuts in public services.

In a survey conducted a decade earlier than ours, the Institute of Economic Affairs, itself an advocate of a market-based system for the provision of health and other social services, found only about a fifth to a quarter in favour of a policy that would 'take less in taxes, rates and national insurance, concentrate on people in need leaving others to pay or insure privately' (Harris and Seldon, 1971). Enthusiasm for this view was greater among lower socio-economic groups, suggesting either a realistic recognition of the failure of the welfare state to be truly redistributive (see, for example, Kincaid, 1973, Chs 5 and 6) or 'false consciousness'. More recently the Institute has collated a series of such surveys to suggest that popular opinion has been 'over-ruled' on welfare (Harris and Seldon, 1979). In other words, a public hungry for a free market system of welfare services has been frustrated by the uncontrollable expansion of expensive state bureaucracies as myopic politicians outbid one another with unrealisable promises. This research is riddled with methodological and logical fallacies.[4] Most importantly, it extrapolates one of the contradictory strands in popular thought and assumes it to be dominant. What their evidence, and ours, suggests is a widespread acquiescence in the dominant view that expenditure is too great. But this needs setting in context.

Antipathy to increased spending among our respondents was stronger among older groups, among lower occupational groups, and among the less educated. Those willing to see more spending financed from rates and taxes were even more concentrated among those who felt themselves to be better off than average than among those in the high income group.[5] Generally it seems there is considerable suspicion of additional public expenditure on social security and welfare among groups who feel they have more to lose as tax-payers than to gain as beneficiaries. The fairly uniform response may reflect the increasingly orthodox belief that personal taxation has become too high, a view that has been widely canvassed in recent public debate, in much of the media, and in the mainstream political parties, while at the same time it has been attached to the related view that rising taxation is a burden imposed by excessive public expenditure, notably in the field of social services and social security.

The kind of concern voiced by some middle-class respondents is captured in the following two quotes from our survey:

We seem to be spending too much on the social security side than on the management/industrial side which we need to live.
[40-year-old male social worker]

The higher income groups have been so badly knocked by taxation and contributing to the welfare state. Professional people have been squeezed to help the poor. The poor are helped more than they used to be with welfare benefits and things.
[47-year-old teacher's wife]

The contradictory nature of popular beliefs is illustrated by people's responses to statements about conditional welfare and the insurance principle. While 45.7 per cent agreed that 'people should only get money from the government if they've paid in for it in the past', nearly as many (41.7 per cent) agreed that 'everybody who's poor should be given help regardless of why they're poor'. Attitudes on both these issues harden noticeably down the occupational hierarchy.

This concern to make welfare conditional so as to contain expenditure becomes particularly sharp when mingled with racism and xenophobia:

This welfare spending's all wasted. They give these handouts to natural scroungers, especially foreigners. If they made them live here for two years before getting anything that would be alright.
[Age 24, male decorator]

There's too many gets help. Wogs, spades, any foreigners. Anybody with a black face. The blacker you are the more you get. They're just natural scroungers.
[Age 54, storeman]

Concern about social welfare expenditure very often reflects economic insecurity and disadvantage. When forced by circumstances to account for their economic distress people will use the explanations commonly available to them. As our content analysis has shown, these explanations, or at least those provided by the media, have prominently related economic problems with the excessive cost and scope of social security.

THE NATIONAL BACKBONE: ATTITUDES TO THE SOCIAL EFFECTS OF SOCIAL SECURITY

Much of the force in ideological opposition to welfare spending has been directed against the social as distinct from the economic effects of social security. Although there is still clearly a strong vestigial feeling that 'the welfare state in this country is something we can really be proud of', a view agreed with by two-thirds of our respondents, we found that this view was more widely held among older, low income, and lower occupational groups, the very people who elsewhere express considerable suspicion of the welfare apparatus and its clientele. It may well be the hint of patriotism rather than altruism that evokes this favourable response. Four people out of five thought that too many people depend on welfare, and seven out of ten agreed that welfare has made people lazy.[6] It was noticeable that unskilled manual workers were the group responding most positively to the statement that 'if there wasn't so much social security people would learn to stand on their own two feet',[7] a view shared by 38.9 per cent of people with current or previous experience of claiming one of the main benefits.[8]

These concerns were spontaneously expressed in a variety of ways, mostly drawing on the standard clichés about national decline and personal inadequacy:

It takes away incentives. It's all easy come and easy go.
[Age 57, female clerical worker]

What we tend to do is to feather bed. It affects the moral outlook of the nation and the whole thing has tended to weaken our national outlook.
[Age 47, male teacher]

When presented with the fairly harsh view that 'poor people have only themselves to blame, so there's no reason why society should support them' (an outright denial of the minimum moral basis of a welfare system), one in six people (16.3 per cent) still agreed with the statement. Perhaps a proportion of this can be explained by 'yea-saying'—the commonly observed inclination of questionnaire respondents to agree with statements offered to them in this way. It is to check for this that we set such statements variously in pro and anti welfare terms in the questionnaire. Nonetheless this explicit opposition to social welfare is a striking finding. The figure was highest for unskilled manual workers, pensioners, the low paid, and welfare recipients themselves. Those most in need of support, yet least likely to feel they derive any benefit from the welfare state, are thus driven to express most vehemently rejection of even its weakest claims. Exposed to a culture that stresses self-help and the 'burden model' of welfare, their own poorly rewarded efforts in the economic struggle leave little room for an abstract sympathy for those whose deprivation can only be explained by inadequacy.

In order to evaluate overall attitudes to social security, we constructed a thirteen-point scale of various attitudes and questions in the questionnaire. The construction and checks of validity of the scale are described in the notes to this chapter.[9] Taking a score of 8 or more on this scale as high (an arbitrary cut-off), just over a third of our respondents had high anti-welfare attitudes. Scores were significantly higher among older people. Anti-welfare scores were also higher among manual workers. Whereas roughly four out of ten of the professional classes (A: 41.4 per cent; B: 40.8 per cent) had low scores, this dropped to only just over a quarter for manual workers. The highest proportion of high scorers was among unskilled manual workers, of whom over a third (34.2 per cent) had high scores. Low wage earners were similarly distinct, 28.7 per cent receiving high scores compared with only 8.0 per cent of high wage earners.

The association between class[10] and attitudes to welfare is thus a significant one, showing the extent to which living on the edge of the welfare state induces fears that are easily aroused by economic recession, and that are most easily articulated in terms of the most readily available mythologies. In Britain over the last few years, and indeed over a much longer period, the welfare scrounger and immigrants have been the main victims of these mythologies. Both welfare and race freely tap veins of myth, stereotype and scapegoating that make the burden of economic decline easier to bear. Lacking an alternative explanation, it is those most seriously hit by the recession who have greatest need to mine this vein, so readily exposed for them by the institutions of public agenda-setting.

ABUSE AND THE ABUSED

Attitudes to claimants: a culture of contempt

The essence of welfare legislation is classification—of the eligible and non-eligible, the deserving and undeserving. The same is true of popular perceptions of the claiming classes. People's understanding of the welfare system is understandably sketchy, and their attitudes to it are based on fairly imprecise notions of present arrangements. The only certainties are about the traditional categories of people who receive help. When asked about this it was the old and the sick who came most readily to mind—the unambiguously deserving poor. As we shall see, this limits the range of people perceived either as poor or as needing help to these most eligible groups. Even in answering a preliminary question about 'who can get help' from welfare or social security, 18.5 per cent of men, 21.6 per cent of skilled manual workers, 21.0 per cent of unskilled manual workers, and 22.3 per cent of low-income earners mentioned 'scrounging' or people not wanting to work when asked to name groups who receive financial assistance. Notably these answers also came rather more from those who themselves had experience of welfare benefits than from those with none.[11] One in five of the people who felt their own circumstances to have deteriorated in the past three years gave this kind of answer. Clearly, even an open-ended question such as this evokes considerable hostility and a readiness to complain about welfare dependency. This is especially true for the lower paid and those in unskilled jobs, who feel most resentful of the apparent failure of their labours to provide a noticeable advantage over those outside the labour market.

Confirmation of this comes from people's views about who should receive welfare assistance. When asked who they 'think most deserve to get money from the welfare' people again nominate the old and the sick. Only 5.9 per cent mentioned the unemployed (even though up to three answers were coded). One in ten made a point of mentioning the 'really needy' or 'genuine' cases. Only 2.4 per cent mentioned the low paid. The need to distinguish the really needy was mentioned by 25.0 per cent of people who felt their own circumstances to have declined, and by 27.7 per cent of low wage earners (of whom only 5.3 per cent mentioned the low paid as a deserving group). The low paid more than any other income group were likely to think that many claimants do not deserve any help, a view also strongly shared by those who feel themselves to be worse off than average.

In postal surveys carried out in 1972 and 1976, Norris (1978) has shown how sympathy for the old and sick actually increased in the four-year interval, while the unemployed remained an unpopular cause, down at the foot of the table with tramps, drug users and gypsies.[12] Assessment of those in need immediately evokes classification of those over-generously treated. We asked our respondents about 'people who shouldn't really get money from the welfare'. Answers focused far more on the moral legitimacy of claims for assistance than on a purely financial means test. The largest category of answers by far concerned the lazy—people who won't work, the work-shy, layabouts and so on. A quarter of our respondents gave answers of this kind—over twice the proportion that fell into any other category of answer. The second most popular answer was in any case the related theme of people who could work if they wanted to, who were fit and able to work, and so on:

> The people who shouldn't get help are all those who can't be bothered to look for work, and all those who earn too much money and have council houses.
>
> [Age 46, male biologist]

The emphasis on the 'work-shy' and 'layabouts' was strongest among skilled manual workers, the young and, once again, in Southwick. It was also mentioned by 30.4 per cent of people who themselves had experience of benefits. This emphasis took two forms. One was to distinguish particular groups who received benefits but should not have done so. As a research report prepared for the DHSS concluded:

> It was the almost universally declared belief of informants of all types that those who were in least need would be the most likely to claim, and the most successful in obtaining Supplementary

Benefit; while those who were in most need, and most deserved to receive help, would be the most reticent in claiming, and the least likely to receive help. This belief is the lynch-pin of attitudes towards the Supplementary Benefits scheme. [Schlackman, 1978, p. 34]

Resentment of blacks or immigrants receiving benefits is seldom far beneath the surface in this context. In the Leicester 'middle-class' area, 13.5 per cent mentioned immigrants as an undeserving group and 12.8 per cent mentioned people who 'had just come into the country' or similar phrases. This last group was especially of concern to low wage earners. This concern was often expressed in particularly virulent terms.

> The people who get help are the blackies and the wogs and those who can do without it. The old people who need it don't get it yet the blackies get all they can and more. The darkies have never paid stamps yet they can get it.
>
> [Age 70, female retired home-help]

The other side to this concern was the supposedly corrosive effect of benefits on the work motivation of claimants. This was set by many in a rosy historical perspective, current indolence being contrasted with the tougher, more industrious spirit of an earlier age. This was as true of younger respondents as of those who could fairly claim experience of 'the good old days':

> When there wasn't so much welfare people would put themselves out to work. They should be encouraged to work and not to take welfare as an alternative.
>
> [Age 33, male truck driver]

A very high proportion of our respondents felt people should be encouraged to be self-sufficient, and that the existence of welfare and social security blunts motivation and independence. These views were most common among low wage earners and unskilled workers. Nearly a quarter of the total sample agreed that 'people who claim social security should feel guilty about living off taxpayers' charity', a statement with which 35.5 per cent of unskilled manual workers, 30.0 per cent of people in Southwick, and 29.0 per cent of low wage earners concurred.[13]

It takes very little to shift from a concern about the effect of welfare services on claimants to a more comprehensive suspicion of the moral fibre of the claiming population as a whole. We have shown in chapters 3 and 4 to what extent social security and welfare are reported by news media as lax systems exploited by the unscrupulous. Not surprisingly, this is reflected in popular attitudes, though to a degree we could not have anticipated. Only 2.3 per cent of respondents denied that some people receiving social security are scroungers.[14] It may be surmised that, posed in this form, agreement is almost inevitable. However, three out of ten people who estimated what proportion of claimants are scroungers gave a figure over 25.0 per cent, and nearly one in ten said half or more.[15] It is difficult to credit even such an energetic campaigner as Iain Sproat with a result like this. Clearly he was voicing, and of course giving legitimacy to, the well-nourished suspicions of large numbers of people. The highest estimates were given by younger people, manual workers, welfare recipients and the low paid. High estimates were given also by more women than men, and by inner-city residents. The massive moral panic about scroungers reached its highest pitch among those with the greatest need to stress the social distance between themselves and the pauper stratum. 'There but for the grace of God go I' soon becomes 'there but for hard work and honesty go I', in a culture that places such a central stress on the equation of economic success with diligence, endeavour and obedience to the rules of the economic game.

The majority of people claimed their knowledge of such extensive scrounging was based on personal experience—seeing them around, knowing of someone who had claimed fraudulently or excessively:

I go down the road and see 40 or 50 of them in the pub [estimated 60%].

[Age 55, male, slaughterhouse worker]

I know quite a few personally [estimated 30%].

[Age 37, single parent on SB]

More diffusely, evidence was distilled from the currents of popular opinion in a vague but undeniably plausible way:

I don't know, it's a matter of people talking about how easy it is to live off the state [estimated 50%].

[Age 31, male lorry driver]

In fact, twice as many people referred to personal observation as referred to the media. Nonetheless, 15.7 per cent of respondents mentioned the media as a source of their certainty about the extent of scrounging, usually in such terms as 'you read about these cases all the time':

> There are some genuine ones but the majority just bleed the country dry. The ones who have not worked for a long time should be made to do some kind of work and not claim benefit. 80% are scroungers. It's just what you hear, what's on TV, what's been in the papers over the last few weeks.
>
> [Age 31, fitter's wife]

> People who are on the dole who have refused two jobs should not be helped any more [estimated 30%]. From press cuttings, gossip, talk, looking about, seeing the ones buying beer and gambling.
>
> [Age 43, housewife]

Quite clearly, media coverage of the kind we have analysed in chapters 3 and 4 provides a vocabulary and a set of explanations that can focus inexact personal observations into cogent social theory. That this is derived in part from the media has been observed in many American studies. Adams notes how critical articles about unemployment insurance in the 1960s 'probably convinced those people who were already critical of the UI program that they were right, and it probably persuaded others that the system was in need of an overhaul' (1971, p. 30). Waxman notes the stigmatisation that results from the fact 'that the mass media persist in presenting singular instances of irregularities . . . and fraud as if they were the norm' (1977).

Imprecision about the sources of information about scrounging is matched by uncertainty about the kind of behaviour described by the term. Its connotations range from outright illegality—most commonly, working while claiming benefit—to the unacceptable though legal dependence of some claimants on benefits that they could well do without, a judgement based very often on observations either about their ability to work if they could be persuaded to, or their relatively comfortable life-style and apparently imprudent, even extravagant, expenditure patterns. These cross-cutting streams flow most furiously when discussing the unemployed, and before drawing together some of the survey finding we need to look specifically at attitudes to this group.

Return of the sturdy beggar: attitudes to unemployment

We initially asked people to estimate the level of unemployment. People are not generally familiar with percentages and it may be that this explains the inaccuracy of responses to this question. However, there was a very consistent pattern in that a large number of people considerably overestimated unemployment levels. Over four out of ten people estimated unemployment to be over 10 per cent, and one person in five put it at over 20 per cent. By mid-1977, unemployment in the East Midlands was 5.0 per cent and in the Northern region 7.8 per cent. The national figure at the time of the survey was 5.7 per cent. Unemployment had increased by over a million people between 1973 and 1977. The East Midlands, traditionally an area of low unemployment, was hit, psychologically if not economically, as much as anywhere else, with textiles and footwear among the worst-affected industries. The shedding by manufacturing industry of nearly 600,000 jobs in the two years to mid-1976, the increase in numbers entering the labour market, constraints on consumer spending power and consequent falls in distributive trade employment, the cut-back in public service employment, and recession in the construction industry, all accelerated the rise in unemployment, and with it a chronic awareness of the 'problem of unemployment' (see Hughes, 1978).

The highest overestimates of unemployment were made by manual workers, women and benefit recipients. Among unskilled manual workers, 56.2 per cent put unemployment at over 10 per cent and 27.4 per cent thought it was above 20 per cent. There was a similar level of overestimation among people living in the inner-city wards. Awareness of unemployment is, not surprisingly, thus highest in those areas and among those groups most vulnerable to it.

The commonest answer to the question 'Who do you think is unemployed at the moment?' was along the lines that it is 'a cross section', 'all sorts', and so on. Nearly a quarter of answers were of this kind. The unskilled or less educated were mentioned in 15.4 per cent of answers and 14.6 per cent mentioned the young or school leavers. But the only other major category of response was that which suggests the 'work-shy' or people who won't work—a style of answer provided by 10.0 per cent of respondents. Lacking any clear picture of the causes or differential impact of unemployment, people are as likely to focus on the individual inadequacies or lethargy of the workless as on the economic basis of their condition:

> There's not many genuine unemployed. The social security don't check properly.
>
> [Age 36, male caulker]

> I know there is no shortage of jobs, I've had no trouble. The majority are wasters, drinkers, that type of man.
>
> [Age 37, male lorry driver]

Answers in this vogue—suggesting 'that type of man', the idler, waster, sponger or ne'er-do-well was the typical unemployed person—came especially from manual workers and the low paid. In looking at these results we should remember five points. First, unemployment does disproportionately affect the young and late middle-aged: 'Of 1,622,000 unemployed in Britain in July 1977, 313,000 were under 18 and 708,000 under 25' (Townsend, 1978, p. 9).[16] Second, given the better qualification levels on the whole of younger people, 'if we were to claim that unemployment was the result of deficient skills we would have to impugn the present system of education and industrial training' (*ibid.*). Third, notified vacancies at the time of our survey were roughly a tenth of the number of unemployed. Fourth, unemployment is especially high among the unskilled and low paid, and among manual workers generally (Barratt Brown *et al.*, 1978, *passim*). Fifth, in 1977, at the time of the survey, the weekly rate of unemployment benefit for a married couple with two children was only 41.3 per cent of average earnings of male manual workers (H. C. *Hansard,* Written Answers to Questions, 2 February 1978), and between a sixth and fifth of the unemployed were drawing no benefit, either unemployment or supplementary. In May 1977, 16.0 per cent of the unemployed were in this position (*Department of Employment Gazette,* November 1977, Table 112). It is noticeably high-income, better educated and higher occupational grades who stressed lack of skill and education as the essential failing of the unemployed. Few respondents mentioned the low paid or non-unionised as particularly vulnerable groups.[17] The popular portrait of the unemployed is thus far closer to the cruder stereotypes of popular journalism than to the revealing statistics of the Department of Employment. Once again, however, we find that contradictory and complex beliefs lie behind these caricatures.

When asked to explain unemployment, the commonest answers were the general decline in British industry, usually expressed as a vague recognition that the nation was in a bad way, a matter of national decline as much spiritual or moral as industrial.[18] Equally common were references to world recession and to the ineptitude of government policies. Explanations were either in these vague *deus ex machina* terms, or in terms of the wilful idleness of the unemployed. Unemployment thus seemed either a malevolent visitation of impenetrable world forces plaguing a once great nation, or the aggregate result of a million individual acts of indolence and cynicism by a pampered and ill-disciplined work force. The machinations of the unions and the greed they articulated were seen as central in this unhappy state of affairs:

> All sorts of people are unemployed. They have only themselves to blame because they keep striking and the bosses will only stand for so much.
>
> [Age 57, male machine operator]

> I blame the unions. They keep pressing for rises and I think it's terrible when the country's in such a state.
>
> [Age 47, male printer]

Particular blame was attached to groups believed to have earned a privileged rank in the pay league by their selfish militancy:

> It's all these high wages and the unions. I think it was started by the miners when they wanted such high·wages.
>
> [Age 64, female retired catering cook]

> I think the car workers started it, and it upset the whole country.
>
> [Age 69, female retired dress factory operative]

On the other side was the widespread belief in the disincentive effects of over generous or laxly monitored welfare benefits, a point we return to in the following chapter:

> It's the trade unions and the social state. There's no need to

work because of what the welfare will give them. There are lots of people doing two jobs or working and drawing unemployment.

[Age 44, male restaurant proprietor]

It's the Beveridge Report, because of it many people who are capable of working choose not to work.

[Age 27, male solicitor]

More pressure should be put on people to get work. We spend too much supplementing the families of strikers.

[Age 55, male unemployed]

The high rate of unemployment benefits was mentioned as a cause of unemployment by 11.7 per cent of respondents, and 11.4 per cent used the phrase 'work-shy' or some close synonym. Bad or unskilled management was mentioned by only 4.4 per cent. By far the most common explanation was that offered by a 52-year-old man, himself unemployed through disablement, who said 'I think there's plenty of jobs, but people won't work. Social security pay, too much dole, there's no incentive to work'. The low paid were the most likely to mention the 'work-shy' or 'the idle' when identifying the unemployed (20.2 per cent of the low paid, 17.6 per cent middle incomes, 14.7 per cent high incomes), and more welfare recipients (18.6 per cent) than non-recipients (15.3 per cent) volunteered this category.

These complementary views—that unemployment is frequently voluntary and no great hardship financially—were the twin pillars of a general lack of sympathy for, and indeed disbelief in the genuineness of, the unemployed. Whereas only 5.9 per cent of respondents mentioned the unemployed as a group who should get financial assistance, 25.2 per cent referred to those who won't work or are too lazy to work, and a further 12.0 per cent to those who could work if they wanted to, in naming groups they thought should not get such help. The low paid were the least likely to think the unemployed should get help, and clearly the mythology that unemployment can reap rewards close to, if not better than, the worst paid jobs, has struck home among the low paid. In fact, analysis shows that 'about 40% of the unemployed were losing more than 30% of their net income as a result of being unemployed' (Layard *et al.*, 1978, p. 79). Further, 'it is only where there are at least four children that the total income support of the man on

benefit can exceed 90% of his total income support when working .
. . . the proportion of the unemployed who actually get more
money in benefit than in work is very small. (DHSS, 1978, pp. 117,
120).[19] As the 1978 review of supplementary benefits pointed out,
'some gap between incomes in and out of work is expected by
public opinion, reflecting the desire to prevent unnecessary
dependence on supplementary benefit and encourage, wherever
possible, those in the employment field to support themselves'
(*ibid,* p. 37).[20] This is clearly true, and in seeking this gap it is not
the inadequacy of low wages to which public opinion has been
directed. Recurrently appearing in different guises in dominant
mythology, it is resentment of the 'sturdy beggar' that has fuelled
the economic misery of recent recession.

CONCLUSION: KEEPING PAUPERISM AT BAY

Despite the complex range and social differentiation of attitudes
to welfare and social services, perhaps the most striking finding is
the overall virulence and nature of hostility to welfare claimants. It
is strongest among the low paid and unskilled—those most
threatened by economic gloom and looming unemployment. But it
is also voiced by claimants themselves. Indeed, claimants and the
low paid are frequently the most bitter and hostile of commentators
on welfare recipients. There are two important threads to untangle
here: one is the specific concern of welfare claimants; the other is
the prevailing antipathy to welfare among the low paid and other
groups (for comparable evidence see Bowles and Holmes, 1979,
pp. 47, 92; or Ritchie and Wilson, 1979, pp. 42—3). The hostility of
claimants should not be underestimated:

> We had to work for it when we were young and now they get it
> far too easily these days.
>
> [Age 64, pensioner]

> You hear about these people say they know where they can go
> and get money and then go and play bingo all night.
>
> [Age 70, retired home-help]

With many areas of belief, knowledge derived from the media
and knowledge derived by direct experience are at odds, and
cleavages in public attitude result from variation in such direct

experience. Research on attitudes to 'race' (see Hartmann and Husband, 1973) and to 'industrial relations' (Hartmann, 1976, 1979), shows how direct experience shapes behaviour and specific attitudes, even though the media provide the rhetoric and general framework within which social issues are couched. Thus black immigrants are seen as 'a problem', especially in areas of low immigration where imagery is derived, by default, from the media. Direct experience can provide a counter, so that, for example, it is commonly found that trade union members concur with the view that unions are too powerful, though they will support militant activity by their own union for a pay claim. Parkin has summarised this phenomenon by suggesting a revision of Rodman's 'lower class value stretch', that is 'that the lower class person, without abandoning the general values of the society, develops an alternative set of values' (Rodman, 1963, p. 209). Parkin's reformulation is that 'in situations where purely abstract evaluations are called for, the dominant value system will provide the moral frame of reference; but in concrete social situations involving choice and action, the negotiated version—or the subordinate value system—will provide the moral framework' (Parkin, 1972, p. 93).

For claimants, these 'concrete situations' arise in dreary, individualising, stigmatising and frequently punitive experiences in the institutional apparatus of welfare administration. There is thus no source of oppositional values in situational experience to challenge dominant views. The attitudes we have found to be shared by claimants and non-claimants alike are institutionalised in our social security system.

> The abolition of the wage stop removed the most blatant example of the institutionalisation of the less eligibility principle from our supplementary benefit statutes in 1975, but the principle still exists in the denial of the long-term supplementary benefit rate to the unemployed'. [Lister and Field, 1978, pp. 67—8]

The unemployed are the only claimant group never to receive the higher long-term rate of supplementary benefit. The gap between the two rates has steadily risen: it was 10 per cent in 1973, 20 per cent in 1976, and by November 1980, when new legislation reduced the period for eligibility for the long-term rate from two years to one, the gap had risen to 25 per cent (£8.75 per week for a couple). The extension of fraud investigation, heightened use of Unemployment Review Officers and the sheer bleak and hostile climate of most Social Security offices, all add clearly punitive connotations to the claiming experience.[21] Moore, quoting a leaked internal DHSS report, notes that 'The officials are abrupt, even discourteous'. More importantly,

> concern to prevent abuse was probably the single most significant influence on staff's attitudes to and dealings with claimants. The prevalent view was that abuse, whether trivial or serious, was rife throughout the scheme. Staff had seen enough of it, visited homes of long-term claimants which suggested much higher standards than SB would allow, come across it (and been deceived) often enough to have become fairly hardened. It was also the more outrageous cases of fraud or abuse that had become the common gossip of the office, and so further infected the general attitude . . . Questioning a claimant with one eye on his welfare needs and the other on the possibility of fraud, was an impossible schizophrenic role. And with some staff, the suspicious eye became much the sharper of the two. [Moore, 1980, pp. 68—9][22]

It is in this specific way, then, that social security differs from race and industrial relations.

The mythology that facilitates these administrative controls also acts potently on those most susceptible to the threat of imminent unemployment. Sustaining an acceptable distance between the deprivations of poorly paid jobs or inadequate housing and the morally culpable status of unemployment produces an assessment of the motives of the unemployed of a particularly sceptical kind. By extension, the welfare state, which colludes in such behaviour, is seen as a cause of mendicancy rather than a palliative for immiseration. It is the lack of secure employment for the low paid on the one hand, and the flow of a steady stream of mediated mythology supporting such explanations on the other, that maintain both the mythologies and their legislative consequences.

For unskilled, older and low paid workers the potential threat of unemployment and fear of disposal to the welfare scrap-heap prompt redefinition of those already there; a cultural pauperisation of claimants that finds ready support in the dominant values of our culture (cf. Alston and Dean, 1972). Conversely, there is no source of oppositional values in situational experience to challenge the dominant or mediated views. On the contrary, exposure to the situational realities of welfare claiming or unemployment is likely to mean exposure to institutions and situations that will reinforce the dominant hostile and unsympathetic view. A historical survey of public attitudes to social security published by the American Social Security Administration notes how very similar anti-claimant attitudes were between classes and over time. As the author notes, the idea that welfare makes people lazy was but a restatement of Roosevelt's remarks in his annual message to Congress in 1935 that 'continued dependence upon relief induces a spiritual and moral disintegration fundamentally destructive to the national fibre'. The report suggests that 'conviction that the "dole" is inimical to self-esteem and to the American way of life is an essential of American social ideology' (Schiltz, 1970, p. 158; see also Betten, 1973).

The same may well be true of Britain. Shielded from any broader view of social injustice, those crushed by inadequate and censoriously administered welfare benefits on the one hand, or by poverty wages on the other, find their fears and resentments readily channelled into a bitter and divisive contempt for those alongside them at the bottom of the economic ladder. In the phrase Beveridge borrowed from Bronte, we have clear evidence here indeed of the 'misery that generates hate'.

NOTES

1. Income groups here, and in subsequent references, were defined as: low—up to £40 per week; medium—£41 to £70 per week; high—£71 or more per week. According to figures in the *New Earnings Survey,* in April 1977 2.4 per cent of full-time men over 21 and 28.8 per cent of full-time women over 18 earned less than £40 per week, while 45.7 per cent of men and 86.7 per cent of women earned less than £70 per week. The average male wage was £78.60 per week including £6.80 overtime (Department of Employment, 1977, Table A5).
2. After 1979 the Conservative government asked the Commission to reduce its efforts in estimating take-up levels, and figures were not published in 1979 and 1980.
3. cf. Piachaud (1974) who found 80 per cent of people willing, so they said, to be worse off so that pensions could go up.
4. The following points among many others could be raised about the IEA studies:
   (i) The series of surveys use quota samples, which are distinctly less reliable than random probability samples. This poses particular

problems for claims to detect shifts in opinion over time—for which a panel study or rigorous controls over the consistency of the sample would be required.

(ii)   Evidence is used selectively. For example (Harris and Seldon, 1979, p. 24), 63 per cent of this sample were against a 'California' style reduction of taxation resulting in fewer services. The authors are forced to pursue their object by changing the question (ignoring the effect on services) to get the result they are after.

(iii) The logic is inconsistent. If the argument is to allow a greater power to popular demand over unrepresentative government, why ignore the massive vote in their survey to deflect public spending from defence to social services (1979, p. 130)? The answer is to chop-logic over definitions. This finding is explained away by arguing that people do not really know what they want in such an area, since 'The benefits of defence spending to each individual are intangible and remote . . . That respondents were anxious to increase spending on these [health, education, housing, pensions] services strongly suggests that, as we have argued, they are not public goods' (1979, p. 130). This unlikely piece of special pleading sits oddly with calls to 'trust the consumer'!

(iv)   Explanations are attached to findings arbitrarily. Finding that a desire to limit income taxation was strongest among lower income groups, the authors explain this as related to rapid increases in income in this group. It might be equally persuasive to look at the evident regressiveness of taxation over certain income bands, notably those caught in the 'poverty trap' (p. 36).

(v)   Questions constantly invite people to choose among hypothetical alternatives that neither exhaust the options possible nor offer explanations of the social and financial implications of any given choice (e.g. pp. 44—5). Among the missing options is improvement in welfare provision financed by a more progressive taxation system, for example (see pp. 54—5).

(vi)   Many of the conclusions are *a priori* arguments for limited welfare provision not research findings, e.g. the statement (p. 66) that 'we should be on guard against pushing standards too high so that they raise costs . . .'

(vii) There is much confusion between needs, wants and choices. Much welfare provision is to meet unpredictable and unavoidable need (sickness, loss of employment). It is totally inappropriate therefore to employ the Friedmanite notion that 'There ain't no such thing as "want" without price!' (p. 80) All the questions assume the opposite.

There are many other difficulties with the research that are too legion to discuss in detail here.

5. In answer to the question 'Do you think we spend too much, too little,

or about the right amount on welfare and social security?' 46.8 per cent said 'too much', 32.2 per cent said 'about right', and 21.0 per cent said 'too little'. Of this last group 67.5 per cent said 'yes' to the question 'Would you be willing to see more spent on welfare and social security, even if it meant more rates or taxes?' Cross-tabulation with a question asking people to assess their own relative circumstances showed that 81.3 per cent of those feeling themselves 'better off than average' said 'yes' to the more rates and taxes proposition.

6. The concern with laziness is widespread, a tribute to the staying power of the work ethic in periods of large-scale unemployment. This is not, it should be noted, the 'protestant ethic'. A survey by Clifford in Ireland (1975) found that 84 per cent thought welfare encouraged laziness, a figure the author reasonably describes as showing 'overwhelming support' for the work ethic.

7. 50.0 per cent of occupational group D agreed with this statement as compared to 32.1 per cent in group A and 27.9 per cent in group B (higher and intermediate professional groups respectively).

8. cf. Form and Rytina's finding (1969) that 24 per cent of their sample of poor respondents felt the government had done too much for the poor (see also Rytina, Form and Pease, 1970).

9. The components of the scale were:
   1. Do you think we spend too much (too little, or about the right amount) on welfare and social security?
   2. Many people who should get social security in fact don't get what they're entitled to (disagreement).
   3. Nowadays too many people depend on welfare.
   4. Poor people have only themselves to blame so there's no reason why society should support them.
   5. There's so much welfare now it's made the people of this country lazy.
   6. The trouble with welfare benefits is it's too easy to get them.
   7. Welfare benefits are too generous.
   8. People who get social security get too dependent on it and stop trying to help themselves.
   9. Many people who get social security don't really deserve any help.
   10. People who claim social security benefits should feel guilty about living off tax-payers' charity.
   11. Poor people who have only themselves to blame are not entitled to help.
   12. If there wasn't so much social security people would learn to stand on their own two feet.
   13. People should only get money from the government if they've paid in for it in the past.

All respondents could thus receive a score between 0 and 13. Scores were distributed as follows:

Score	%	Score	%
0	4.0	8	13.2
1	6.8	9	8.0
2	6.6	10	5.1
3	8.3	11	5.7
4	8.5	12	1.8
5	10.9	13	0.6
6	10.8	N=650	
7	9.7		

For cross-tabulation, scores of 0—4 were grouped as 'low', 5—8 as 'medium' and 9—13 as 'high'. The construction of the scale was checked by running non-parametric correlation coefficients of all items with each other, and of each item with the scale scores. Using Kendall's Tau, all items were significantly correlated with the scale at the 0.001 level.

10. In the empirical work reported here we have restricted ourselves to the term 'occupational group' rather than pretend that we have operationalised 'class' in any conceptually rigorous way. The complex relationship between class and the occupational structure is of course a central issue of contemporary sociology. For a very useful discussion see Wright (1980).

11. Here and elsewhere we defined welfare recipients as those with current or previous experience of receiving supplementary benefits, unemployment benefit or Family Income Supplement. Of this group (N=237), 24.0 per cent spontaneously mentioned scrounging or 'work-shyness' compared with 14.3 per cent of 'non-recipients' (N=413).

12. cf. Askham's finding that many would be willing to see pensions increased but unemployment benefits reduced (Askham, 1975, p. 109). Even in the early 1960s when welfare expenditure was more generally supported it was pensions that received most support (see Butler and Stokes, 1971, pp. 413—17).

13. Many surveys have shown a similar pattern of suspicion about the diligence of the welfare recipient. Feagin's research in the United States found 84 per cent who thought there were too many welfare recipients who could and should be working (Feagin, 1972a, 1975). In a study in Boston in 1972 Williamson found massive suspicion of welfare recipients, and opposition to increased benefits. These he found correlated with self-assessed ideological positions on a liberal—conservative continuum (Williamson, 1974). However, this may be misleading as his sample was predominantly female, and he

does not examine in detail the grounds for opposition to increased benefits, which we would argue have structural not psychological roots.

14. That is, 97.7 per cent answered 'yes' to the question 'It is sometimes said that some people who get social security are just scroungers. Do you think there are people like that?'

15. This was in response to a follow up to the question quoted in note 14. It was thus not addressed to 2.3 per cent of our sample. Of those who answered 'yes', 23.9 per cent did not offer an estimate of the proportion of scroungers.

16. However, it is important not to overstress youth unemployment, to which much attention has been given. By July 1980 the under-20s made up 29.4 per cent of the 1.9 million unemployed, but of these only 3.2 per cent had been out of work for a year or more. The over-50s made up 19.0 per cent of the unemployed, but of these 154,577 or 43.0 per cent had been out of work for over a year (compared to 19.2 per cent of all unemployed persons). For the middle-aged, and especially unskilled, unemployment has become chronic, though it may be the sporadic political militancy of the young unemployed that has provoked the greater administrative response (figures calculated from *Department of Employment Gazette,* Vol. 88, no. 9, September 1980, p. 954).

17. cf. Williamson's findings (1974) that in a survey in Boston in 1972 massive numbers overestimated the percentage of 'able-bodied' employable males on welfare, while on average 41 per cent of benefit claims were believed to be fraudulent.

18. Gallup poll findings suggest that, in 1963, 32 per cent blamed the government for unemployment, 25 per cent said people do not work hard enough, and 18 per cent blamed management. By 1971, 27 per cent were blaming trade unions and wage claims; in 1975 this figure was still at 26 per cent (Gallup, 1976, passim). See also Redpath (1979), Deacon (1978), Deacon and Sinfield (1977).

19. See also Burghes (1980) for a full summary of relevant evidence.

20. A study by Freeman (1979) found 30 per cent who thought the unemployed should not get benefit at all. See also Bowles and Holmes (1979).

21. With growing pressure on the service, a higher proportion of interviews take place in offices rather than people's homes. Nearly two-thirds of all benefit claims were dealt with by office interviews by 1977. Both benefit claims and decisions to award discretionary exceptional needs payments are dealt with by office interview most often for the unemployed, least often for pensioners (see DHSS, 1977a).

22. See also the account by Whitfield and Jordan (1979).

CHAPTER 7

The Residuum Rediscovered

Ever since the happy sixteenth-century custom of chopping off the ears of vagabonds, rogues and sturdy beggars, the British have had some difficulty in distinguishing poverty from crime. The poor have been a nuisance, a threat and a financial burden throughout our history, and explaining their continuing and irritating presence has been a persistent problem for the ideologists of capitalism. Earlier centuries have classified, victimised and criminalised the poor. The supreme achievement of 'welfare capitalism' has been to render the causes and conditions of poverty almost invisible. The attitudes to the welfare state we discussed in chapter 6 can only be understood in this broader context. In this chapter we explore this theme by presenting the findings of our survey insofar as it investigated people's attitudes to poverty.

LESS ELIGIBILITY: THE INCOME ILLUSION

Since the new poor law, a core concern of income maintenance schemes has been to protect work incentives by ensuring a considerable gap between income in and out of employment. In recent years the size of this gap has been the object of much discussion, and belief in its gradual erosion (by low wages, dropping tax thresholds, and generous welfare benefits) has been central in the rising swell of anti-welfare feeling. We asked our respondents to estimate family income requirements. A majority (58.9 per cent) gave a figure under £50 for an average family with two children. Respondents were also asked to estimate the same family's income if they were on social security. A majority (57.1 per cent) gave a figure over £35, although the supplementary benefit scale rate for the family described was only £29.35 at the time, so that even allowing for a rent addition a large majority of people overestimate benefits. Indeed, nearly a quarter (22.7 per cent) gave a figure at least a third higher than the scale rates.

It is interesting that people underestimate family requirements and overestimate welfare benefits.[1] One possible explanation, we would suggest, is that people have not caught up, psychologically, with inflation. That is, people judge low incomes against outdated notions of the value of money. A low income is perceived as having more value than its true purchasing power, while the upward drift of wage levels is widely underestimated. This may explain much of the hostility to welfare benefits, whose periodic upratings are given considerable publicity, so that the gap between the visible value of benefits and the underestimated level of average incomes is itself underestimated. It is interesting, too, that though the overestimate of benefits is greatest among manual workers and the young, those with experience of benefits are as likely to overestimate their value as anyone else. The validity of this 'psychological lag' effect of inflation is indicated by the tendency for older people to underestimate incomes more than those perhaps more accustomed to the rapidly changing value of money. A similar point was made by Behrend in some research conducted in the 1960s, who pointed out that 'stable prices are remembered more easily than prices liable to fluctuation', a point equally true of incomes (1966, pp. 276–7).

The same phenomenon appeared when we asked people to estimate average industrial wages. Of those who offered a figure, 58.2 per cent gave one under £60 a week, and 25.4 per cent gave one under £50 a week. Only 3.9 per cent gave a figure over £70 a week. In fact average gross weekly earnings for all occupations at the time of the survey were £78.60. Thus most people were underestimating wages and overestimating welfare benefits, very probably a contributing factor in the generally hostile reception given to welfare benefit upratings. We also asked people to estimate average earnings in a range of occupations. There was a general tendency to underestimate earnings in lower paid jobs and overestimate those in higher paid jobs, at least by comparison with Department of Employment statistics. In part, however, this might be explained by the extent to which higher incomes are understated in such statistics. It was notable that the low paid in particular gave low figures for manual jobs, again suggesting one root of this group's particular hostility to welfare benefits.

Table 7.1 shows people's estimates of the distribution of incomes, together with official estimates. A high proportion of people overestimate the number of families with very high incomes, whereas over half underestimate the number of families with low incomes. These results should be seen together, and probably reflect a belief in a more symmetrical and egalitarian distribution of incomes than is actually the case. The general implication of these results is to suggest the very important effect of inflation on mental monetary values. People clearly lag behind psychologically in periods of rapid inflation, and thus over-evaluate smaller sums of money; hence the apparent adequacy, even largesse, that seemed to be provided in welfare benefits whose values are widely discussed publicly yet consistently overestimated by the majority of people.

TABLE 7.1 ESTIMATES OF INCOME DISTRIBUTION
'WHAT PROPORTION OF FAMILIES WOULD YOU SAY HAVE MORE THAN £200 A WEEK (LESS THAN £30 A WEEK) TO LIVE ON?'

Answers in range	Over £200		Under £30	
	No.	%	No.	%
None	11	2.2	43	7.8
5% or less	170	33.8	168	30.6
6—10%	135	26.8	111	20.2
11—30%	150	29.8	169	30.8
31—50%	27	5.4	40	7.3
50% +	10	2.0	18	3.3
No answer	147	—	101	—

N=650
Note:
Percentages are of those who offered an answer.

Official figures
Households with income up to £30: 13.7%
Households with income over £200: 4.8%

(*Source:* Family Expenditure Survey as summarised in *Social Trends* Vol. 9, HMSO, 1979, p. 99.)

JUST A LITTLE BIT OF LUCK: WHO'S RICH, WHO'S POOR?

When asked to describe who they have in mind when thinking of the rich, the largest number of people mentioned businessmen, managers, tycoons, executives and so on. However, this category was only mentioned by one in five respondents. One in eight thought of royalty, especially the Queen, or 'Lords and people like that'. The other major category of answers was that of pop stars or sports celebrities, either mentioned by name or generically. Only 6.2 per cent mentioned inherited wealth and 6.9 per cent mentioned owners of big business, shareholders or possessors of wealth as distinct from high incomes. Riches were generally seen to accrue from an unpredictable slice of good fortune ('One just has to look around, after all you read in the papers about people winning premium bonds or football pools'—age 57, female clerical worker), from the due rewards for merit or effort, or from a skill with money and things financial beyond the scope of the less able:

It's all those people whose thinking is financially better. They can handle money well. It's not worth worrying about.
[Age 45, male machine operator]

When asked a similar question about the poor, it was the old who were most frequently mentioned (by 17 per cent of people). This is rational enough, as at the end of 1978 nearly 60 per cent of supplementary benefit claimants were pensioners—about 1.74 million people or about a fifth of all retired people. However, nearly half the unemployed are on supplementary benefit and nearly half of lone parents. Only 6.9 per cent of people mentioned the unemployed and only 4.6 per cent single parents. By contrast, 5.3 per cent denied there were any poor people now and 6.4 per cent referred to large families. The emphasis on the elderly and on the contemporary absence of poverty tended to be expressed in terms of the successful abolition of poverty:

Nobody is really poor apart from people too old to manage the little money they have. But this is an age problem rather than a financial one.
[Age 44, male, shopkeeper]

You don't see so much poverty about as you used to. You used to see children in London with no shoes on but you don't now.
[Age 69, female, retired dressmaker]

It's only old people who are poor nowadays—mainly people who haven't earned enough to save up for their retirement . . .

there's less gap between rich and poor now. From what I read and hear on television, wealthy people like Lady Churchill are having to sell things to make ends meet. Rich people are getting a big salary, but they probably have a lot of expenses.

[Age 70, female, pensioner]

The low paid were not thought of to the same degree as the old as a category of the poor: 8.8 per cent mentioned lack of earning power because of inadequate skills or education, and 7.2 per cent made other references to low pay. In fact, the number of workers receiving less than the gross income needed to give them the same living standard as a two-child family on supplementary benefit at the time of our survey was 3.8 million, or 4.5 million if overtime earnings are discounted (*Low Pay Unit Bulletin* no. 18, December 1977, Table 3, p. 5). However, the low paid were the most likely to deny that there is any poverty now,[2] and least likely to mention the low paid as a category of the poor. This finding will make more sense in the context of our discussion of relative deprivation below.

In as much as people recognised that poverty still exists, they identified it primarily with old age. Inequality of condition was only dimly conceived and was construed as an accident of individual fortune. These evaluations were fairly uniform through the population, and were strongly held by those at the lower end of the reward structure. Wealth, on the other hand, was seen in the context of high incomes, particularly as expressed by consumer spending, or as a windfall. Runciman's use of the concept of relative deprivation in a study in the early 1960s remains a seminal attempt to explain, historically and social psychologically, the persistently acquiescent response to objective inequalities among those least favoured by the structured distribution of rewards. He argues that the inter-war depression 'reduced rather than heightened the magnitude and intensity of relative deprivation because few of its victims felt it to be obviously avoidable' (Runciman, 1972, p. 71). Although the Second World War led to mobility and wider social contacts, media portrayals of wealth were not such as to encourage comparison or resentment. Runciman concludes:

most men's lives are governed more by the resentment of narrow inequalities, the cultivation of narrow ambitions, and the preservation of small differentials than by attitudes to public policy or the social structure as such. Inequalities which are scarcely visible and difficult to remedy will have little influence on the day-to-day emotions of any but those whose political consciousness is unusually militant or sensitive, and envy is a difficult emotion to sustain across a broad social distance if gratification is nowhere within view. [Runciman, 1972, p. 336]

As we shall now briefly show, our findings confirm Runciman's very largely. However, we wish to argue that this does have implications for attitudes to public policy, and indeed that limited perceived inequality is a substantial prop of attitudes of the kind we have explored throughout this chapter.

The majority of people (62.0 per cent) felt the gap between rich and poor is smaller than it used to be. This view was more prevalent among the higher occupational groups, older people, high-income groups and those who assess their own circumstances as well off. In response to the statement 'Some people say there are no really rich or poor people any more — we're all about the same', only 9.9 per cent of respondents agreed, mainly people who mentioned the progressive effects of taxation. People do not believe an egalitarian utopia has arrived, merely a relative economic equalisation as grosser inequalities have been smoothed down by progressive taxation, generous social security and militant wage bargaining. All three of these were prominently discussed. Taxation:

> The high income groups have been so badly knocked by taxation and contributing to the welfare state. Professional people have been squeezed to help the poor. The poor are helped more than they used to be with welfare benefits and things.
> [Age 47, teacher's wife]

> The gap's much smaller because of the way the rich have been taxed to relieve them of their wealth plus the fact I read it in the newspaper recently so it's official.
> [Age 44, male shopkeeper (*Daily Mail* reader)]

At the other end, social security has granted generous advances to the poor:

> There's no need for anyone to be poor if they go and ask for help.
> [Age 63, female pensioner on £22 per week]

Well I think them on social are better off these days. They seem
to get all they want.

[Age 67, retired housekeeper]

And of course the bargaining power of the major unions is believed
to have massively privileged the working class in post-war
redistribution, with particularly publicised groups seen as emblematic of major economic revolution.

People who work in large car industries get whatever they want.
It's always on the news. I feel very bitter about it.

[Age 32, male unemployed welder]

There are some rich people—look at the miners. The price of
coal goes up and everything goes up.

[Age 47, male printer]

Of those who believed there are still rich and poor, a very large
number (22.9 per cent of all respondents) spoke resignedly about
the inevitability of the given order, the gap between rich and poor
being a fact of life or of nature. Very many people illustrated their
point by reference to variations in conspicuous consumption: the
larger cars and houses, and bigger and better possessions of the
rich. Indeed, as we have seen earlier, this is the defining
characteristic by which the rich are identified. Quite often this
advantage was seen to accrue from the innate familiarity with
things economic enjoyed by the rich. One respondent suggested
that 'they [the rich] can often go to wholesalers and buy goods at
wholesale prices, while we have to go and pay proper retail prices.
When I say goods, I mean food, clothing, and all household goods.
This is what makes some people rich'. There is, of course, the
glimmer of a truth in this. Economists have identified 'massive
consumer detriment for poor consumers', caused by lack of money-
saving capital equipment, travel facilities and so on, the costliness
of buying small quantities, poor access to services, discriminatory
tariff and other policies, and lack of information (Williams, 1977,
p. 235). But no economist seriously uses 'consumer detriment' to
explain the wealth structure of British society.

We can begin to see the relevance of Runciman's arguments
when we look at people's assessments of their own circumstances.
Four out of ten felt worse off than three years previously, though
among the better paid this proportion rose to 49.3 per cent. But

one in ten of the low paid felt themselves to be better off than
average and only a quarter of them felt worse off than average
(Table 7.2). People are generally not overwhelmed by an awareness
of others doing better. An insurance salesman thought 'there must
be' such people, but could only think of 'show biz people. And
there's a bloke in Saudi Arabia working in the oil fields'. Older
people quite often referred to younger people in the same job
doing better than themselves, and retired people referred to those
in work. But clearly the range of reference was limited and based
on the occupational ladder.

TABLE 7.2 ASSESSMENT OF OWN RELATIVE CIRCUMSTANCES AMONG
DIFFERENT INCOME GROUPS

	% feeling themselves to be:		
Income group	Better off than average	About average	Worse off than average
Low	9.6	64.9	25.5
Medium	16.0	74.9	9.1
High	50.7	45.3	4.0

Most people (87.6 per cent) did in fact feel that 'there are some
sorts of people doing much better than' themselves. But when
asked who these people were, most referred to people in only
slightly better paid jobs.

It's car workers, miners, people who keep getting pay rises.
From what you hear in the country they're always demanding
pay rises.

[Age 25, male greengrocer]

People with high incomes referred rather more to professional
groups, but among low wage earners reference was more often
made to two-income families. Only 1.7 per cent of respondents
made reference to unearned income, inherited wealth and so on.

People were rarely disturbed by the feeling that others are doing
better than themselves. Over four in ten used phrases like 'I'm not
bothered' and 13.2 per cent used the phrase 'Good luck to them'.
Clearly, if the social structure is seen to be open to mobility, and
both meritocratic and just, then success will seem fairly distributed

and will therefore be little resented. Only 8.5 per cent expressed some resentment of their own disadvantage, and only 3.4 per cent expressed any concern about the relative advantage of those they thought better off than themselves. There is at work here a thoroughgoing individualism—'it suits me, every man for himself I say'. Relative material deprivation is simply bad luck or just deserts for lack of effort or merit. The more distant reaches of wealth are invisible or believed to have been dismantled by the bulldozers of modern fiscal policy. How does this imagery arise?

Most people knew of the existence of people better off than themselves from personal experience. This claim was supported particularly by reference to the observed spending or consumption habits of the privileged. This accords with the theory that people will only make limited comparisons—the smart shopper in town, the big car in the next street, the Riviera tan on the next door neighbours. Less than 10 per cent referred to the media. What seems to be happening is that the media are providing the interpretative frameworks and ideology in which people's direct observations of inequalities are couched. Thus the picture they provide of an openly mobile, relatively egalitarian society prevents the translation of observable inequalities into a social resentment.

As Runciman argues, the consequence of this is that 'the frequency of relative deprivation among the manual stratum is considerably lower than would be consistent with the actual position of its members' (1972, p. 265). In turn, this means that support for the welfare state as a redistributive mechanism is itself muted, and 'the proportion of manual respondents who are opposed to any state provision whatever is high enough to suggest that their sense of relative deprivation on these topics is neither very widespread nor very intense' (*ibid.*).

Not surprisingly therefore, given our earlier analyses, such resentment as there is is turned down—to the unemployed and welfare claimants—rather than up to an invisible privileged stratum or to relatively adjacent groups whose advantages are seen to be both limited and fairly achieved.[3]

BLAMING THE VICTIM: HOW PEOPLE EXPLAIN POVERTY

Barbara Wootton has recently written:

Attitudes to poverty are changing. Years ago the well-heeled middle classes tended to accept poverty as a normal social phenomenon to be lightly dismissed as largely the fault of the shiftlessness of the poor themselves. But now that social investigators have thrust the facts under our noses, we have become ashamed and guilt conscious. The well-to-do critics of today are, therefore, less disposed to blame the poor for their poverty than to pretend that no-one is still poor. In their imagination, yesterday's poor have become the spoilt darlings and the cheats of the welfare state. [Wootton, 1978, p. 554]

We believe our findings show this to be a misleading half-truth. Yesterday's poor may well have become today's spoilt cheats, but beliefs about the causation of poverty have persisted in a way that belies Baroness Wootton's remarks.

We asked people in general terms about reasons for poverty. The largest category of answers made reference to the financial ineptitude of the poor: not managing household budgets very well, incurring ill-advised HP commitments, not saving, and so on. Far more than any other reason poverty was seen to result from the failure of the poor to control money going *out* of the home, rather than from society's failure to get a decent income *into* the home—a classic case of 'blaming the victim'. The second most popular explanation was in meritocratic terms: the poor just do not have the skills, intelligence or training to command a good wage in the competitive labour market. Unemployment was mentioned by only 5.8 per cent of respondents, though by rather more among younger people. Those on high incomes and skilled manual workers, two groups who in recent years have complained more than most about the erosion of their differential advantages, were more likely than others to mention low pay. Lack of skill or intelligence were most frequently invoked by those on high incomes, the better educated and those who assessed their own circumstances as relatively well off. Financial ineptitude and wastefulness were stressed by women and by people in Southwick, where there was least opportunity to sell labour of any kind but, equally, the most intense competition to do so.

In order to examine people's underlying understanding of poverty we offered a variety of statements about the causes of poverty derived from pilot research. A factor analysis of responses to these statements gave the results summarised in Table 7.3.[4] Four clear underlying clusters of explanations were derived. These were produced both by a total matrix of items and by predicting clusters

TABLE 7.3 EXPLANATIONS OF POVERTY: FACTOR MATRIX

	Factor			
Poor people are people who:	*1* Prodigality	*2* Injustice	*3* Ascribed deprivation	*4* Fatalism
Don't manage their money properly	.64	−.10	−.11	−.10
Are just unlucky individuals	.03	.07	.10	.53
Work in jobs which are poorly paid	−.02	.15	.14	.21
Waste their money on drink and other things like gambling	.66	−.07	−.04	.02
Just aren't very bright or talented	.26	−.03	.28	.09
Never stood a chance because their parents were poor	−.02	.16	.60	.22
Just don't make any effort to get on in life	.59	−.08	.03	.00
Come from places where there's little opportunity for most people	−.02	.12	.49	.11
Are taken advantage of by rich people	.00	.68	.09	.09
Have too many children	.30	.08	.14	.11
Do badly in life because rich people get more than their fair share	−.17	.70	.15	.07
Have had a bad break at some point in their lives	.03	.00	.13	.47
EIGEN VALUE	2.23	1.98	1.19	1.03

Note: The technique used was a varimix rotated factor matrix (after rotation with Kaiser normalisation). Boxes show the items loading significantly on each factor.

of items. The first factor we called prodigality, being to do with the wasteful spending patterns, financial ineptitude, imprudent breeding habits and sheer fecklessness or lack of motivation of the poor. This theme recurred throughout the survey.[5]

It's because they've never appreciated the value of money. They've never looked ahead. They go out drinking when they've got it with no thought for the future.
[Age 56, male machine operator]

Poor people are people lacking spirit and initiative or the guts to go out and earn a little money to make things easier.
[Age 73, female pensioner]

The second factor was injustice, a positive explanation of poverty as the converse of wealth and a direct consequence of the exploitative or unfair distribution of financial reward. The third and fourth are variants of a single factor that Feagin, in his comparable research, identifies as fatalistic. We found two separate versions of this. The first (factor 3) is to do with the bad luck involved in choosing one's parents unwisely, or being brought up in places where there's little opportunity for most people. It is the cycle of deprivation thesis, which we have labelled ascribed deprivation, and includes the notion that rewards are fairly distributed according to talents and merit that the poor unfortunately lack.

Poor people often have foolish parents, those who don't encourage industry and thrift, they have confused priorities.
[Age 40, male teacher]

The remaining factor was the individualistic version of fatalism, poverty being seen to descend randomly on people anywhere in the social structure as a result of sheer bad luck—perhaps a bad illness or some such unpredictable bad break.

How are these four types of explanation spread across the population? By allocating a score of 1 for each statement agreed to, 0 for each disagreed with, and ½ for any for which no answer or uncertainty was the response, we were able to give each respondent an average score for the group of items contributing to each factor.[6] After subjecting these scores to an analysis of variance with each of several criterion variables, eight relationships significant at better than the 1% level were discovered.

Prodigality was distinctly more likely to be mentioned by women and by people in the two middle-class neighbourhoods. Perhaps isolated domestically or protected by suburban comfort, they are most prone to explain poverty as a matter of reckless wastefulness. Surprisingly, pensioners were also substantially more likely to give this kind of explanation. Explanations of poverty as structural injustice were only accepted by about 26 per cent of respondents in all. However, this explanation was significantly more likely to come from those with experience of receiving benefits, from manual workers and from people in the two inner-city areas. Initially, this appears to indicate an unexpected radicalism of spirit among the groups who have seemed in other aspects most likely to adopt dominant values to explain their own disadvantage, and to visit most vehemently their resentment on the pauper stratum beneath them. However, as our discussion of relative deprivation suggested, perceived injustice as between rich and poor is a relative matter, and a great deal rests on who is identified as the advantaged group. Although manual workers were more likely than other groups to attribute poverty to distributional injustice, this was more a perception of small injustices over a limited range than an oppositional view of the iniquities of class inequality. Ascribed deprivation did not produce a statistically significant breakdown demographically, though it was mentioned more often by people in the inner-city areas and by high-income groups. Fatalism pure and simple was subscribed to more by women than by men, by low earners and very much more by pensioners (cf. Feagin, 1972a,b; Huber and Form, 1973; Alston and Dean, 1972).

These results should be contrasted with some research conducted for the Commission of the European Community. The authors of this research derive a series of not dissimilar sets of explanations of poverty, basically on the divide between individualistic and structural explanations. They conclude, however, that 'the striking thing about these results is not, of course, that some people rather than others tend to perceive poverty and attribute it to social causes . . . Properly speaking, the added value of these analyses is that they show the predominance of subjective factors over objective factors' (Commission of the European Communities, 1977, p. 91). They argue that personality factors—degree of cynicism, self-satisfaction and the like—are the major concomitants of explanations of poverty. Our results expose this reductionist view for the unlikely simplification it is.[7] It is interesting, however, that their research does show Britons to be significantly tougher minded, and more likely to ascribe individualistic explanations of poverty than any other European nation, an interesting cultural variation that would be worth probing further. Most particularly it suggests the ease with which the values we detected historically in chapter 2 became quickly resurrected when the British economy is in recession, suggesting that these make up not the ideology of a social formation in crisis but its core values, only thinly covered over even in periods of expansion.

CONCLUSION: 'HUNGER AND SIN, SIN AND HUNGER'

Stedman Jones (1976, Chs 5, 14, 15) has shown how the Victorians in the 1870s still saw the lowest group of the 'casual poor' as an unthreatening 'residuum', a view that did not turn to alarm until the sensationalist revelations of the 1880s. Explanations were varied and plentiful, but most focused on the individual 'viciousness', and the need for remoralisation, of the poor. When General Booth came to seek the way out of Darkest England, the scale of the problem was vast, ensuring that 'without some extraordinary help, they must hunger and sin, and sin and hunger, until having multiplied their kind, and filled up the measure of their miseries, the gaunt fingers of death will close upon them and terminate their wretchedness' (1890, preface).

The thin veneer of the Keynesian welfare consensus has barely covered these two views. Poverty remains invisible. On the one hand it is widely believed that little or no poverty persists, other than an unavoidable degree of hardship in old age. On the other hand, where poverty is recognised, it is explained in terms of the individual culpability of its victims. Firmly wedded to an absolute rather than a relative standard of deprivation, most people deny that serious poverty exists, and see little gap between the circumstance of those on the lowest incomes and the rest of the population. Considerable faith in the redistributive consequences of income taxation and social security buttresses a conviction that those left at the bottom of the pile must have wilfully evaded the largesse of the new egalitarianism.

Structural explanations of poverty are largely absent. Poverty, like wealth, attaches to individuals and has no visible relation to larger movements or processes in society. Far more people relate poverty to the inefficient consumption of incomes rather than to their inegalitarian distribution in the labour market and from the ownership of wealth.

While this ideology has such a tight grip it must be improbable that opposition to welfare measures could be reduced, or seriously fundamental changes in notions of social policy made acceptable. Here, in these broader understandings of poverty and inequality, is the root of the kind of hostility to both the welfare system and claimants we described in the previous chapter. If blaming the victim is a deeply entrenched philosophy, a system of positive redistribution, or even income maintenance, will always be viewed with suspicion, especially by those who earn their poverty or face its worst consequences despite their best efforts to escape its clutches in the crumbling squalor of our inner cities.

NOTES

1. See also Freeman (1979) who similarly found people to underestimate wages and overestimate benefits.
2. cf. Townsend's finding that 38 per cent of his respondents who felt themselves to be 'always poor' believed there was no real poverty in Britain in the late 1960s (Townsend, 1979, p. 427).
3. cf. Coates and Silburn (1970) Ch. 7 and Townsend (1979) p. 426. The latter shows that among his poorest respondents those who said they never felt poor were more likely to have stable circumstances and greater social contacts. However, as the author stresses, 'The myth of the contented poor is not borne out by the data' (p. 431).
4. This procedure was suggested by and adapted from the work of J. Feagin; see Feagin (1972a and b, 1975).
5. Lack of effort as a cause of poverty has figured highly and increasingly in public opinion surveys. But this may be because people have been offered a simple choice of explanations. For what it is worth, Gallup surveys showed the following progression (Gallup, 1976):

Poverty is caused by:	1964 %	1968 %	1970 %	1971 %
Lack of effort	28	35	27	32
Circumstances beyond people's control	38	30	32	32

6. These are not factor scores; no attempt was made to weight scores by the loading of each item on the factor. Tabulation has been omitted here for reasons of space.
7. For a full discussion and critique of this research see Golding (1980b).

IV Conclusion

It is no exaggeration to say that the shape of Britain today owes more to Tory principles of the nineteenth century than to the ideas of Karl Marx and Friedrich Engels. [*Milton Friedman*, Free to Choose, *1980*]

CHAPTER 8

Welfare, Ideology and the Mass Media

In this chapter we attempt to draw together some of the threads left hanging from the empirical work described earlier. There are many complex theoretical and historical issues that, though relevant, we can scarcely touch on here. Much work remains to be done on that triangular relationship between the state, the mass media and popular ideologies that frames thinking about the legislation and administration of social policy.

The argument in this conclusion is a tentative sketch of themes to be explored. In outline it is as follows. The early promise of the 'welfare state' has not been fulfilled. Poverty persists and the welfare apparatus has more enemies than friends. The failure of the welfare state is common ground across the political spectrum. However, of the available diagnoses, those that emphasise the damaging burden of welfare expenditure and the abuse of social security and services by much of their clientele have received privileged exposure and authority, especially in the mass media. Although alternative views have been available they have lacked a political or cultural carrier. On the one hand, the major potential political voice for such views, the Labour Party, has largely conceded the argument either wilfully or by default. On the other hand, the systematic decline and exclusion of a mass left press has cleared the field for the promulgation of a conservative critique of welfare via the major available cultural apparatus.

With the end of the post-war period of economic growth, always relatively modest and contradictory, economic crisis has liberated a full-scale assault on the welfare consensus, which was in fact never very firmly attached to popular consciousness. This assault came ready armed with a neo-liberal critique always present in post-war writing and thinking on social policy among the radical right. The media helped jerk this critique into prominence by a burst of 'scroungerphobia', which reasserted a moral and social theory whose impact through the development of welfare administration has been consistent and remains undiminished. Contradictory attitudes in working-class thought were thus orchestrated around this theory in popular form, at the expense of alternatives, though the role of the media was to interpret and organise rather than to create attitudes and myths.

These arguments all pose problems of theory and evidence. They are presented here with due caution and a wary appreciation of the frequent fate of ambitious generalisations, in the hope that the findings reported in the earlier parts of this book have more than particular or ephemeral significance.

THE RETREAT FROM UTOPIA

When the Beveridge Report on Social Assistance and Allied Services (Cmnd. 6404, HMSO, 1942) was published in December 1942, a nation desperate for visions of a better tomorrow grasped at its promises with fervour. Shrewd and energetic publicity by Beveridge himself and his aide Frank Pakenham (later Lord Longford) ensured that few were unable to warm their hands by the glow of the report's heady proclamations that the giants of Want, Disease, Ignorance, Squalor and Idleness would be banished from post-war Britain. Despite the scepticism of some industrialists and the rather qualified support of the Coalition government, to the public at large (already euphoric with news of the turn of the military tide in North Africa) the report was a statutory blueprint for utopia.

The report got a 'big press': 'Freedom From Want' (*The Times*); 'Beveridge Report Plans to Abolish Want' (*Daily Telegraph*); 'New-Era-For-All Beveridge Plan' (*Daily Sketch*). Pakenham wrote later 'In my own experience I can recall no burst of acclamation remotely resembling it' (1953, p. 126). Beveridge became a national hero. Over half a million copies of the report were sold and the BBC broadcast details of its contents in twenty-two languages. 'The People's William' had given a war-weary Home Front fresh purpose for victory.

The story of post-war welfare administration is one of repeated retreat from the aims of the Beveridge Report, itself in hindsight a fundamentally conservative document, firmly wedded to the insurance principle, cautious about income redistribution, anxious to promote thrift, reverberating with echoes of an earlier period's concern with national efficiency, and shot through with reactionary attitudes to the role of women.[1] From the start, the government refused to accept Beveridge's plan for subsistence level benefits, and the rates eventually agreed were well below such a minimum. By 1948 flat rate benefits were only 19 per cent of average wages. In the long 'White Paper Chase' between 1942 and the implementation of National Insurance after the war several further lumps were eroded from the grand design. The report itself had drawn back from adequate provision for housing costs, for the congenitally disabled and for married women. Treasury pressure further suppressed the level of family allowances, limited the period of time for which benefits would be paid and reduced the value of benefit allowances for children.[2]

None of these inadequacies caused much disquiet as the long post-war boom and economic growth kept unemployment well within actuarial provisions. The post-war 'settlement' between capital and labour allowed a managed, if not a planned economy, in which the newly learned Keynesian techniques of demand management seemed to produce the goods. When the Tory Butler succeeded Labour's Gaitskell as chancellor in 1951, continuity seemed effortless; 'Butskellism' was enthroned and the sweet smell of post-war affluence displaced the stale aroma of austerity. The Labour movement shrugged off the 1948 wage freeze and the effects of the 1949 devaluation, even the end of free prescriptions. Full employment, as a fact and a policy commitment, was too rich a reward to worry about pinpricks like these. Marshall Aid of £2,000 million provided a helpful cover to underlying economic fault-lines that were not to reappear for over a decade. In 1950 Labour went to the country with a manifesto declaring 'destitution has been banished'. The economy was hungry for workers, immigrants were sedulously welcomed and the only witch-hunts were for the 'drones' of the leisured classes.[3]

Virtually full employment from 1950 to 1963 drew from social democrats a chorus of satisfaction. Government, in Rose's phrase, was now the business of 'fine-tuning heaven' (1978, p. 3). The victory was triumphantly proclaimed by Anthony Crosland in 1956: 'Primary poverty has been largely eliminated; the "Beveridge revolution" has been carried through; and Britain now boasts the widest range of social services in the world, and, as a result, the appellation "Welfare State" . . . The historic objective has, in Britain, largely been attained' (1964, p. 59). The very concept of the 'welfare state' entered popular vocabularies as a comforting condensation of the varied achievements of post-war Britain, projected in cameos of 'working-class embourgeoisement' and the 'managerial revolution'. Unemployment between 1948 and 1966 averaged 1.7 per cent, and Macmillan as prime minister from 1957 to 1963 could persuasively, and for the majority, accurately argue that we had 'never had it so good'.[4]

Every silver lining has its dark cloud. While Britain gazed with satisfaction at domestic prosperity, in most other major industrial countries productivity and investment accelerated away from British levels, while British exports were artificially and temporarily protected in the Sterling Area. Real wage levels rose as did company taxation, and capital investment remained low. As doubts crept in, new systems of planning were introduced, spurred by a balance of payments crisis in 1960 (only the second year of deficit since 1949) and a sterling crisis in 1961. The National Economic Development Council was set up in 1962 as part of the Conservatives' last effort to keep the momentum going, together with reorganisation of fiscal control through the Public Expenditure Survey Committee (PESC) system. But years of 'stop—go' and the increasing burden of tax on wage earners (the tax threshold dropped from 218 per cent of average earnings in 1952 to 110 per cent in 1965—Field *et al.,* 1977, p. 41[5]) were the prelude to growing unease and the return of a Labour government in 1964.

The new government came in bursting to unleash the 'white heat of the technological revolution' and put an end to 'thirteen wasted years'. Proving the efficiency of the Labour national plan was too obsessive a task to allow more than an irritated glance at the 'rediscovery of poverty' being publicised by academics like Richard Titmuss and 'the Titmice', and by new vociferous pressure groups like Shelter and the Child Poverty Action Group.[6] Other more urgent problems were at hand: a large balance of payments deficit—the legacy of the Tory push for growth in 1963/4—and growing pressure on the pound, whose standing became the abiding obsession of the Wilson years. Deflation in 1966 and eventually devaluation the following year turned round the balance of payments, though not till 1969, while the introduction of the Industrial Reorganisation Corporation was a further throw of the dice to reconstruct an increasingly moribund British industry whose profits as a proportion of output fell from 23.0 per cent in 1960 to 14.8 per cent in 1970.

Along the way the commitment to full employment slipped from view. By 1969 unemployment was 2.4 per cent. The notion of 'unemployables' returned and much ink was spilled over the problem of incentives and the 'work-shy'. The new bogy of inflation arose to haunt economic thinking, which concentrated efforts on controlling wage levels, industrial discipline and public expenditure. At the return to power of the Conservatives in 1970 unemployment was 2.6 per cent and had become a tool of economic policy rather than the rock on which it foundered.[7]

Initially the Tory government, in its 'Selsdon Man' persona, launched Edward Heath's 'quiet revolution'. Cuts in corporation and general taxation were accompanied by increases in school meal prices and the end of cheap welfare milk and of free school milk for the over-sevens. Yet expenditure on health and social security rose 5.2 per cent in 1970/1 to cope with unavoidable expansion of dependent populations, not least the growing number of unemployed (crossing the million barrier by January 1972), and reorganisation. Britain was clearly out of line with Europe, on whose activities the gaze of the Heath government was enviously fixed. By 1972 expenditure on income maintenance programmes in Britain was lower by far than in most European countries (OECD, 1976).[8] European examples also prompted the expansion of a coordinating corporatist apparatus including the introduction of Programme Analysis and Review, Programme Planning Budgeting Systems and the Central Policy Review Staff. This was ostensibly the spirit of the end of ideology made flesh.

By the summer of 1972 'the quiet revolution was dead' (Bruce-Gardyne, 1974, p. 100). Statutory wage controls were the first step in a manic spiral of confrontation that climaxed with the three-day week and the defeat of the Conservatives in 1974. Chancellor Tony Barber's frantic dash for growth in 1972—4, fuelled by tax cuts and propelled by a floating exchange rate (from June 1972), demand expansion and increases in the money supply of up to 30 per cent per annum (in 1972), eventually crashed into political ruin in the aftermath of the 1973 oil crisis. The road was clear for the return of the ideologues of sound money and reduced public expenditure.[9]

Public expenditure had risen throughout this period, though neither so fast as frequent admonition suggested nor so much as in many other countries. Between 1956 and 1966, for example, public expenditure grew as a proportion of Gross Domestic Product from 34 per cent to 38 per cent. Between 1950 and 1975 there was a secular rise in this ratio from 34 per cent to 50 per cent, a significant rise of 5.6 per cent having occurred in 1973/4, though this figure was in part magnified by the drop of GDP in real terms in 1974.[10]

However fast this growth, there is no question that the increase in expenditure on social security and social services was a major component. Between 1950 and 1978 the average annual growth rate at constant prices of the social security programme was 4.9 per cent and for personal social services 5.7 per cent (though the latter started from a very small base). Social security spending in 1977 was 20 times its 1950 level and personal social services had grown 45 times in the same period. Between them they accounted for 26.1 per cent of public expenditure by 1977. Public expenditure on all social services (including social security, health, education, housing and personal social services) rose from 48 per cent of government expenditure (14.5 per cent of GDP) in 1950 to 58.1 per cent (25.1 per cent of GDP) in 1974. In the same period, social security alone rose from 16.4 per cent of government expenditure (5.0 per cent of GDP) to 19.3 per cent (8.3 per cent of GDP) (Gould and Roweth, 1980; see also Gough, 1975).

Despite this growth however, the social security system was roundly condemned from all sides and with growing vehemence. Three indicators illustrate the problem. First the numbers in poverty continued to increase, a cruel riposte to the premature claims of the 1950s. The National Insurance scheme had become a frail safety net through which fell an ever-multiplying number onto means-tested National Assistance (renamed supplementary benefits in 1966). The numbers on National Assistance, intended originally as a last resort for the exceptional few, rose from just over a million families in 1948 to 1,857,000 in 1960 and to 2,680,000 in 1974. The number of people dependent on supplementary benefits rose from 2,048,000 in 1951 to 4,092,000 in 1974, or 7 per cent of the population (H. C. *Hansard* Written Answers, 28 July 1977).[11] Secondly, because of the proliferation of means-tested benefits, large numbers of people were failing to claim considerable sums of money to which they were entitled. By 1975 an estimated 930,000 people, including 600,000 pensioners, were failing to claim £240 million of supplementary benefits alone (H. C. *Hansard* Written Answers, 7 April 1977; see also SBC, 1978; Lister, 1974, 1976). The value of other unclaimed benefits probably equalled this sum. As a result, vast numbers of people have been living below the official poverty line. To this group should be added those in full-time work whose income falls below the supplementary benefit level. By 1975 this group comprised 210,000 families or

630,000 people (H. C. *Hansard* Written Answers, 1 August 1978). The total number of people living below supplementary benefits standards grew from 1.26 million in 1960 to 1.84 million in 1975, while in the same period the total number living at up to 10 per cent above supplementary benefits level rose from 4.64 million to 6.67 million (Townsend, 1979, p. 908).[12]

The third indicator is the failure of the welfare state to effect that material redistribution for which it has been mistakenly condemned by its opponents and applauded by its friends. The redistributive potential of progressive and rising taxation together with income maintenance schemes is the fulcrum on which the ideological equation of welfare state with socialism has rested. To explore the empirical extent of redistribution is beyond our brief here. But three points are relevant. First, the value of welfare benefits has kept up with and indeed exceeded price inflation. However their value has, at best, only kept pace with earnings. National Assistance scale levels were 29.4 per cent of average earnings in 1948, 28.5 per cent in 1973 and 31.8 per cent in 1977 (*Social Security Statistics,* DHSS, 1981, Table 46.07). Other benefits show a long-term improvement in this period, but this is partly due to significant increases in 1965, and their relative value has declined since 1977. Transfer payments have remained a fairly constant proportion of public expenditure, at about 43 per cent of the total from 1957 to 1966 and at about 45 per cent of the total from 1967 to 1977 (Gould and Roweth, 1980, p. 343). Secondly, income distribution has remained resolutely unequal throughout the post-war period. In 1949 the share of all after-tax incomes received by the top 10 per cent was 27.1 per cent while for the top 20 per cent the share was 41.6 per cent. In 1974/5 the share accruing to these two groups was still 23.2 per cent and 39.0 per cent respectively. For the bottom 30 per cent, after-tax income only rose from 11.6 per cent of the total in 1954 to 12.8 per cent in 1974/5 (Royal Commission on the Distribution of Income and Wealth, Table A.2). As Field *et al.* conclude,

> For the great bulk of the tax payers . . . the system of income tax is a proportional one. The only element of progression is introduced through the system of tax allowances. But as we have seen these are themselves regressive in their effects, being of greatest benefit to high income groups . . . We conclude therefore that the belief in the progressive system of income tax is more firmly rooted in myth than in reality. [1977, p. 69]

Putting taxation and benefits together, the picture becomes more complicated. However, most studies suggest that since the early 1960s the distribution of final incomes after taxes and benefits has been stable, with a slight downward distribution to the rich from the very rich (Royal Commission on the Distribution of Income and Wealth, 1978a, pp. 141–5; also 1979, Tables 3.5 and 3.6). Finally, the continuity of inequalities of wealth is even more striking than in the distribution of incomes. In 1951 the top 5 per cent owned 68 per cent of total wealth; by 1972 this had slipped to 56 per cent, but almost entirely to the benefit of the next richest 5 per cent.[13] In these three ways, then, the welfare state has remained an inegalitarian social system: through the failure of benefits to provide claimants with increases in living standards comparable with those in work, through the failure of taxation and benefits to dent final income inequality, and through the persistence of wealth inequality.

The social security apparatus thus 'failed' on three fronts: firstly because of the increase in numbers in poverty, secondly because of the failure of means-tested benefits, and thirdly because of the lack of any serious redistribution of income or wealth. By the mid-1970s the 'failure of the welfare state' was common ground. Despite the radicalism of the February 1974 Labour election manifesto, both major parties agreed that inflation was the major problem and that the size of public expenditure was part of the cause. Of the available critiques of the welfare system two were given privileged exposure, one emphasising the burden of welfare expenditure, the other its unnecessary expansion by abuse and by undue dependence on public assistance. Missing from popular debate were at least two other forms of critique. One radically reconceived the welfare apparatus as part of the infrastructure of an industrial system—'the ambulance service of capitalism'. The other was a technical critique explaining the expansion of welfare expenditure as in large part the result of demographic changes (especially the increase in the elderly population) or the relative price effect (by which some of the increased cost of social services represents their imperviousness to productivity improvements and thus the increase in expenditure they require over and above general inflation to sustain service standards and volume). The point here is not to explore the basis or validity of these or other arguments. More simply it is to contrast their limited exposure with the trumpeted deficiencies of the welfare state as a burden (creeping socialism) or as a source of bounty for the indolent. To look at this further we need to examine the channels available for alternative views.

MESSAGE WITH NO MESSENGER

Two carriers that might have kept aloft a banner for the poor and welfare are the Labour Party and the left press. We can briefly look at each of these in turn, though their history is more sensibly considered jointly within the complex history of socialist thought and organisation in Britain.

The Labour Party

The Labour Party has spent long years basking in the afterglow of having 'created the welfare state', a comforting charter myth that has often absolved today's compromises by virtue of yesterday's triumphs. Yet those glorious years of 1945—1951 were essentially the fruit of post-war consensus (Hess, 1981). For the Attlee generation, any advance in working-class conditions, especially full employment, was tantamount to social revolution. Trusting in the lingering conviviality of wartime social unity, they only intermittently perceived the cold glint of exploitation and inequality that still lay beneath the surface accord. Productive thinking within the Labour Party on social policy had frozen to a standstill in the 1930s. The moderate if broad Beveridge proposals would have been anathema to the radical party conferences of a quarter century earlier. In Marwick's considered verdict,

> In passing the major acts that established the contemporary welfare state, Labour was governed not only by its own recent pronouncements but also by attitudes formed over a much longer period . . . When Labour fell from office in 1951 it left behind several imposing chunks of masonry instead of the complete welfare edifice it had hoped to build. [1967, pp. 401, 403]

Out of office in the 1950s the party endorsed the prevailing conclusion that poverty had been conquered. Aside from some routine 'pensioneering', the Butskellite consensus fused around the solid congratulatory core of affluence and consumerism. The left found itself devoid of social policy battles to fight, and the hunt for public squalor amid private affluence was brief and tentative. Gaitskell emerged in 1955 as leader of a party desperate to return to power and convinced 'that the essential condition for that success was to present the Labour Party as a moderate and respectable party, free from class bias, "national" in outlook, and whose zeal for reform would always be tempered by its eager endorsement of the view that Rome was not built in a day—or even in a century' (Miliband, 1972, p. 339).

With creeping doubts about the endurance of post-war economic growth, the party slipped into a cautious posture. The poor could only benefit to the extent that the whole community prospered. A recurrent metaphor was that used by Richard Crossman at the 1962 party conference, suggesting that the poor 'must have an escalator, a moving staircase which moves at the same pace that the worker marches up the steps of prosperity' (Labour Party Annual Conference Report, 1962, p. 105).[14] Poverty was not thought to be widespread and was no longer conceived in relative or structural terms. The party's 1963 *New Frontiers for Social Security* speaks only of a 'defenceless minority', 'chiefly concentrated among those who through infirmity, ill-fortune, or old age' were in an isolated, individual and redeemable state of hardship (Labour Party, 1963, p. 6).[15]

Back in power, the defence of sterling and the stark facts of economic deceleration deflected the party further from a radical consideration of social policy. As Peggy Herbison told the 1965 party conference, 'The key factor in determining the speed at which new and better levels of benefit can be introduced will be the rate at which the British economy can advance' (Labour Party Annual Conference Report, 1965, p. 123).[16] Impatience among the party rank and file was doused by the cold water of Wilsonian pragmatism.[17] Callaghan as chancellor, like Wilson, made the defence of sterling a priority, and the party leadership lost hold of any commitment to redistribution, indeed accepted the redundance of such a shibboleth in a low-growth economy. The Labour victory in 1966 proved, said Wilson, that Labour was the party of national unity, rejecting 'the Conservative concept of cynical conflict between class and class' (Labour Party Annual Conference Report, 1966, p. 162). The record of 1964—70 left a mountain of outrage on the left of the party beneath which was buried a mausoleum of forsaken promise (see, for example, Coates, 1972; Bosanquet and Townsend, 1972). Housing and education targets were cut, the 'wage-stop' extended, tax thresholds dropped, school meal charges rose and the provision of free school milk was reduced. Unemployment rose and was the major cause of increased social security spending. By 1970 'the aspirations of the 1950s, to use State power to redress the uneven distribution of social privileges and rights, had been abandoned; and the search for the conditions under which sustained economic growth could be achieved had been allowed to drown completely any vestigial interest in social reform' (Coates, 1975, p. 115; see also Banting, 1979). Occasional eruptions of angst within the party were easily contained, as for example over the wage-stop.[18] The uneasy wedlock of the Labour Party with social reform had been totally severed by the pressures of managing an economy quite unable to generate the surplus that might have rendered redistribution and welfare expansion painless.

By 1974, four years in opposition had recharged the batteries of radical rhetoric, but they were to be irreversibly run down by the sheer scale and ferocity of recession. More significantly, radicalism in welfare policy was by now merely the icing on the cake. The manifesto promise to 'eliminate poverty wherever it exists' was lip-service to a priority long superseded in the power centres of the party. Whether one views the Labour government in 1974—79 as the hapless victim of capitalism in crisis (or more simply of the Treasury), or as a cynical collaborator in the containment of working-class ambition, the dissolution of the party as a source of radical thinking on social policy was complete.

The Healey budget in 1975 launched a deflationary strategy that was already well down the slip-way when given a massive shove by the Olympian visit of the IMF at the end of the year. The February 1976 cuts in public expenditure reduced previously planned programmes by £4,595 million. The hospital building programme was cut from £378 million in 1975/6 to £298 million in 1979/80. Capital expenditure in social services was cut from £115 million in 1975/76 to £54 million in 1979/80. School meal subsidies were cut, so were food subsidies. Short-term social security benefits remained roughly constant relative to average earnings, but the number of supplementary benefit recipients increased by 310,000 between 1974 and 1977. The Labour government initiated a review of the supplementary benefits scheme whose brief was the Treasury dictum that any change should be at nil cost. Child Benefits were dragged onto the statute book only after a reluctant Cabinet was manoeuvred by hostile publicity and press leaks.

Surrounded by a sea of industrial stagnation, rising unemployment, the legacy of a massive balance of payments deficit in 1973/4, and rates of inflation that stubbornly refused to obey the laws of economics and come down, the Labour Cabinet compromised on its pension scheme, quietly swept the promised wealth tax under the carpet and presided over an increase in unemployment of three-quarters of a million while in office. While the wealth tax vanished over the horizon, other taxes on wealth declined and mainstream corporation tax virtually disappeared. In Roy Jenkins' words, the party was indeed over.[19]

At the rhetorical level, the Labour government seemed to be making a virtue of necessity. Keynesian techniques and commitment to full employment and public expenditure were discarded with a brazen flourish and evident scorn for the naivety of past promises and present regrets (see Coates, 1980).

A party committed to battling for the centre of the road is bound to stumble when the road surface cracks up. More or less throughout the post-war period the Labour Party has endorsed the orthodoxy that the elimination of poverty would be achieved by growth not by redistribution. The national interest is defined by this view as requiring sound money and economic growth as preconditions to increased expenditure on welfare. Transfer payments are included as public expenditure not redistribution. It is an ideology flanked on one side by work incentives and labour discipline, on the other by lean, minimal public services and self-help. Our point is not that no welfare advances or social policy initiatives have been achieved by Labour in office, or designed by the party in opposition. It is rather that poverty and welfare have simply been left to one side in the party's considerations. A careful reading of party conference reports reveals only rare discussions of poverty, and few on social security other than pensions. As Field has noted, this is reflected in the writings of party leaders who have found little time or inclination to dwell on what has become a marginal area of policy (1981, pp. 220—2). Hooked for years on the beguiling myth of post-war affluence and the elimination of destitution, 'the rediscovery of poverty' found the Labour Party committed to the permanent postponement of redistribution in the interests of 'the economy'. It was not a platform from which a vigorous assault on the principles and practices of the welfare state could be resisted.

The press

The British national press has lurched from crisis to crisis since the war, and no fewer than three Royal Commissions have examined the entrails in the search for solutions. From a circulation plateau of between 16—17 million in the 1950s, national daily circulation fell to 14.07 million in 1976. National Sunday circulations fell from 28.3 million in 1947 to 19.6 million in 1976. These aggregate figures mask an important distinction. While popular newspapers suffered a major decline, the 'quality' or up-market titles increased circulations by 14.5 per cent between 1961 and 1975. At the same time, the surviving titles became concentrated into fewer hands—increasingly large, conglomerate multinational groups (Murdock and Golding, 1978, pp. 132—4).[20] By 1981 three groups controlled 73.5 per cent of the national daily circulation and 89.6 per cent of the national Sunday circulation.

The evolutionary process that produced this result, and that reduced the number of provincial dailies from 41 in 1921 to 17 in 1975, did not strike randomly. The deaths were almost entirely among the Labour or left press. At the simplest level of partisanship, as the most recent Royal Commission noted, 'There is no doubt that over most of this century the Labour movement has had less newspaper support than its right-wing opponents and that its beliefs and activities have been unfavourably reported by the majority of the press' (Royal Commission on the Press, 1977b, pp. 98—9). In circulation terms the imbalance has not been massive. In elections between 1945 and 1970 Labour-supporting dailies generally accounted for 35—45 per cent of circulation. Conservative-supporting dailies 50—57 per cent (Seymour-Ure, 1974, pp. 166—7).[21] The imbalance in the number of titles has been more marked, though with a roughly 2 to 1 advantage for Conservative over Labour support (Curran, 1981, p. 103). However, explicit partisanship flourishes only at election periods and, as we have seen, advocacy of the Labour cause would not necessarily have included an energetic defence of welfare policies. More important has been the obliteration of a left and social democratic tradition in the press, which has occurred in three ways: through the death of individual titles, through the deradicalisation of the surviving working-class press, and through the rise of economic barriers to entry by new titles.

The second Royal Commission was in part prompted by the death of the *News Chronicle* in 1960. The paper closed with a circulation of over 1 million, more than double that of *The Times* and *Guardian* combined. The *News Chronicle* had been the voice of a liberal radical tradition with a strong hold on the loyalties of its readers. It had not made a loss until 1957, but in that year it lost a sixth of its circulation (Glenton and Pattinson, 1963, pp. 215, 158). Its real problem was a lack of financial reserves and a readership far less affluent than other 'small'-circulation 'quality' titles. The *Sunday Citizen* (formerly *Reynold's News*), child of the Co-Operative movement, closed in 1967. In many ways a paper past its natural peak it nonetheless suffered unduly from low advertising income, receiving only a tenth of the advertising revenue per copy of a paper with a more attractive clientele like the *Sunday Times*.

Perhaps even more significant was the *Daily Herald*. Launched initially as a strike-sheet, the *Herald* became the major socialist paper. Relaunched as a daily in 1919, however, it found itself at odds with the new newspaper economics, and in 1922 it was taken over by the TUC jointly with Odhams, the latter acquiring control of the paper in 1929. Its subsequent commercial success took it to the heights, but in the post-war period the *Herald* paid the price for loyal support and consistent politics, with a readership becoming too old and too narrowly working-class to attract advertisers. Its net advertising revenue dropped by 19 per cent between 1955 and 1964 even though the annual volume of advertising in its pages rose by 10.4 per cent during these years, while its share of national daily circulation fell only slightly, from 10.8 per cent to 8.1 per cent (Curran, 1978, p. 251). The *Daily Herald* was bought not by too few people but by the wrong people. In 1963−4, 39 per cent of its 4.6 million readers were in the advertisers' pariah caste, social groups D and E, and another 48 per cent in social grade C2 (*ibid.,* p. 253). Its Labour commitment was unshaken, but the TUC lost editorial control when Odhams was acquired by the Mirror Group in 1961. They relaunched the paper as the *Sun* in 1964, aimed it at a broader readership, but failed to attract new readers and lost the old ones. In 1969 the *Sun* was sold to News International whose chairman Rupert Murdoch soon stamped his own brand of popular journalism on the paper, exploiting the traditional attractions of sex, sport and sensation, which in a few years made the paper the country's leading popular daily. Since 1974, when it supported the Heath government in the February election, it has moved steadily to the right of the political spectrum.

These three papers alone (*News Chronicle, Sunday Citizen,*

Daily Herald) had an average readership of over 9 million in their last full year of publication (Curran and Seaton, 1981, p. 121). Their disappearance decimated the left commercial press, which at the end of the war had accounted for nearly 9 million copies, not including the well over 4 million readers of the socially radical *Picture Post* (*ibid.,* p. 100).[22] By the 1960s a vast sweep of liberal and social democratic opinion had been erased from the pages of British journalism.

Perhaps more significant in the long term is the narrowing of the available range of views in the surviving press that has resulted from post-war economic pressures in the newspaper industry. The trend to oligopoly has produced a textbook example of a crush in the centre of the market, which, as the economists Hirsch and Gordon have argued, has not only diminished the range of newspaper opinion but moved the centre of the range, since 'the centre of the market in terms of newspaper revenue is not the centre of the market in terms of newspaper readers' (1975, p. 45). In parallel with this hunt for the affluent reader has been the gradual dilution of explicit politics in an attempt to avoid antagonising potential or existing readers. For this reason the whole daily popular press has become more entertainment oriented and less concerned with traditional news in general, and political news in particular. This trend has been accelerated but certainly not caused by competition from television news. An analysis conducted for the third Royal Commission shows that between 1947 and 1975 there was 'a general fall in attention given to "political, social, and economic" news' (McQuail, 1977, p. 20). The expansion of sport, features, entertainment and general interest material created a situation where, as another analysis shows, 'By 1976 none of the seven popular papers that were examined devoted more than 20 per cent of their editorial content to public affairs' (Curran and Seaton, 1981, p. 123; see also Curran, 1981, p. 100).

The resulting 'depoliticisation' of the popular press is illustrated by the *Daily Mirror*. In the words of Cecil King, chairman of the Mirror Group from 1951 to 1968, the 'formula was social realism though served up with buckets of sentiment'. Politics became populist in mood: 'If the *Mirror* was sensational and sexy it also had a nagging social conscience. It was firmly on the side of the underdog . . . Always it was necessary to attack the Establishment, to denounce blunders in high places, the selfishly complacent, the unimaginative and stupid old men who had too much power' (lecture given in 1966; quoted in Smith *et al.,* 1975, pp. 140−1). It was a stance of jaunty optimism, feeding on post-war confidence. In its own favourite self-image the paper was brash, celebrating the new prosperity with aggressive and bubbling enthusiasm. Recognising its own best interests, *Mirror* rhetoric rotated the main social axis from class round to age, and sought to represent the bright young new Britain against the tired old men of yesterday. While poverty provided the infrequent occasion for bursts of indignation and voyeuristic exposé, 'to have gone on talking about poverty in a period marked by rising consumption might have seemed like dismal harping' (Smith *et al.,* 1975, p. 149). The paper was now caught up in, indeed an important creator of, the buoyant mood of consumerism and the 'new working-class'. Rare excursions into deprivation mostly appeared as intermittent outcries on behalf of the pensioners, other than in election rhetoric, notably in 1959, but even then the misfortunes of the unemployed were diagnosed as local. 'In their isolation from the general prosperity, they are as discontinuous, just unlucky, as the lucky pools winners who grin from other pages' (*ibid.,* p. 162).

The *Mirror*'s radicalism was neither partisan—its support for the Labour Party has been consistent since 1945 but frequently lukewarm as in 1955—nor doctrinaire. Politics was a series of postures and attitudes. 'In King's estimate the Left was a state of mind, independent, liberal, critical, socially compassionate and tolerant of human behaviour—except perhaps of humbug' (Edelman, 1966, p. 192).[23] While not likely to echo the explicit hostility to the welfare state of its main rival, the *Daily Express,* the *Mirror* was unlikely to dwell on poverty or welfare policies in the course of its frenetic enthusiasm for the new, technocratic, consumerist, youthful Britain.

The kind of radicalism that results from this brew is a particular construction of working-class beliefs: hedonistic, materialist, impatient of bureaucrats and busybodies, hard-working, decent, ambitious but in a modest and individual way, blunt and bluff but never insurrectionary, politically agnostic and intolerant of 'doctrine and dogma'. It serves well the twin needs of straddling enough fences to corral a large and diverse readership, while identifying sufficient targets for the occasional demonstrative fusillade to impress an image of pugnacious independence. In its celebration of one side of working-class materialism it accords well with scepticism about the welfare apparatus, and is an ideology easily translated to this purpose.[24]

The third problem for the left press is that of entry to the market. While a number of socialist newspapers have been started, the list of short-lived and long-forgotten titles is lengthy and cautionary. Those that survive do so because of the support of the minority parties to which they are linked, which subsidise production and distribution costs. In practice, as the third Royal Commission noted, 'although anyone is free to start a national daily newspaper, few can afford even to contemplate the prospect' (Royal Commission on the Press, 1977b, p. 9; see also Golding and Murdock, 1978, pp. 82—4). The need not merely for the initial capital but for sustained and massive investment in the early period of a new title is illustrated by the *Daily Star,* launched in 1978 as the first new national daily in nearly 60 years. Forced to create a corner in the market with a cover price lower than the *Sun* and *Mirror,* it sustained heavy losses in its first two years, and spent three-quarters of a million pounds on the initial promotion campaign alone. It could only do this because its proprietors were Trafalgar House, the massive shipping, engineering and investment combine that already owned the *Daily* and *Sunday Express.* The fate of the *Scottish Daily News,* kept alive as a workers' cooperative for just a few months after the withdrawal of the *Scottish Daily Express* from Glasgow in 1974, illustrates the problem in a different way, despite a government loan of £1.2 million (see McKay and Barr, 1976). No new provincial paper has been set up in competition with another for over 60 years.

The problem is that while sales have fallen production costs have soared, especially after the ending of newsprint controls in 1958. At the same time, advertising revenues have been uncertain, cut by reduced expenditure in periods of recession, marginally by competition from television, and by the growing power of advertising agencies to hold down rates.[25] The problematic profitability of working-class papers has exaggerated tendencies to depoliticisation, the drift to the political centre, and to conglomerate ownership. One result, as Hirsch and Gordon perceive it, is that 'At the crucial divide in modern British politics—between left and right within the Labour Party—the mainstream British press, and regular television commentators along with it, are all on the same side' (1975, p. 31).

Market forces have expunged from British national journalism a whole tradition of socialist and social democratic responses. That these could or would have provided a different view of social security or welfare from that documented in chapters 3 and 4 of this book can only be speculation. That the contemporary press is predetermined to lack a political commitment to the poorest and weakest in society is an inescapable result of the political economy of the newspaper industry.

DROPPING THE MASK:
THE TRIUMPH OF NEO-LIBERALISM

The social and political dislocations of the 1970s have received varied diagnoses, which we cannot rehearse or evaluate here. Two approaches are relevant to our argument, however, both seeing the mid-1970s as a period of crisis. To describe a social system as in crisis is not to fall prey to a millenarian or 'big-bang' view of change. Crisis is a condition rather than an event. A fruitful analysis of this condition is provided in an influential work by O'Connor (1973), who argues that the state in modern capitalism is in 'fiscal crisis' (see also Mosley, 1978). The state, suggests O'Connor, tries to fulfil two potentially contradictory roles. On the one hand, it attempts to sustain conditions for successful capital accumulation, while on the other it tries to create conditions of social stability and harmony to permit its first aim to succeed. The state spends money to achieve these ends. To foster accumulation the state provides 'social investment' to assist industrial productivity (for example transport and communications) and 'social con-sumption' to reduce the cost of reproducing the labour force (for example through state-managed national insurance). To ensure social stability the state provides 'social expenses', which are not productive but buttress the legitimacy of the social order by supplying welfare schemes of various kinds. O'Connor suggests that because these state functions expand and become increasingly costly while the profits they facilitate are appropriated privately, a structural gap appears, a 'fiscal crisis' whereby the state's spending increases more rapidly than the revenues to finance it.

In Britain this fiscal crisis is a response to a more secular 'crisis of accumulation' in the private sector to which alternating policies have been applied with varied degrees of failure. Whatever the causes, the rate of accumulation (measured as rate of growth in the stock of capital per worker) has been considerably lower in Britain than in most major industrial nations for much of the twentieth century (see, for example, Glyn and Harrison, 1980, p. 37, Table 2, or Gomulka, 1979, Tables 9.1 and 9.2). Public expenditure has increased steadily in the post-war period, though never 'explosively' or 'critically' except in 1973/4 when it rose by 28 per cent in money terms (though inflation in 1974 was itself 28 per cent) (Gould and Roweth, 1980, p. 342). The consequent expansion of the Public Sector Borrowing Requirement (from a budget deficit of £4.6 billion in 1973/4 to £10.8 billion in 1975/6) has become the dominant symbol of the fiscal crisis in recent political debate, producing totally polarised views about the role of public expenditure in recession in which the Keynesian view that it might be largely self-financing has fallen into disfavour. Public expenditure dropped 6.5 per cent at constant prices from 1975/6 to 1977/8, and only unavoidable increases interrupted this trend before the more aggressive reductions introduced by the Thatcher government after 1979 (Public Expenditure White Paper, Cmnd. 7841, March 1980).

However terms are defined and the accountancy juggled, the undeniable extension of state involvement is the dominant feature of the economic landscape after the war.[26] Wartime planning became, in diluted form, the post-war Keynesian welfare state, with significant extensions of nationalisation in 1945—50. The period of 'stop—go' growth under the Conservatives saw a further extension of state involvement, partly through the demands of armaments manufacture. By 1958 'three-fifths of total research expenditure went to the atomic energy, aircraft, and electronics industries, and three quarters of this was financed by the state' (N. Harris, 1972, p. 63). The growth of corporate planning and its apparatus of para-statal bodies and 'quangos' meant a significant transformation in the form and presentation of the state. During the period of Conservative government the state employed roughly a quarter of the labour force and provided roughly 40 per cent of national investment (*ibid.,* p. 228). This trend continued right through the 1960s.

The Heath experiment in 1970—72 was an interruption that failed. It was too soon for the 'neo-liberal counter-revolution' and the experiment in planning marched on into a more divisive and openly confrontational phase. The Labour government in 1974—9 was crucial in preparing the ground for a more widespread social base for a neo-liberal revolt, with a further shift in the balance of state expenditure away from O'Connor's 'social expenses'. This both required and precipitated the drift into the 'strong state' with a dirigiste executive, frequently through powerful central direction from Cabinet alone, and the disarray and fragmentation of traditional party politics.

The second approach to crisis has preferred to read it as a crisis of the legitimacy of state power, which in turn is understood to have grown either as the result of bad political decisions or because of economic necessity. The first view, largely provided from the political right, has perceived the growth of public expenditure as a threat to democracy; indeed doomsday predictions came thick and fast in the mid-1970s with the claim that social stability was about to crumble as public expenditure reached 60 per cent of Gross Domestic Product. In fact this figure was misleading, not least because it included transfer payments in public expenditure, and more realistic figures show public expenditure as 46 per cent of GDP in 1974/5 reduced to 40.5 per cent in 1977/8 (Public Expenditure White Paper, Cmnd 7439, 1979; see also Ormerod, 1980, pp. 51–2). Nonetheless these claims have provoked alarm about 'political overload' and 'ungovernability', suggesting that government has become too big, too complex and too incompetent to fulfil its expanded role. The state, it is suggested, promises too much, provoking an inevitable crisis of rising expectations. 'The hungry sheep look up and reckon that they have at least a reasonable chance of being fed. In so short a time has government come to be regarded, in Britain at least, as a sort of unlimited liability insurance company, in the business of insuring all persons at all times against every conceivable risk' (King, 1975, p. 164).[27]

The alternative version of this approach sees the legitimacy crisis as one of the contradictory outcomes in capitalist development, in which the very attempt by the state to achieve its perilously expanded objectives paves the way for failure to meet those objectives and at the same time ensure its own legitimacy (Habermas, 1976, pp. 46–7). More significantly, the political legitimacy of the state has come to depend on its economic performance, since its economic involvement is now, in Poulantzas' term, 'incompressible' (1978, p. 169).[28] The reverberations of this 'fiscal crisis' reach deep into the political and ideological process.[29]

These various interpretations of crisis have tended to obscure the lengthy pedigree of the political rhetoric that emerged as a response. The seeds of the neo-liberal attack on the welfare state have long been germinating in the soil of post-war economic uncertainties, even though not finally transplanted into the sunlight of popular debate until the 1970s. At one level this was a simple continuation of the philosophical defence of the individual against the state.[30] Its fullest development has been in the work of Hayek, arguing for the restoration of individual liberty and reduction of the role of the state to providing 'security against severe physical deprivation, the assurance of a given minimum of sustenance for all' (1960, p. 259). Social insurance involves compulsion, he argues, and rapidly becomes a totalitarian tool for redistribution. The social security apparatus mushrooms and becomes its own most powerful propagandist. It also fosters unreasonable demands and unjustifiable 'rights'. In a remark that ironically might have been culled from the Webbs, Hayek contends that

> the objection against discretionary coercion can really provide no justification for allowing any responsible person an unconditional claim to assistance and the right to be the ultimate judge of his own needs. There can be no principle of justice in a free society that confers a right to 'non-deterrent' or 'non-discretionary' support irrespective of proved need. [1960, pp. 303–4]

Hayek's views have been canvassed and supported widely over the years, particularly in this country through the work of organisations like the Institute for Economic Affairs.[31] Whatever the genesis of these views in the work of mid-European academics or fringe groups, they have not remained peripheral, but on the contrary have been fully incorporated within the mainstream of social debate. This has occurred at two levels. Firstly these views have been rehearsed and refined within the Conservative Party since the war, particularly among the men and factions who were to become dominant after the Heath era. Secondly they have maintained a popular presence, if only by default of alternatives, sufficiently influential to cast serious doubt on the notion of a deeply entrenched post-war 'welfare consensus'. We can briefly illustrate these two points, looking first at the Conservative Party, which by 1974 had been in office for eighteen of the previous 25 years.

Many of the arguments had already surfaced by the time of the return of the party to office in 1951, with a manifesto promising to 'foster the ancient virtue of personal thrift'. Some in the party were by now arguing that the cost of social services was a major cause of inflation, and a prescient Walter Elliott was writing in 1949 that the value of the social services could only be guaranteed by cutting public expenditure to restore the value of the pound. Through the 1950s the party rode the wave of affluence to arrive at the triumphant conclusion that the welfare state had been 'built to repel an enemy who has vanished into the footnotes'. To continue with a redundant Beveridge plan was 'to swallow the drug after the disease has gone'.

> For primary poverty has now almost disappeared . . . The Beveridge assumptions have governed our national outlook for a decade and a half. But there is nothing sacred or immutable about them. They postulate a Britain in which the great majority of citizens are too poor to provide for themselves. It is the business of Toryism to thrust that Britain into the history books, and to thrust the politics of poverty into the dustbin. [Curran, 1960, pp. 25—6]

Since the poverty problem inconveniently refused to disappear in quite this way, it had to be reinterpreted. This raised from temporary torpor the spirits of individualism, moral pathology and efficiency, which we have earlier suggested are the props for dominant explanations of poverty. The individualistic strand in social policy thought has been 'the mainspring of the Conservative belief in social legislation . . . Conservatives insist that the collective provision of social security must be the "springboard and not a sofa". It must not detract from the self-reliance of the individual' (Clarke, 1950, pp. 34—5). The loss of initiative and self-respect due to welfare 'are consequences far more potent than the immediate loss of income' (*ibid,* p. 35).

The moral cost is not borne merely by the individual however. 'A state which does for its citizens what they can do for themselves is an evil state . . . In such an irresponsible society no-one cares, no-one saves, no-one bothers—why should they when the state spends all its energies taking money from the energetic, successful, and thrifty to give to the idle, the failures, the feckless?' (Boyson, 1971, p. 5). For many the answer was simple. 'The welfare state is not the boon it is supposed to be; it is an undigested lump on the collective stomach, constipating the entire nation. It must go' (Crozier, 1979, p. 190).

With growing concern about cost came further arguments on the grounds of efficiency, especially after 1964 when it was recognised that in its last four years in office the party had presided over a 25.1 per cent increase in social security spending and a 26.9 per cent increase in all welfare spending (at 1963 prices). Firstly, large-scale social services were unnecessary, when all that remained were small 'pockets of need and poverty . . . in spite of the leap in real earnings and general prosperity since the war' (Joseph, 1966a, p. 5). Secondly, therefore, far more rigorous selectivity must be reintroduced since, quite simply, 'the more that is spent on those not in need, the less will be available for those who are' (Joseph, 1966b, p. 18).[32] As the 1966 manifesto argued, it was time to 'remodel' the welfare state 'to concentrate better care and the biggest benefits on those most in need'. This neutral proposition only thinly veiled a moral argument that came more and more into prominence, as metaphors old and new were minted to justify further selectivity. 'State welfare has become an end in itself,' suggested Ian Gilmour; 'The welfare state must be pruned in places, and pruning it will strengthen it like roses' (1977, p. 152; see also Coleraine, 1970). More colourfully, Boyson returned to the fray to suggest that 'The welfare state has really become a treacle well and not a lifebelt'. 'To help without corrupting the recipient to some degree is impossible unless the state is prepared to distinguish sharply between those deserving support from the undeserving who could support themselves if they chose to make the effort' (Boyson, 1978, pp. 106, 105). All kinds of schemes were devised for sorting out, as one Bow Group pamphlet put it, the 'unemployed sheep and goats'. Such schemes would 'tighten the screws on the long-term unemployed' by providing differential benefits based on the adequacy of work records (Harvey, 1977). Thirdly, calls for efficiency could be voiced in the venerated language of inequality and incentives:

> . . . rich and poor are united in a common brotherhood, humanity . . . The incentive of inequality, if inequality corresponds to skill and energy, is one of the main means whereby new wealth can be created . . . So far from being the cause of poverty Conservatives believe it demonstrable historically that the most decisive steps which have been taken in the past towards a higher standard of living for the mass of the people have in fact been taken as the result of this incentive operating on the minds of the few. [Hogg, 1947, quoted in Conservative Political Centre, 1950, p. 137][33]

Quintin Hogg's thesis came to command a vital part of party ideology in the 1970s as yesterday's marginal figures drew the centre of the party towards them with an increasingly pertinent use of an ancient rhetoric.

Consistent throughout the period was a lingering concern with abuse. By 1970 the issue was central. Indeed, of five pages on 'Conservative Aims' in the Campaign Guide 1970 chapter on social security, two deal with abuse and fraud. In the 1970 manifesto, moves were promised to 'prevent the whole system being brought into disrepute by the shirkers and scroungers'.

By the 1970s, therefore, there was an extensively canvassed and clearly argued case against the welfare state on grounds of philosophy, morality and economics, well established in the party that had formed the government for most of the post-war period. At the same time, as we have seen earlier, there was a marked absence of any popular coherent alternative. To what extent had similar views become rooted in more popular debate?

Marshall has suggested that a period of initial appraisal set in as early as 1952, as 'a system obsessed with the ideas of poverty and subsistence began to look out of place in a society enjoying the first fruits of a new prosperity' (1965, p. 92). The mood of retrenchment in public expenditure focused on welfare; symptomatic were two articles in *The Times* in 1952 (25 and 26 February) headed 'Crisis in the Welfare State' and demanding a reappraisal of 'what principles and attributes of the welfare State are essential, and what are mainly accidental or convenient' (*The Times,* 25 February 1952). In the same year the *Daily Telegraph* warned that 'the most prolific source of waste is the provision of social security for the socially secure' (18 September 1952), and *The Economist* (27 September 1952) welcomed the Labour Party's recognition, in its discussion document *The Welfare State,* that welfare would have to be held back to the growth rate of the economy as a whole. In the following year the Oxford Union voted down the view that 'cuts in social services should play no part in any solution to our economic problems', and Lord Denning warned of the dangers of welfare 'breeding selfishness and ingratitude among the people' (*The Times,* 2 October 1953).

Public opinion took these warnings to heart. Sceptical affection for the health service apart, pensions were a frequently isolated object of public approval. Butler and Stokes show how easily such credit could be lost. Their 1963 survey tapped a broadly expansive mood toward welfare, particularly on issues like pensions and housing. By 1966 the proportion who thought more should be spent on pensions and social services had dropped from 77 per cent two years previously to 54 per cent (1971, p. 417). Though the authors explain this as a sign of widespread satisfaction with pension increases in the first two years of the Labour government, it can also be interpreted as an indicator of the weak attachment of large numbers of people to the cause of welfare and social services, especially when confronted with powerful arguments about the need for public spending restraints. The tougher side of public attitudes has been consistently sceptical about many of the provisions of the social security scheme. Runciman's 1962 survey, in the middle of Butler and Stokes' expansive mood, found 40 per cent opposed to any form of family allowance for a first child, 27 per cent opposed to any form of subsidised rent, and 19 per cent opposed to unlimited unemployment benefit (1972, p. 265).

By the late 1960s the tentative attachment of a large proportion of the population to many aspects of the welfare state was frequently stretched to breaking point. Behind a diffuse and lingering loyalty to the notion of 'the welfare state' as in some sense a good thing (a benign paternalism writ large reflecting a national genius for civilised administration), lurked more severe views readily tapped in political wrangling. Commenting on a 1968 poll finding that 33 per cent thought too much was spent on social services, the *Financial Times* political editor noted that 'Judith Hart scrounger bashing is more fruitful than Crossman saying they are within their rights . . . Both major parties are being asked to reappraise their attitudes to the welfare state in an atmosphere in which rational inquiry is being poisoned by a sudden irrational wave of ungenerousness and envy in the country' (Watt, 1968). The same year, an ORC poll found 89 per cent thought too many people would not work because the dole was too high, and 78 per cent thought 'we have so many social services that people work less hard than they used to' (see Klein, 1974, p. 412). In 1971, 32 per cent told a Gallup poll that poverty was due to lack of effort, and by 1975 twice as many (34 per cent) thought unemployment benefit was too high as thought it too low (Gallup, 1976, p. 1456).

Obviously such superficial, scattered and methodologically dubious evidence, together with similar findings, provides only the sketchiest impression of the complex and shifting nature of 'public opinion', that most nebulous and evasive of political concepts. However, in the absence of convincing contrary evidence, our argument is that the so-called 'welfare consensus' has never taken deep root, and was therefore relatively easy to dislodge by the return of an incisive neo-liberal rhetoric in the wake of the significant material shifts in working-class experience in the mid-1970s (supervised at crucial stages by a Labour government vociferously committed to trimming public expenditure, especially in the social services, spending on which declined from 25.6 per cent to 24.1 per cent of GDP between 1975 and 1978).

This rhetoric was all the more powerful for being backed by a full-blown ideology of the 'social market economy'. Hall has argued that this marked a significant lurch to the right, around a set of values that translate into popular form the theorising of Hayek and Milton Friedman. These 'social market values' include 'the restoration of competition and personal responsibility for effort and reward, the image of the over-taxed individual enervated by welfare coddling, his initiative sapped by handouts from the state' (Hall, 1979, p. 17). The tendency to view this creed as 'Thatcherism', however, has sometimes obscured its deeper origins. Gamble (1979, *passim*) has insightfully explored these roots and the twin doctrines of 'free economy and strong state' that have grown from them. As he notes, to concentrate on 'Thatcherism' is to mistake the flower for the roots, the populist ideology for the material and historical background. On the one hand, social market doctrines promote liberty over democracy, law above bureaucracy, and the market above planning, while advancing technical solutions—notably the control of the money supply—to guarantee the proper workings of the market to which state intervention, public expenditure and trades union power are serious obstacles. On the other hand, social market theory is a form of 'corporate liberalism', requiring a strong state to police the labour market (particularly as unemployment is allowed to rise), guarantee the security of property, actively promote 'self-help' and supervise technological change.

The welfare state is central in this reconstruction of political orthodoxy because it is seen as both the major drain on scarce resources as well as an institutional source of weak and prodigal attitudes towards a dependent, improvident and often morally or legally dubious sector of the population (Gough, 1979, p. 7). The economic doctrines of 'Thatcherism' then—the reduction of public expenditure, reprivatisation of services and industries, the achievement of price stability by control of the money supply, and control of the labour market to facilitate these ends—are all at odds with recent Conservatism in its phase as 'the party of protection, imperialism, paternalism, and intervention' (Gamble, 1980, p. 15). But, in the rediscovery of the liberal arguments of an older Conservatism, 'Thatcherism' has been able to draw on a critique of the welfare state already clearly argued within the party and immediately recognisable in popular prejudice and mythology.

Since Britain lacks a unified bourgeoisie and is too locked into the international economy to rely on the corporatist solution, the relatively modest onslaught of the Thatcher government[34] could proceed by attaching itself to the real grievances of an economically depressed population, thus appearing more radical in deed than in effect. This broad conclusion should not disguise, however, the very real impact on the particular population group with which we are concerned here, social security claimants, rediscovered as the scapegoats for hard times.

THE WHIPPING-BOYS OF RECESSION

The 'scroungerphobia' we documented in chapter 4 was quite specific to the mid-1970s, though we have tried to illustrate its parallels and rhetorical origins.[35] The widespread antipathy to social security and to claimants reflected in the press clearly resonated with deep anxieties and indignation felt by many working-class people. As the Chairman of the Supplementary Benefits Commission observed, 'Those letters which arrive by the hundred each month, complaining that we hand out too much in social security benefits and support too many layabouts and scroungers, rarely come on headed notepaper from the leafy suburbs. Most are written by ordinary voters and taxpayers' (Donnison, 1976a, p. 624). A number of relatively short-term shifts in material experience contributed to this explosion of rancorous hostility, and to the cruel choice of target.

The first factor is the drop in real incomes experienced by many on low or average wages. Real average weekly take-home pay for a couple with two young children fell from £73.90 in 1973/4 to £68.50 in 1977/8 (at December 1978 prices) (H. C. *Hansard*, Vol. 961, Written Answers, cols 287—8, 26 January 1979). Looked at another way, personal disposable income per capita fell from £1341 in 1973 to £1283 in 1977 (at 1975 prices) (*Economic Trends* Annual Supplement, Central Statistical Office, 1981, Table 45). Tarling and Wilkinson (1977) suggest net real incomes fell by about 10 per cent between 1972 and 1976. The impact of incomes policies, the deepening slump, fiscal changes and inflation began to cut deeply into working-class living standards. Inflation averaged 18.9 per cent in 1973—76, but this was in any case experienced differentially, with those on the lowest incomes hit by the higher inflation rates for those goods on which they spent the greater part of their incomes.[36]

Secondly, the tax net was dragging in more and more of the low paid, so that large numbers of ill-rewarded people found their pay packets irritatingly rifled for dubious purposes. Wilensky (1976) has argued, on the basis of comparative statistics, that high and rising levels of 'visible' taxation (income tax and social security contributions) correlate significantly with the likelihood of a welfare backlash.[37] We have noted the secular fall in tax thresholds earlier, from 62.8 per cent of average earnings in 1949/50 to 44.6 per cent in 1975/6 for a married couple (Field, Meacher and Pond, 1977, p. 32). The drop was quite rapid in the first half of the 1970s: for a two-child family the threshold fell from 58.6 per cent of average earnings in 1971/2 to 44.0 per cent in 1975/6 (H. C. *Hansard* Vol. 971, Written Answers, cols 557—8, 27 July 1979). Thus more and more low-paid workers were losing more of their income to the state. This was exacerbated by increases in National Insurance Contributions, a clearly identifiable tax on the worthy for the benefit of the unworthy. National Insurance contributions provided 14.1 per cent of government revenues in 1971 rising to 17.4 per cent in 1977 (Barratt Brown, 1979, p. 69). Despite the effect of graduated contributions, the low paid continued to contribute a higher proportion of their incomes than those on median or high incomes, while average contributions had in any case steadily risen since 1961.[38]

Thirdly, there had been real, visible and irreversible rises in the costs of welfare. The most important reason was demographic. Between 1951 and 1976 the number of people of pensionable age rose by over 40 per cent (from 6.7 million to 9.4 million) while the working age population rose by less than 4 per cent. The ratio of the latter to the dependent population (pensioners and children) fell from 1.8 to 1.5 in the same period (Office of Population Censuses and Surveys, 1978). To this chronic problem was added the acute distress of unemployment, which rose from 2.7 per cent in 1973 to 5.8 per cent in 1976, an increase of three-quarters of a million people. Within these figures long-term unemployment itself increased. By 1976, 25.5 per cent of the unemployed had been so for over a year, adding significantly to the number of claimants receiving non-contributory social security benefits. For these various reasons, total expenditure on social security nearly trebled from 1973/74 to 1978/79, an increase of about 30 per cent in real terms (Piachaud, 1980, p. 172—3). Most of the increase was accounted for by the growth in the number of claimants, most obviously the unemployed. In fact after 1974/5 resource spending, and especially capital expenditure, in the social services as a whole was severely curtailed. The rise in expenditure was now due almost entirely to the soaring number of people receiving transfer payments.

Thus social security benefits were the most obvious result of public spending excesses and could be easily identified as their 'cause'. While wage levels were being held back by the Social Contract and reduced in value as we have shown by taxation and inflation, social security benefits were being manifestly protected. Between 1971 and 1974 sickness and unemployment benefit fell slightly in value relative to average earnings (from 19.5 to 18.6 per cent) (DHSS *Social Security Statistics,* 1981, Table 46.06; figures for a single person). However, between 1974 and 1979 there were six upratings that kept benefits increases at least as high as the rise in prices or earnings. Between 1973 and 1978, while average earnings rose 107.9 per cent, benefits rose 114.3 per cent, and prices 109.6 per cent (Piachaud, 1980, p. 174). Between 1975 and 1977 the value of benefits as a percentage of average earnings rose slightly, from 39.4 per cent to 41.3 per cent (H. C. *Hansard* Written Answers, 2 February 1978; figures for a couple). The fact that these figures were, firstly, low in absolute terms, secondly less advantageous for those with children, and thirdly much less positive if viewed from a longer perspective (levels were relatively lower than in 1966—71) is beside the point here. In the period of the worst slump since the war, and with falling living standards for those in work, especially on lower incomes, benefits were being claimed by larger numbers of people and were being increased or protected in value.

The experiences created by these changes required explanation, and were wide open to selective interpretation. Four major examples illustrate this point. First, the debate on the gap between benefits and wages leant inextricably towards the problem of 'incentives' rather than towards low pay. The deprived in work were invited to invest their energies in observation of the public affluence below them rather than on private privilege above. In fact extensive research showed an improbable degree of attachment to the work ethic, and only a very tiny number who could be better off out of work.[39] Nonetheless little attention was given to the 6 million whose basic wage fell below the level necessary to keep their net income above the poverty line in 1976. Secondly, the increases in social security spending featured far more prominently than the decline in capital expenditure until the 'anti-cuts' campaigns of 1976 onward. However, by 1977 central government capital expenditure had been cut for four years. Thirdly the growing burden of taxation and social security contributions was far more evident than the narrowing of the tax base. Two points are pertinent here. First, while the level of taxation as a whole is no higher in the UK than in most industrial countries, the proportion of direct to indirect taxation was, by the mid-1970s, unusually high.[40] Second, the contribution of capital taxes to Inland Revenue receipts has fallen continuously in recent years, for example from 8.2 per cent of all receipts in 1973/4 to 4.1 per cent in 1980/81 (*Financial Statement and Budget Report,* HMSO, 1980). Over the period since the war as a whole the burden of taxation has shifted to income taxation, and onto lower incomes in particular (Field, Meacher and Pond, 1977, Chs 2 and 3).[41] The final example of selective interpretation relates directly to social security abuse, which, however estimated, is dwarfed financially by the scale both of tax evasion and of unclaimed benefits. In 1975/6 the official estimate of social security fraud was £2.6 million, about 1½p in every £50 paid out (H. C. *Hansard* Written Answers, col. 745, 7 December 1977). By contrast, in 1976/7 the Inland Revenue wrote off £28.2 million of evaded tax as not worth the expense of pursuing; in 1978 this figure was £61.7 million (Board of Inland Revenue, 1978, p. 44; 1980, p. 37). Less easy to calibrate is tax loss through unreported earnings, estimated by civil service unions as between £5,000 million and £11,000 million per annum (*Guardian,* 30 October 1980). The value of unclaimed benefits has risen steadily. In 1977 an estimated £340 million of supplementary benefits alone was not received by those entitled to it (Supplementary Benefits Commission, 1978). Take-up rates for other major benefits vary from under 2 per cent for free welfare milk, to under 30 per cent for rent and rate rebates, adding another £150 million or so in 1977 on top of the supplementary benefits figure (Townsend, 1979, p. 892; National Consumer Council, 1976, p. 35).

Public concern cannot, of course, be expected accurately to reflect the arithmetic of national finance. However, these examples show a remarkably consistent process of problem definition according to preferred and dominant constructions of causes and effects. The preoccupation with containment of abuse has inevitably conditioned the administration of social security, which in turn confirms in public sentiment the validity of the initial concern. The number of prosecutions for social security offences doubled between 1970 and 1975 (from 7,700 to 15,400) and then rose by a further 69 per cent in the following two years (to 26,100 in 1977) (DHSS, 1977b, p. 12; 1979, p. 1). The rate of prosecution of suspected fraud cases rose from under 30 per cent in 1970 to 48 per cent in 1977 (DHSS, 1979, p. 4). The emphasis on fraud was reflected in staff deployment. The number of special investigators grew from 248 in 1970 to 398 in 1977, and 447 in 1978 (H. C. *Hansard* Written Answers, 25 January 1978). Redeployment of local office staff produced an increase in those working on fraud from about 600 in 1975 to over 1,000 in 1978. The number of Unemployment Review Officers, the officers concerned with rooting out 'work-shyness', has been rapidly enlarged to 300 in 1978 and to 880 by 1980. In 1978, 116,181 long-term unemployed claimants were interviewed, of whom 43,738 ceased to draw benefit shortly after the interview. The process was accelerated in February 1980 when the Conservative administration announced a number of anti-fraud measures including the redeployment of 450 staff and an additional 600 staff to work in fraud and abuse investigation.

Not only the mechanics but the whole tenor of social security administration has moved further towards a primary obsession with abuse. This has steadily deepened since the appointment of the Committee on the Abuse of Social Security Benefits by Sir Keith Joseph in 1971. The committee, which reported in March 1973, could find no evidence of widespread abuse. Nonetheless it concluded that 'Although the percentage of claims which are known to be fraudulent is not great, substantial sums of money are misappropriated each year. We have no doubt that a considerable effort should be devoted to preventing and detecting abuse' (Committee on the Abuse of Social Security Benefits, 1973, p. 224). It was. In 1976 the Co-ordinating Committee on Abuse was set up to increase effort and promote measures to reduce abuse in the Departments of Health and Social Security and of Employment. As a result of its recommendations, a series of 'fraud drives' was instigated and a 'Fraud Awareness Package' distributed to all local offices. The specialist DHSS fraud branch at headquarters, C3, was bolstered and strengthened its liaison with the police through their Regional Crime Intelligence Conferences. The Rayner Report on unemployment benefits appeared in 1981 against a background of soaring unemployment, with an even greater enthusiasm for what it candidly refers to as 'a policing mechanism in the benefit system'. It noted that in the year ended February 1980 there were

1713 man years spent on fraud in the DHSS and 477 in the Department of Employment, plus 534 man years of special investigation in the two departments (Department of Employment/ Department of Health and Social Security, 1981, p. 61).

In the wake of each initiative the amount of discovered fraud and abuse remained small. As a proportion of benefits paid out, fraud was roughly 0.027 per cent in 1978/9 (Field, 1979b, p. 755). The stated target of a saving of £53 million by anti-fraud measures in 1980/1 was cast into severe doubt by late 1980 when leaked figures suggested the figure would be much lower (*Observer* 3 August 1980). The government was forced to reject the Rayner Report's arbitrary suggestion of an 8 per cent fraud rate among the unemployed as statistically dubious.[42] Nonetheless the institutional and administrative attention to abuse and fraud had been expanded through the 1970s to the point where the system of checks and controls made the provision of social security an apparently endless obstacle course for the potential felon rather more than a 'featherbed for every hardluck case around' as it had been caricatured by the press. The 'disreputable poor' (Matza, 1966) made the perfect sacrificial scapegoat in a process of social 'redemption through victimage'.[43] The frequently brutal policing of large numbers of claimants has provided 'absolution' of the social order through a colossal ritual purge of the 'guilty'.[44]

IMAGES OF WELFARE AND THE MEDIA: THE CONTINUOUS PERFORMANCE MORALITY PLAY

The media are implicated in social policy on at least two levels, in its creation and in its administration. Firstly they frame public debate, advancing priorities and a sense of issues in a way that media researchers have labelled 'agenda-setting'. Policies may often be designed to manage such an agenda in that complex political commerce in which the media are the wholesalers of demands and responses. Policy may be produced to quieten apparent popular 'outrage' or antipathies. It may also be a 'placebo policy', which satisfies a demand for action while avoiding the riskier business of serious attention to the underlying problem.[45] At a second level the expectations, mythologies, stereotypes and elisions of media creation influence the day-to-day administration of policy. Moore (1980, 1981) has shown, for example, the deteriorating relationships between social security officials and claimants as the climate of 'scroungerphobia', always latent in the system, has become more prevalent and openly sanctioned. Such attitudes are, of course, rooted in the history and structure of the social security apparatus and are promoted by the expansion and changing character of its clientele and the increasing pressure on and material disadvantages of its junior officers.[46]

The media may precipitate or provide the form and vocabulary for these agendas and attitudes. They do not, however, create them. One view of their role is that the media locate and label deviant behaviour, then thrust it into prominence by a process of 'amplification' that sensitises public response and mobilises the forces of order to contain the threat thus identified, in turn provoking further deviant behaviour (see Wilkins, 1964, and, for illustrations, Young, 1971; Cohen, 1971). A variant of this analysis has portrayed the media as instigators of 'moral panics' in which public hostility is focused on 'folk devils' to explain and solve underlying unease. There are many difficulties with such analyses, not least that they are unable to explain why some amplification works while at other times the process remains dormant. Nor does this analysis explain how and when these cycles of panic or amplification occur, in other words where the cycle begins and what are its material roots. In sum, they tend to lack a material or a historical dimension.

Hall has suggested an important distinction between 'primary definers'— those in positions of power and privilege who have easy access to channels of public opinion formation— and the media as 'secondary definers', which reproduce and reinterpret the logic and values of those to whom they turn as 'accredited witnesses' (Hall *et al.*, 1978, pp. 57—9). We have illustrated how this privileged access works in chapter 5, suggesting that definitions of both poverty and social security are persistently derived from the authors of policy rather than its clients. These authors are themselves, of course, entwined in a more complex web of interests that envelops the state and the economy. The media are inserted in this process in two ways that we can very briefly outline.

Firstly, the media act as the 'switchmen of history', in Weber's sense that 'the "world images" that have been created by ideas have, like switchmen, determined the tracks along which action has been pushed by the dynamic of interest' (1948, p. 280). As social change accelerates or throws up disorders or dislocations the media divert attention to a limited range of the available metaphors and explanations. In this sense the media do not create or impose attitudes. They orchestrate or selectively reinforce among the contradictory attitudes that people hold towards institutions and processes.

For example, alongside the tough, individualistic, artisanal condemnation of much in the welfare state remains a fertile if subdued tradition of welfare communality in working-class sentiment. These elements in a 'residual culture', as Williams has termed it (1980, pp. 40—4), derive from the organisation of mutual help in the working-class response to industrialism. They were 'microscopic welfare-states', in Titmuss's phrase (1974, p. 34), which ran as a powerful counter to the paternalism of philanthropy and the punitive discrimination of the poor law. The Friendly Societies, for example, with their origins in burial clubs, and before that in the guilds, were providing mutual insurance through 21,875 societies in 1855, and by 1905 had 14 million members. Alongside their story runs the rich history of co-operatives, working-men's clubs, mechanics institutes, building clubs, and the like, with roots back into the mutual aid of, for example, the 'tramping system' of hospitality among guilds and trade societies in the eighteenth and early nineteenth centuries (see Gosden, 1973; Baernreither, 1889; Pollard, 1960; Leeson, 1979). Frequently male-dominated and authoritarian, such movements were at one level the appropriation by the 'aristocracy of labour' of Victorian values of thrift and self-help, which did more to incorporate the working class than to establish an alternative ideology (cf. Yeo, 1980). They nevertheless created a space for a set of oppositional and mutually supportive values that has survived to provide house-room for alternative senses of 'anti-statism' and 'welfare' to those now dominant. Some would even see their survival in practices that look forward rather than backward, as 'prefigurative forms' of radical welfare practice in community activism, the women's movement and elsewhere. However confused, faded or contradictory these experiences and memories, they have clearly not been favoured by the ideological switchmen of history.

The second role of the media is to connect contemporary material experiences and anxieties with particular cultural legacies. A major mechanism for this is through the resurrection of 'social types' or characters. The media act as directors of a continuous morality play, reasserting the core elements of dominant social values by their personification in the daily drama of media output. The recent period, for example, has seen the raising of several such spirits: the sturdy beggar, the rogue, the stranger (the alien presence) on one side; on the other, the shopkeeper-hero distilling a mixture of thrift, enterprise and decency neatly caricatured by *Guardian* columnist Michael White as 'providing the incentive to rekindle British industrial genius in the toolsheds and cellars of the nation. A potent combination of Heath Robinson and moral rearmament'. The strength of the rhetoric of the Thatcher administration has been to couch its message in terms that conjure up these types so readily for the media to act as cheer-leaders.

Laclau has shown how the populism that thrives on this stylisation of public life is a movement reasserting the national as distinct from the antagonistic, partisan or class nature of a ruling ideology. The reassertion of basic values of national unity, the work ethic, self-help, traditional family life, anti-welfarism and moral rectitude at times of crisis for the prevailing social order has brought in from the wings those social types now rampant in centre stage. Their presentation appears a form of radicalism because of the very antagonistic character of populism (see Laclau, 1977; also Hall, 1980). Anti-welfarism is difficult to resist against a backlash so solidly based in the dramatic types of folk memory and the real privations of current recession.

The particular characterisations and concerns we have been examining have been 'fixed', we have suggested, in two periods when social dislocation synchronised with major innovations in social policy and with rapid advances in the form and social penetration of popular media. Following the construction of the new poor law in the early nineteenth century, these periods were, first, roughly 1890—1920, which saw the state organisation of conditional welfare and also the creation of a cheap daily press, and second, the inter-war period when mass unemployment provoked an increasingly corporatist and consensual state to broader and more costly measures of containment and palliation, while the mass popular daily press first reached a more complete working-class readership.

Three presentational devices have been forged in these periods. The first is the invisibility of structural poverty, an illusion of crucial importance, as we have seen, in the first 15 years of the post-war welfare state. This illusion has been sustained by the notion of a 'culture of poverty', a set of behavioural patterns by which the inadequate are presumed to reproduce their kind. It suggests the creation of poverty by and from within the world of the poor, a land untouched by any hint of relational disadvantage to the rest of society or to social structures of power and privilege. This vision has been recharged in recent years, notably by Sir Keith Joseph's frequent explication of the 'cycle of deprivation',[47] which has at times taken him emotively close to eugenics in his emphasis on excessive birth rates among the lower orders. The notion has in turn framed much recent explicatory and investigative work, with occasional bizarre results.[48] It reaffirms an image of poverty as a congenital defect of individuals rather than as a relational aspect of social structure. A more direct technique for 'primary definition', or rather primary erasure, of poverty has been the recent trend to reduce its official documentation. In 1979 the government halved the frequency with which calculations of the numbers in poverty would be published, and the DHSS was requested to discontinue estimates of the underclaiming of means-tested benefits. The government also dropped an innovation developed in some departments of accompanying policy proposals with estimates of their impact on income distribution, alongside the usual statements of financial and manpower implications that accompany policy papers submitted to Cabinet.

The second device involves the reiteration of those concepts that, we have argued, have in one form or another formed the lenses through which poverty has been perceived—namely efficiency, morality and pathology. Each dovetails neatly with the rhetorical needs and production exigencies of journalism. The criterion of efficiency in the social services and welfare meshes with the guiding principle of the national interest that is at the core of any ruling ideology but is also central to the imagery of a journalism seeking the crown of the road on the political highway. It meets too the self-image of popular journalism as tribune of the people against the overweening state and its sprawling, smothering bureaucracy (see Murdock and Golding, 1974, pp. 226—30). The powerful legacy of morality in perceptions of the poor resonates with the strain in journalism that proclaims a guardianship of core values of decency and the work ethic, providing a referee for the public calculus of effort and reward.[49] The pathology of the poor, the keynote to poor law policy for centuries, is only explicable in individualistic terms. Again this fits the necessary individualism of journalism, dependent as it is on a vocabulary of the concrete and the personal. Even sympathetic coverage of the poor will tend to deflate the problem by concentrating on the exemplary case, unavoidably compressing a generic problem into individual misfortune.

The third device is the packaging of the welfare state. There are many definitions of the welfare state, and they are inevitably contradictory. Is it, for example, 'capitalist fraud or working-class victory' (Gough, 1979, p. 11)? The welfare state has increasingly come to be seen as a thing apart, not so much an inherent characteristic of the kind of society in which we live, contradictory in the same way that other institutions are contradictory, but as a distinct appendage, harmful or redundant in one view, essential and remediable in another. The 'subversive' character of the welfare state lies on the one hand in its displacement of services from the market to a supervised assessment of need by statutory public authorities, and on the other in its detachment of income from labour, that is it debases the defining character of capitalist society—the wage relation (cf. Müller and Neusüss, 1978). The ideological separation of the welfare state from the rest of society cauterises this subversive potential by preventing further contamination. The damage is seen to lie within the welfare system, diagnosed as the cankerous defect in an otherwise healthy social organism. At an administrative level, as seminal work by Titmuss (1958) demonstrated many years ago, this has masked the 'social division of welfare', particularly the benefits derived from the fiscal system and from occupational welfare by already advantaged groups (see also Sinfield, 1978; Field, 1981, Chs 7 and 8). At the same time it has assisted the 'recapitalisation of capitalism' (Miller, 1978), that is the return of marginal, and potentially more crucial, areas of welfare provision to the private sector, and the replacement of service for need by service by market demand.

All three devices suggest the importance of 'primary definers', yet also the crucial orchestrating and interpreting role of popular media. Professor William Robson has suggested that 'whether the prevailing attitudes and outlook in Britain today are compatible with the principles and policies of the welfare state . . . is at once the most intangible and the most important issue of our time' (1976, p. 34). Two processes at the heart of contemporary social change are likely to reinforce his assessment, relating to changes in the nature of work and in the social security system.

With recent and unprecedented increases in levels of unemployment has come a dawning realisation that notions of full employment and indeed of the relation between work and nonwork may have to change. Most indications suggest that the levels of growth required to restore full employment in any real sense are beyond the likely capabilities of the economy, however buttressed by oil or technological change. Demographic changes alone will increase the working age population by more than three-quarters of a million by 1986. At the same time, the limited prospects for growth suggest that any form of redistribution will have to come from positive policies to achieve more egalitarian distributions of income and wealth rather than from the illusory hope that they will accrue from growth itself. After all, to achieve the limited aim of bringing those below the poverty line up to such a minimum standard would require barely 1 per cent of GNP. Thus structural change rather than growth has to be the major fount of income redistribution or of any serious attack on poverty (cf. Jolly, 1977, Field, 1979a).

If growth is unlikely to restore full employment, there is also the further problem of the changing nature of production, creating 'technological unemployment' on an unpredictable scale. The official view remains sanguine, suggesting that there will be a change in the nature rather than the volume of unemployment, and that the shrinking of the industrial base is quite a separate issue from the separation of the industrial base from employment (see, for example, Sleigh *et al.,* 1979). Others have suggested that the accelerated shift in the distribution of occupations will be towards precisely those sectors most prone to technological replacement of labour, precipitating 'the collapse of work' (Jenkins and Sherman, 1979; see also Hines and Searle, 1979). Between 1961 and 1978 manual jobs decreased by nearly 2½ million, from 15.6 million to 13.2 million, while non-manual jobs increased from 9.3 to 11.4 million. This first phase of 'deindustrialisation', however, was probably little to do with technological advance. But a second phase precipitated by innovations in microtechnology and computer science is likely to affect just those sectors of white-collar employment that have so far been expanding. The construction of a so-called 'information economy' poses, at the very least, serious questions about the future of work patterns and thus of the structure of employment and incomes (cf. Hirschhorn, 1979).

The second change is the increasingly problematic role of National Insurance within the social security system. Although since 1945 there has been a drop in the proportion of social security paid in non-contributory benefits, in recent years this proportion has been rising again. Between 1969/70 and 1979/80, non-contributory benefit payments increased from £967 million to £6,118 million (or from £613 million to £3,191 million if family allowances/child benefits are excluded). This represents an increase from 26.4 per cent to 31.3 per cent of expenditure on social security benefits (calculated from *Annual Abstract of Statistics* no. 117, HMSO, 1981 Table 3.5). National Insurance contributions have consistently increased however, while the contribution from taxation to the National Insurance Fund has declined. Large and increasing numbers of beneficiaries are excluded from entitlement to National Insurance benefits or receive reduced benefits because of incomplete contribution records, while the number receiving non-contributory benefits has increased. More fundamentally, the insurance principle is open to the radical charge of being wholly mythical, since 'the range and levels of social security benefit available at any time are determined not by the record of past contributions of an individual or even of a whole generation, but rather by the month to month decisions of the Government in power' (Kincaid 1973, pp. 200–1). These trends prompt a more fundamental conjecture, namely that recipients of benefit may perforce be advancing claims to income support on grounds of citizenship or need rather than actuarial soundness.

Such demands would need to be articulated and constructed within a political rhetoric fully alive to the growing integration of the fiscal and social security systems, and thus of income distribution both in and out of work. It would thus become impossible meaningfully to introduce the heady claims of personal equality, citizenship or need into a debate about income distribution and maintenance in isolation from broader questions about property relations and social structure (cf. Rose, 1980). Frequently this articulation has been muted and fragmented, a series of abortive slogans whose intelligent reconstruction has been retarded by the absence of any serious or committed vehicle for the rethinking of welfare and social policy. We have tried to illustrate in this chapter the nature of this 'absence', and throughout this book have stressed the contribution of the popular media. One tragic result has been the frequently virulent divisions between the poor in and out of work.

Peter Townsend has suggested three distinct principles for tackling poverty (1979, pp. 62–3). The first is conditional welfare for the few, the guiding maxim of the new poor law and its Victorian legatees. The second principle, minimum rights for the many, emerged in the Liberal legislation of 1902–11 and reached full fruition in the Beveridge Report and the ensuing period in which it was believed the stain of poverty had been removed from the social map. His third principle, distributional justice for all, 'has not yet been clearly articulated or tried' (*ibid.*, p. 63).

It would not be possible to derive conclusions about social justice from research. It is possible to demonstrate the sources and nature of widely held attitudes to poverty and to situate them historically and socially. Our findings suggest public debate about poverty and social policies does rather less than exhaust the possible. Insofar as the media expound this debate, it would seem that claims to comprehensive pluralism in our mass communications media are demonstrably exaggerated. Townsend's third principle, however interpreted, is not yet on the agenda. Our contention is that the victims of this process are precisely those least rewarded by other channels of material distribution. For many this is a fact of daily and bitter experience. A society so firmly anchored in an ethic of competition and reward will only with difficulty dispose of scarce resources to these conspicuously unsuccessful in a system ostensibly offering equal opportunity to all. For success to glisten seductively to the winners, the failure of poverty must display its burden of guilt and shame. While blaming the victim remains the cornerstone of our conceptions of poverty, the grinding and enduring misery of the poor is unlikely to evoke other than contempt, malign distrust or a corrosive pity. That these remain the principles of our welfare system is in no small measure the inheritance of our images of welfare.

NOTES

1. On this last point see Bland *et al.* (1979).
2. For a concise summary of the dilution of Beveridge's proposals see Field (1981) Ch. 4.
3. See Deacon (1980) for this curious interlude of post-war 'scrounger-bashing' in reverse. Deacon's conclusion, that this suggests that a witch-hunt could be initiated as readily by left as by right, would need careful qualification.
4. At the same time countless studies were produced to show a purported trend toward income equalisation. For a summary and crucial critique see Titmuss (1962).
5. For a two-child couple the tax threshold as a percentage of average earnings fell from 107.3 in 1952/3 to 78.1 in 1964/5 (Field *et al.*, 1977, p. 32).
6. A critical publication was Abel-Smith and Townsend (1965) calling into question the 'legitimacy of the national insurance scheme', demonstrating that about 2 million people were living on 'exceptionally low incomes' and 7½ million in poverty, and calling for a 'radical

review of the whole social security scheme'. More generally see Banting (1979).

7. Unemployment rates were amplified by the growth in the absolute size of the working population, a factor thrown into recurrent apologia for unemployment levels. The working population grew from 23.55 million in 1950 to 25.31 million in 1970 (*Economic Trends & Annual Abstract,* HMSO, 1981, Table 99).

8. As a proportion of Gross Domestic Product, income maintenance programmes were as follows in 1972: Austria 15.3%, Belgium 14.1%, Denmark 9.9%, France 12.4%, Germany 12.4%, Italy 10.4%, Holland 14.1%, United Kingdom 7.7% (OECD, 1976).

9. The literature on this pivotal period is now enormous. Among those we have found useful here are Blackaby (1978), Bruce-Gardyne (1974), Jessop (1980).

10. For a summary of these movements see Gould and Roweth (1980). On a slightly different calculating basis, public expenditure as a proportion of Gross National Product dropped from 44.9 per cent in 1951 to 42.1 per cent in 1961, but then rose to 57.9 per cent in 1975 (Gough, 1979, p. 81).

11. Figures are given annually in *Social Security Statistics,* DHSS.

12. All these figures worsen considerably from 1974—1979 but we are concerned here with the period leading up to the explosion of the welfare backlash in 1976—77. For later figures see, *inter alia*, Lister (1978, 1979) and annual reports of the Supplementary Benefits Commission (until 1980). Estimates of non-take-up were discontinued by the Conservative government after 1980. By December 1977, 2.02 million people (including 1.27 million below pension age) were on incomes below supplementary benefit levels; a further 4.16 million were dependent on supplementary benefits (*Social Security Statistics,* DHSS, 1981, Table 47.07).

13. Apart from the data in the Royal Commission reports, the available details are contained in Atkinson and Harrison (1978).

14. See Crossman's more candid version confided to his diary six years later: 'What the national superannuation plan does is to ensure that instead of surrendering year by year to political pressure we have an escalator to carry the old-age pensioner up at a fixed speed in relation to the increase in national wages. We shall proclaim this as a great social advance but I know very well that . . . the escalator will not be moving any faster than it has done . . . in the last fifteen years. My pension plan is not in fact wildly extravagant but unfortunately we dare not say so' (Crossman, 1977, p. 137).

15. For the sense of a loss of momentum on welfare issues in this period see Thompson (1960).

16. She was quoting verbatim from the 1964 manifesto.

17. See Wilson (1971) pp. 53, 64, etc. on the problems caused by the pressure on sterling for advocates of rapid pension increases.

18. The wage-stop was designed to prevent benefits exceeding wages, in

other words it was the modern implementation of 'less eligibility' (see chapter 2). It was opposed at the 1968 party conference 'against the platform'. However this resolution, in Minkin's words, 'simply disappeared from view' (Minkin, 1978, p. 304).

19. For details see the post-mortems in Bosanquet and Townsend (1980), Coates (1979), Kerr (1981).
20. For more general elaboration of this trend in the media see Murdock and Golding (1977) and articles referred to in this and in Murdock and Golding (1978).
21. In 1974 the gap was much more marked, with the pro-Conservative press commanding 71 per cent of circulation.
22. The 9 million figure is the 1945 aggregate circulation of the *Daily Mirror, Sunday Pictorial, Daily Herald, Reynolds News* and *Daily Worker.*
23. The extent to which partisanship becomes muted or confused was illustrated by a MORI poll during the 1979 election that found that more of the *Mirror*'s readers thought it biased to the Conservatives than to Labour. A higher proportion still thought it unbiased. Between a third and a half of the readers of all the popular dailies thought their paper unbiased (*New Statesman* Vol. 97, 27 April 1979, p. 586).
24. For expert advice on how this is done see Gale (1978).
25. For details see Masson (1970) and other material cited in that paper.
26. Excellent brief summaries from contrary viewpoints appear in Jessop (1980), Middlemas (1979) Part Three, Budd (1978).
27. Compare the arguments about the political danger of pauper votes in the 1920s (Deacon and Briggs, 1974). For complementary views see Brittan (1975, 1977), R. Rose (1980).
28. For an interesting discussion in the context of the mid-1970s see McDonnell (1978).
29. We have stopped short here from entering the now tangled theoretical thicket that recently reawakened interest in theories of the state has nurtured. For an acute overview see Jessop (1977).
30. For an influential statement see Nozick (1974). See also Plant *et al.* (1980) pp. 82—9, 227—43.
31. See the discussion of Harris and Seldon (1979) in chapter 6, note 4, above.
32. See similar arguments in McLeod and Powell (1952).
33. Cf. Ian Gilmour's view that 'because of its effect on the economy greater equality hurts the poor as well as the rich and indeed everybody else in the country' (Gilmour, 1977, p. 180).
34. In the sense that, despite spending cuts and major attacks on the social services and social security, there has been no radical programme of denationalisation, no plan to end the NHS, only marginal favours to private education and, despite promises, no really major cuts in income taxation for the majority. The assault on 'quangos', though loudly trumpeted, is expected to save £23 million of a total cost of £6000 million by 1983 (*Guardian* 22 April 1981).

35. The etymology of terms like 'sponger' and 'scrounger' is puzzling. The former is clearly a well-matured term, and appears in Dr Johnson's *Dictionary* (1755), where to sponge is defined as 'to gain by mean arts' and a sponger is 'one who hangs for a maintenance upon others', both recognisable usages. 'Scrounger', however, is of less certain or metaphorically obvious origin. The word does not appear in the 1914 edition of the *Oxford English Dictionary*. The 1933 OED Supplement gives to scrounge as 'to acquire by doubtful means' or to steal (especially apples, suggesting an onomatopaeic origin in the sound of apples being eaten!). Partridge's *Dictionary of Slang* (1937) suggests 'to steal' or 'to get by wheedling', and Klein's *Comprehensive Etymological Dictionary of the English Language* suggests 'to pilfer'. Several sources suggest the old dialect word 'to scringe' or to steal, and most locate the origin of modern usage in the First World War (the OED offers 'a slang term for a soldier with plenty of resource in getting what he wants'). The specific connotation of welfare abuse seems to be of very recent origin. We have been unable to trace its use in this sense before about 1960. Oddly the term now seems to have acquired a narrow and specific connotation related to welfare that has displaced its other and older meanings. How and when this happened is unclear, though the role of the press was probably critical.

36. For example Piachaud (1978) shows that from 1956 to 1974 prices rose 26 per cent more for the poorest fifth than for all households (p. 101). See also Pond (1978).

37. Between 1966 and 1975 the proportion of taxes on income to taxes on expenditure rose from 1.16 to 1.63.

38. In 1974, NI contributions for the lowest tenth were 6.3 per cent of earnings, for the median 5.8 per cent, and for the highest tenth 5.1 per cent (Winyard, 1979, p. 14). Contributions were 4.9 per cent of average earnings in 1961 and 6.1 per cent in 1974 (*Social Security Statistics* DHSS, 1981, Table 46.01).

39. See summaries in Showler and Sinfield (1981) pp. 42—5 and in Lister and Field (1978) pp. 43—50.

40. In 1975, 56.9 per cent of UK taxation was direct, compared to 50.2 per cent in Germany, 32.2 per cent in France, 43.8 per cent in Italy (H. C. *Hansard,* Written Answers, 19 July 1977, Col. 473). For those on two-thirds average incomes the proportion paid in tax and National Insurance contributions increased from 7.1 per cent in 1970/1 to 12.9 per cent in 1978/9. (H. C., *Hansard,* Written Answers, 5 February 1979, cols 44—6). Recent policies have to some extent reversed the trend, though not so much as intended or claimed. In 1980 income taxation started to rise again as a proportion of total revenue (from 1976 to 1979 it dropped from 37.3 per cent to 29.6 per cent; in 1980 it was 31.8 per cent).

41. In 1964 the richest 1 per cent paid 28.6p in each pound collected in income tax. By 1970/1 this had dropped to 17p and by 1978/9 to 11p.

42. The Government statement is included in the Report. See Department of Employment/Department of Health and Social Security, (1981), p. 5.
43. One important administrative measure confirming the disreputability of the unemployed in the social security system is the persistent refusal to allow the unemployed, uniquely among claimants, to receive the 'long-term' rate after two years (one year since November 1980) on supplementary benefit. By 1980/1 this meant a loss of nearly £10 a week for a couple.
44. The imagery is that of Burke as explicated in Duncan (1968); see pp. 125—35.
45. See Stringer and Richardson (1980) for the notion of a placebo policy and also for a fascinating account of political agenda management.
46. See Stevenson (1973) pp. 125, 141—2 for the pressures that cause antipathy among social security officials towards, particularly, the unemployed and single parents.
47. Joseph (1975) reprints a speech originally given in 1972. See also Jordan (1974) passim.
48. See, for example, Knight and West (1977), who claim to demonstrate 'that taking more than average advantage of welfare payments and neglecting welfare contributions are features which tend to be transmitted from father to son' (p. 67). Sir Keith Joseph's 'initiatives' led to a flurry of research, particularly a series of projects sponsored by a DHSS/SSRC Working Party on Transmitted Deprivation. This became a search for 'causal mechanisms' like family influence, and the possibility that 'deprived families and individuals form a sub-culture of their own' that could be investigated anthropologically (*First Report* of the Working Party, 1974, para 19.3). An attempt to review working definitions suggested that 'the term "deprivation" refers to a number of different aspects of a person's environment: to lack (e.g. of mother love or material resources), to deviation (from society's responses and values) or to excess (e.g. of stressful experiences)' (*Third Report,* 1977, p. 2).
49. Many have, of course, noted the evident hypocrisy of condemning social security scroungers who are in fact making (though necessarily rarely) rational calculations of maximum gain for minimum effort in a society based on precisely this calibration of success.

Bibliography

Place of publication is London unless otherwise indicated.

Abel, E. K. (1978) 'Middle-class culture for the urban poor: the educational thought of Samuel Barnett', *Social Service Review,* Vol. 52, No. 4, pp. 596—620.

Abel-Smith, B. and Townsend, P. (1965) *The Poor and the Poorest* Bell.

Abel-Smith, B. (1959) 'Social security', in N. Ginsberg (ed.) *Law and Opinion in England in the Twentieth Century* Stevens & Sons Ltd, pp. 347—63.

Adams, L. P. (1971) *Public Attitudes Toward Unemployment Insurance* Kalamazoo, Michigan, W. E. Upjohn Institute for Employment Research.

Addison, P. (1977) *The Road to 1945* Quartet Books (first published 1975, Cape)

Alston, J. and Dean, K. (1972) 'Socioeconomic factors associated with attitudes towards welfare recipients and the causes of poverty', *Social Service Review* (USA) Vol. 46, March, pp. 13—23.

Alt, J. E. (1979) *The Politics of Economic Decline* Cambridge University Press.

Anderson, P. (1974a) *Lineages of the Absolutist State* New Left Books.

Anderson, P. (1974b) *Passages from Antiquity to Feudalism* New Left Books.

Anthony, P. P. (1978) *The Ideology of Work* Tavistock Publications.

Ashforth, D. (1976) 'The urban poor law', in Fraser (ed.).

Askham, J. (1975) *Fertility and Deprivation* Cambridge University Press.

Asquith, I. (1978) 'The structure, ownership, and control of the press, 1780—1855', in G. Boyce, J. Curran, P. Wingate (eds) *Newspaper History* Constable.

Association for the Improvement of London Workhouses (1867) *Opinions of the Press upon the Condition of the Sick Poor in London Workhouses* Manchester Central Reference Library, Pamphlets P. 3056/5.

Atkinson, A. B. (1972) *Unequal Shares: Wealth in Britain* Allen Lane.

Atkinson, A. B. (1975) *The Economics of Inequality* Oxford, Clarendon Press.

Atkinson, A. B. and Harrison, A. J. (1978) *The Distribution of Personal Wealth in Britain* Cambridge University Press.

Bacon, R., Bain, G. S., Pimlott, J. (1972) 'The economic environment', in Halsey (ed.).

Baernreither, J. M. (1889) *English Associations of Working Men* Swan Sonnenschein & Co.

Bain, G. S., Bacon, R., Pimlott, J. (1972) 'The labour force', in Halsey.

Banting, K. G. (1979) *Poverty, Politics and Policy: Britain in the 1960's* Macmillan.

Barnett, S. A. (1886) 'Sensationalism in social reform', *Nineteenth Century,* Vol. XIX, pp. 280—90.

Barratt Brown, M. (1971) 'The welfare state in Britain', *Socialist Register,* pp. 185—224.

Barratt Brown, M. (1979) 'The growth and distribution of income and wealth', in Coates (ed.).

Barratt Brown, M. *et al.* (eds) (1978) *Full Employment* Nottingham, Spokesman Books.

Behrend, H. (1966) 'Prices, images, inflation and national incomes policy', *Scottish Journal of Political Economy,* Vol. 13, pp. 273—96.

Behrend, H. (1972) 'Public acceptability and a workable incomes policy', in F. Blackaby (ed.) *An Incomes Policy For Britain* Heinemann.

Behrend, H. *et al.* (1966) *A National Survey of Attitudes to Inflation and Incomes Policy,* Occasional Papers in Social and Economic Administration No. 7, Edutext Publications.

Behrend, H. *et al.* (1970) 'Views on income differentials and the economic situation', *Economic and Social Research Institute,* Papers 56 and 57, Aug/Nov, Dublin.

Benjamin, D. K. and Kochin, L. A. (1979) 'Searching for an explanation of unemployment in inter-war Britain', *Journal of Political Economy,* Vol. 87, No. 3, pp. 441—78.

Benn, T. (1980a) 'The mandarins in modern Britain . . .' *The Guardian,* 4 February, p. 9.

Benn, T. (1980b) *Arguments for Socialism* Harmondsworth, Penguin Books.

Berridge, V. (1978) 'Popular Sunday papers and mid-Victorian society', in G. Boyce, J. Curran, P. Wingate (eds) *Newspaper History* Constable.

Best, G. *et al.* (1977) *Health, the Mass Media, and the National Health Service* Unit for the Study of Health Policy, Guy's Hospital Medical School.

Betten, N. (1973) 'American attitudes toward the poor: A historical overview', *Current History,* Vol. 65, No. 383, pp. 1—5.

Beveridge, W. H. and Maynard, H. R. (1904) 'The unemployed: Lessons of the Mansion House Fund', *Contemporary Review,* Vol. 86, pp. 629—38.

Blackaby, F. (ed.) (1978) *British Economic Policy 1960—1974* Cambridge University Press.

Bland, L., McCabe, T., Mort, F. (1979) 'Sexuality and reproduction: three "official" instances', in M. Barrett *et al.* (eds) *Ideology and Cultural Production* Croom Helm.

Blaxter, M. (1974) 'Health "on the welfare"—a case study', *Journal of Social Policy*, Vol. 3, No. 1, pp. 39—51.

Board of Inland Revenue (1978) *Annual Report*, Cmnd. 7473, HMSO.

Board of Inland Revenue (1980) *Annual Report*, Cmnd. 7822 HMSO.

Booth, C. (1892) *Labour and Life of the People, London* (2nd edn), Macmillan.

Booth, W. (1890) *In Darkest England and the Way Out* International Headquarters of the Salvation Army.

Bosanquet, N., and Townsend, P. (1972) *Labour and Inequality* Fabian Society.

Bosanquet, N. and Townsend, P. (eds) (1980) *Labour and Equality* Heinemann.

Bowles, T. and Holmes, M. (1979) *Report on a Survey of Claimants' Attitudes to Central Issues of the Supplementary Benefit Review* Research Surveys of Great Britain Ltd. for the Department of Health and Social Security.

Bowley, A. L. and Burnett-Hurst, A. R. (1915) *Livelihood and Poverty* G. Bell & Sons Ltd.

Boyson, R. (1978) *Centre Forward: A Radical Conservative Programme* Temple Smith.

Boyson, R. (ed.) (1971) *Down With The Poor* Churchill Press.

Branson, N. (1979) *Poplarism 1919-1925,* Lawrence & Wishart.

Branson, N. and Heinemann, M. (1973) *Britain in the Nineteen Thirties* Panther Books.

Brebner, J. B. (1948) 'Laissez-faire and state intervention in nineteenth century Britain', *Journal of Economic History,* Vol. viii, Supplement viii, pp. 59—73.

Briar, S. (1966) 'Welfare from below: recipients' views of the public welfare system', in J. Tenbroek (ed.) *The Law of the Poor,* pp. 46—61, Chandler Publishing Company, USA.

Briggs, A. (1961) 'The welfare state in historical perspective', *Archives Européenes de Sociologie,* Vol. II, pp. 221—58.

Briggs, E. (1979) 'The myth of the pauper disqualification', *Social Policy and Administration,* Vol. 13, No. 2, pp. 138—41.

Briggs, E. and Rees, A. M. (1978) 'How word gets around', *New Society,* 29 June p. 716.

Briggs, E. and Rees, A. M. (1980) *Supplementary Benefits and The Consumer* Bedford Square Press.

Brittan, S. (1975) 'The economic contradictions of democracy', *British Journal of Political Science,* Vol. 5, pp. 129—59.

Brittan, S. (1977) *The Economic Consequences of Democracy* Temple Smith.

Brown, C. V. (1980) *Taxation and the Incentive to Work* Oxford University Press.

Brown, J. (1968) 'Charles Booth and labour colonies 1889—1905', *Economic History Review,* Vol. 21, pp. 349—60.

Brown, J. (1971) 'Social Judgements and Social Policy', *Economic History Review,* Vol. 24, pp. 106—13.

Brown, J. (1978) 'Social control and the modernisation of social policy', in P. Thane (ed.) *The Origins of British Social Policy* Croom Helm.

Brown, K. D. (1971) *Labour and Unemployment 1900—1914* David and Charles, Newton Abbott.

Bruce, M. (1961) *The Coming of the Welfare State* Batsford.

Bruce, M. (1973) *The Rise of the Welfare State* Weidenfeld and Nicolson.

Bruce-Gardyne, B. (1974) *Whatever Happened to the Quiet Revolution?* Charles Knight and Co. Ltd.

Brunhoff, S. de (1978) *The State, Capital and Economic Policy* Pluto Press.

Budd, A. (1978) *The Politics of Economic Planning* Fontana.

Bull, David (ed.) (1971) *Family Poverty: Programme for the Seventies* Duckworth.

Burgess, K. (1980) *The Challenge of Labour* Croom Helm.

Burghes, L. (1980) *So Who's Better Off on the Dole?* Child Poverty Action Group.

Burkitt, B. and Davey, A.G. (1980) 'Choice and markets; the "new right's" approach to welfare', *Social Policy and Administration,* Vol. 14, No. 3, pp. 257—65.

Butler, D. and Stokes, D. (1971) *Political Change in Britain* Harmondsworth, Penguin Books.

Cameron, C. (1975) *Attitudes of the Poor and Attitudes Toward the Poor: an annotated bibliography* Institute for Research on Poverty, University of Wisconsin-Madison, USA.

Campbell, W. E. (1930) *More's Utopia and His Social Teaching* Eyre and Spottiswoode.

Castle, B. (1980) *The Castle Diaries 1974—76* Weidenfeld and Nicolson.

Chambliss, W. (1964) 'A sociological analysis of the law of vagrancy', *Social Problems,* Vol. 12, pp. 66—77.

Chibnall, S. (1977) *Law-and-Order News* Tavistock Publications.

Clarke, D. (1950) Introduction to *Conservatism 1945-50* Conservative Political Centre.

Clifford, D. (1975) 'Stigma and the perception of social security services', *Policy and Politics,* Vol. 3, No. 3, pp. 29—59.

Coates, D. (1975) *The Labour Party and the Struggle for Socialism* Cambridge University Press.

Coates, David (1980) *Labour in Power? A Study of the Labour Government 1974—1979* Longman.

Coates, K. (1972) 'Dismantling the welfare state', in K. Coates, *The Crisis of British Socialism* Nottingham, Spokesman Books.

Coates, K. (ed.) (1979) *What Went Wrong?* Nottingham, Spokesman Books.

Coates, K. and Silburn, R. (1970) *Poverty: The Forgotten Englishman* Harmondsworth, Penguin Books.

Coats, A. W. (1960) 'Economic thought and poor law policy in the eighteenth century', *Economic History Review,* Vol. 13, No. 1, pp. 39—51.

Coats, A. W. (1976) 'The relief of poverty, attitudes to labour, and economic change in England 1660—1782', *International Review of Social History,* Vol. 21, No. 1, pp. 98—115.

Cohen, S. (ed.) (1971) *Images of Deviance* Harmondsworth, Penguin.

Cohen, S. (1972) *Folk Devils and Moral Panics* MacGibbon & Kee.

Cohen, S. (1973) 'Mods and Rockers: the inventory as manufactured news', in Cohen and Young (eds).

Cohen, S. and Young, J. (eds) (1973) *The Manufacture of News* Constable.

Coleraine, Lord (1970) *For Conservatives Only* Tom Stacey.

Commission of the European Communities (1977) *The Perception of Poverty in Europe,* Document V/171/77-E, Brussels.

Committee on Abuse of Social Security Benefits (1973) *Report,* Cmnd. 5228, HMSO

Conservative Political Centre (1950) *Conservatism 1945—50,* Conservative Political Centre.

Constantine, S. (1980) *Unemployment in Britain Between the Wars* Longman.

Cormack, V. (1968) 'The Royal Commission on the Poor Laws 1905—09 and the welfare state', in A. Lochhead (ed.) *A Reader in Social Administration* Constable.

Corrigan, P. and Corrigan V. (1979) 'State formation and social policy until 1871', in N. Parry, M. Rustin and C. Satyamurti (eds) *Social Work, Welfare and the State* Edward Arnold.

Corwin, R. D. and Miller, S. M. (1972) 'Taxation and its beneficiaries: the manipulation of symbols', *American Journal of Orthopsychiatry,* Vol. 42, No. 2, pp. 200—13.

Craig, F. W. S. (1975) *British General Election Manifestos 1900—1974* Macmillan.

Crosland, C. A. R. (1964) *The Future of Socialism* Jonathan Cape (first published 1956)

Crossman, R. (1977) *The Diaries of a Cabinet Minister. Vol. 3: 1968—1970* Hamish Hamilton/Jonathan Cape.

Crowther, M. A. (1978) 'The later years of the workhouse 1890—1929', in P. Thane (ed.) *The Origins of British Social Policy* Croom Helm.

Crozier, B. (1979) *The Minimum State* Hamish Hamilton.

Cullen, M. J. (1975) *The Statistical Movement in Early Victorian Britain* Sussex, Harvester Press.

Culyer, A. J. (1973) *The Economics of Social Policy* Martin Robertson.

Curran, C. (1960) 'Forward from Beveridge', *Crossbow,* Autumn, pp. 25—6.

Curran, J. (1977) 'Capitalism and control of the press 1800—1975', in J. Curran, M. Gurevitch, J. Woollocott (eds) *Mass Communication and Society* Edward Arnold.

Curran, J. (1978) 'Advertising and the press', in J. Curran (ed.) *The British Press: A Manifesto* Macmillan.

Curran, J. (1981) 'Advertising as a patronage system', in H. Christian (ed.) *The Sociology of Journalism and the Press* Monograph 29, The Sociological Review, Keele.

Curran, J. and Seaton J. (1981) *Power Without Responsibility: The Press and Broadcasting in Britain* Fontana

Curtin, R.T. (1977) *Income Equity Among U.S. Workers* New York, Praeger.

Day, P. (1979) 'Sex-role stereotypes and public assistance', *Social Service Review*, Vol. 53, No. 1, pp. 106—15.

Deacon, A. (1976) *In Search of the Scrounger: the Administration of Unemployment Insurance 1920—31* Occasional Papers on Social Administration No. 60, G. Bell & Sons Ltd.

Deacon, A. (1977a) 'Concession and coercion: the politics of unemployment insurance', in A. Briggs and J. Saville (eds) *Essays in Labour History* Croom Helm.

Deacon, A. (1977b) 'Scrounger bashing', *New Society,* 17 November, pp. 355—6.

Deacon, A. (1978) 'The scrounging controversy: public attitudes towards the unemployed in contemporary Britain', *Social and Economic Administration,* Vol. 12, No. 2, pp. 120—35.

Deacon, A. (1980) 'Spivs, drones, and other scroungers', *New Society,* Vol. 51, No. 908, pp. 446—7.

Deacon, A. (1981) 'Unemployment and politics in Britain since 1945', in Showler and Sinfield (eds).

Deacon, A. and Briggs, E. (1974) 'Local democracy and central policy: the issue of pauper votes in the 1920's', *Policy and Politics,* Vol. 2, No. 4, pp. 347—64.

Deacon, A. and Sinfield, A. (1977) 'The unemployed, policy and Public Debate', Paper given to SSRC Workshop on Social Security, 18 March, University College, London.

Defoe, D. (1704) *Giving Alms No Charity and Employing the Poor a Grievance to the Nation* Booksellers of London and West (Reprint by S. R. Publishers, Yorkshire, 1975).

Department of Employment (1977) *New Earnings Survey 1977. Part A* HMSO.

Department of Employment/Department of Health and Social Security (1981) *Payment of Benefits to Unemployed People* (Rayner Report) HMSO.

Department of Health and Social Security (1977a) 'Local office contacts with the public', background paper for *Social Assistance,* produced by DHSS Branch SB5.

Department of Health and Social Security (1977b) *Report by the Co-ordinating Committee on Abuse* DHSS.

Department of Health and Social Security (1978) *Social Assistance: A Review of the Supplementary Benefits Scheme in Great Britain* DHSS.

Department of Health and Social Security (1979) *Second Report by the Co-ordinating Committee on Abuse* DHSS.

Dicey, A. V. (1914), *Lectures on the relation between Law and Public Opinion in England during the nineteenth century* Macmillan.

Digby, A. (1976) 'The rural poor law', in Fraser (ed.).

Dobb, M. (1969) *Welfare Economics and the Economics of Socialism* Cambridge University Press.

Donnison, D. (1976a) 'Dear David Bull, Frank Field, Michael Hill and Ruth Lister', *Social Work Today,* Vol. 6, No. 20, pp. 622—4.

Donnison, D. (1976b) 'Supplementary benefits: dilemmas and priorities', *Journal of Social Policy,* Vol. 5, No. 4, pp. 337—58.

Duncan, H. D. (1968) *Communication and Social Order* Oxford University Press.

Dworak, J. (1980) *Taxpayers, Taxes & Government Spending* New York, Praeger.

Edelman, M. (1966) *The Mirror: A Political History* Hamish Hamilton.

Edsall, N. (1971) *The Anti-Poor Law Movement 1833—44* Manchester, Manchester University Press.

Eisenstein, L. (1961), *The Ideologies of Taxation* New York, The Ronald Press Co.

Elliott, W. (1949) 'The welfare state', *Tory Challenge,* July.

Emy, H. V. (1973) *Liberals, Radicals and Social Politics 1892—1914* Cambridge University Press.

Epstein, E. J. (1973) *News From Nowhere* New York, Random House.

Evans, P. (1976) *Publish and be damned?* Runnymede Trust.

Fawcett, H. (1871) *Pauperism: Its Causes and Remedies* Macmillan.

Feagin, J. R. (1972a) 'America's welfare stereotypes', *Social Service Quarterly,* Vol. 52, No. 4, pp. 921—33.

Feagin, J. R. (1972b) 'God helps those who help themselves', *Psychology Today,* November, pp. 101—10, 129.

Feagin, J. R. (1975) *Subordinating the Poor* Prentice-Hall.

Field, F. (1976) 'Killing a commitment: the Cabinet v. the children', *New Society,* Vol. 36, No. 715, pp. 630—2.

Field, F. (1978) 'Last word', *Social Work Today,* Vol. 9, No. 34.

Field, F. (1979a) 'Poverty, growth, and the redistribution of income', in W. Beckerman (ed.) *Slow Growth in Britain: Causes and Consequences* Oxford, Clarendon Press.

Field, F. (1979b) 'Scroungers: crushing the invisible', *New Statesman,* 16 November, pp. 754—5.

Field, F. (1981) *Inequality in Britain: Freedom, Welfare and the State* Fontana.

Field, F., Meacher, M., Pond, C. (1977) *To Him Who Hath: A Study of Poverty and Taxation* Harmondsworth, Penguin Books.

Fielding, H. (1751) *An Inquiry into the Causes of the Late Increase of Robbers & Co.,* reprinted in *Works,* Vol. XIII, Frank Cass, 1967.

Fielding, H. (1753) *Proposal for Making an Effectual Provision for the Poor,* reprinted in *Works,* Vol. XIII, Frank Cass, 1967.

Fine, B. and Harris, L. (1976) ' "State expenditure in advanced capitalism"—a critique', *New Left Review,* Vol. 98, pp. 97—112.

Form, W. H. and Rytina, J. (1969) 'Ideological beliefs on the distribution of power in the U.S.', *American Sociological Review,* Vol. 34, No. 1, pp. 19—31.

Foster, J. (1976) 'Imperialism and the Labour aristocracy', in J. Skelley (ed.) *The General Strike* Lawrence & Wishart.

Fraser, D. (1973) *The Evolution of the British Welfare State* Macmillan.

Fraser, D. (ed.) (1976) *The New Poor Law in the Nineteenth Century* Macmillan.

Freeman, I. (1979) 'Public attitudes to social security', Paper given to SSRC Workshop, University College, London.

Friedman, M. and Friedman, F. (1980) *Free to Choose* Martin Secker and Warburg.

Gale, G. (1978) 'The popular communication of a Conservative message', in M. Cowling (ed.) *Conservative Essays* Cassell.

Gallup, G. (ed.) (1976) *Gallup International Public Opinion Polls: Great Britain 1937—75* New York, Random House.

Gamble, A. (1979) 'The free economy and the strong state', *Socialist Register,* pp. 1—25, Merlin Press.

Gamble, A. (1980) 'Thatcher—make or break', *Marxism Today,* Vol. 24, No. 11, pp. 14—19.

Garraty, J. A. (1978) *Unemployment in History: Economic Thought and Public Policy* New York, Harper and Row.

George, H. (1883) *Progress and Poverty* Kegan Paul.

Gershuny, Jonathan (1978) *After Industrial Society? The Emerging Self-Service Economy* Macmillan.

Gilbert, B. B. (1966a) *The Evolution of National Insurance in Britain: The Origins of the Welfare State* Michael Joseph.

Gilbert, B. B. (1966b) 'Winston Churchill versus the Webbs: the origins of British unemployment insurance', *American Historical Review,* Vol. 71, No. 3, pp. 846—62.

Gilbert, B. B. (1970) *British Social Policy 1914—1939* Batsford.

Gilmour, I. (1977) *Inside Right: A Study of Conservatism* Hutchinson.

Ginsburg, N. (1979) *Class, Capital and Social Policy* Macmillan.

Glampson, A. *et al.* (1977) 'Knowledge and perceptions of the social services', *Journal of Social Policy,* Vol. 6, No. 1, pp. 1—16.

Glasgow University Media Group (1976) *Bad News* Routledge and Kegan Paul.

Glasgow University Media Group (1980) *More Bad News* Routledge and Kegan Paul.

Glennerster, H. (1977) 'The year of the cuts', in K. Jones *et al.* (eds) *The Year Book of Social Policy in Britain 1976* Routledge and Kegan Paul.

Glenton, G. and Pattinson, W. (1963) *The Last Chronicle of Bouverie Street* George Allen and Unwin.

Glyn, A. and Harrison, J. (1980) *The British Economic Disaster* Pluto Press.

Golding, P. (1974) 'Media role in national development: critique of a theoretical orthodoxy', *Journal of Communication,* Vol. 24, No. 3, pp. 39—53.

Golding, P. (1980a) 'From Charles Booth to Peter Townsend: poverty research in the U.K.', *Social Policy and Administration,* Vol. 14, No. 2, pp. 169—72.

Golding, P. (1980b) 'In the eye of the beholder: an evaluation of the European Commission Study *The Perception of Poverty in Europe'.* Paper prepared for Vol. II of Report to Commission by ESPOIR, University of Kent.

Golding, P. and Elliott, P. (1979) *Making the News* Longman.

Golding, P. and Middleton, S. (1979) 'Reporting on social security', Letter in *The Media Reporter,* Vol. 3, No. 4, p. 49.

Golding, P. and Murdock, G. (1978) 'Confronting the market: Public intervention and press diversity', in J. Curran (ed.) *The British Press: A Manifesto* Macmillan.

Goldthorpe, J. H. (1962) 'The development of social policy in Britain 1800—1914', *Transactions of the World Congress of Sociology,* Vol. 4.

Gomm, R. (1974) 'The claimant as mendicant', *Social Work Today,* Vol. 5, No. 12, pp. 369—72.

Gomulka, S. (1979) 'Britain's slow industrial growth—increasing inefficiency versus low rate of technical change', in W. Beckerman (ed.) *Slow Growth in Britain* Oxford, Oxford University Press.

Goodwin, L. (1972) 'How suburban families view the work orientations of the welfare poor', *Social Problems,* Vol. 19, pp. 337—48.

Gosden, P. H. (1961) *The Friendly Societies in England 1815—1875* Manchester, Manchester University Press.

Gosden, P. H. J. H. (1973) *Self-Help: Voluntary Associations in the 19th Century* B. T. Batsford Ltd.

Gough, I. (1975) 'State expenditure in advanced capitalism', *New Left Review,* No. 92, July/August, pp. 53—92.

Gough, I. (1978) 'Theories of the welfare state: a critique', *Journal of the Health Services,* Vol. 8, No. 1.

Gough, I. (1979) *The Political Economy of the Welfare State* Macmillan.

Gough, I. (1980) 'Thatcherism and the welfare state', *Marxism Today,* July, pp. 7—12.

Gould, F. and Roweth, B. (1980) 'Public spending and social policy: the United Kingdom 1950-77', *Journal of Social Policy,* Vol. 9, No. 3, pp. 337—57.

Gramsci, A. (1971) *Selections from the Prison Notebooks* Lawrence and Wishart.

Gray, S. (1971) *The Electoral Register* Office of Population Censuses and Surveys, Social Survey Division.

Griffith, J. A. G. (1977) *The Politics of the Judiciary* Fontana/Collins.

Grunig, J. (1972) 'Communication in community decisions in the problems of the poor', *Journal of Communication,* Vol. 22, No. 1, pp. 5—25.

Gulley, E. (1926) *Joseph Chamberlain and English Social Politics* New York, Columbia University Press.

Habermas, J. (1976) *Legitimation Crisis* Heinemann.

Haines, J. (1977) *The Politics of Power* Coronet Books.

Hall, P., Land, H., Parker, R., and Webb, A. (1975) *Change, Choice and Conflict in Social Policy* Heinemann.

Hall, S. (1975) 'The "structured communication" of events', in *Getting the Message Across* Paris, UNESCO.

Hall, S. (1979) 'The great moving right show', *Marxism Today,* Vol. 23, No. 1, pp. 14—20.

Hall, S. (1980) 'Popular—Democratic vs authoritarian populism: two ways of "taking democracy seriously" ', in A. Hunt (ed.) *Marxism and Democracy* Lawrence and Wishart.

Hall, S., Critcher, C., Jefferson, T., Clarke, J., Roberts, B. (1978) *Policing the Crisis* Macmillan.

Halloran, J. D., Elliott, P., Murdock, G. (1970) *Demonstrations and Communication: A Case Study* Harmondsworth, Penguin Books.

Halsey, A. H. (ed.) (1972) *Trends in British Society Since 1900* Macmillan.

Handler, J. F. and Hollingsworth, E. J. (1971) *The 'Deserving Poor'. A Study of Welfare Administration* Institute for Research on Poverty Monograph Series, Chicago, Markham Publishing Co.

Hannington, W. (1938) *A Short History of the Unemployed* Victor Gollancz.

Hannington, W. (1973) *Unemployed Struggles 1919—1936* Wakefield, EP Publishing Ltd (first published 1936).

Hargreaves, R. (1979) 'Television and current affairs', in M. J. Clark (ed.) *Politics and the Media* Oxford, Pergamon Press.

Harris, J. (1975) 'Social planning in war time: some aspects of the Beveridge Report', in J. Winter (ed.) *War and Economic Development* Cambridge University Press.

Harris, J. (1977) *William Beveridge: A Biography* Oxford, Clarendon Press.

Harris, J. F. (1972) *Unemployment and Politics: A Study in English Social Policy 1886—1914* Oxford University Press.

Harris, L. (1980) 'The state and the economy: some theoretical problems', in *Socialist Register,* pp. 243—62, Merlin Press.

Harris, N. (1972) *Competition and the Corporate Society: British Conservatives, The State, and Industry 1945—64* Methuen.

Harris, R. and Seldon, A. (1965) *Choice in Welfare 1965: Second Report on Knowledge and Preference in Education, Health Services and Pensions* Research Report, Institute of Economic Affairs.

Harris, R. and Seldon, A. (1971) *Choice in Welfare* Institute of Economic Affairs.

Harris, R. and Seldon, A. (1979) *Over-Ruled on Welfare* Institute of Economic Affairs.

Hartmann, P. (1976) 'The media and industrial relations', University of Leicester, mimeo.

Hartmann, P. (1979) 'News and public perceptions of industrial relations', *Media Culture and Society,* Vol. 1, pp. 255—70.

Hartmann, P. and Husband, C. (1973) *Racism and the Mass Media* Davis-Poynter.

Hartmann, P., Husband, C., Clark, J. (1974) *Race as News* Paris, UNESCO.

Harvey, R. (1977) *Unemployed Sheep and Goats* Bow Group.

Hay, J. R. (1975) *The Origins of the Liberal Welfare Reforms 1906—1914* Macmillan.

Hay, J. R. (1978) 'Employers' attitudes to social policy and the concept of "social control" 1900—1920', in P. Thane (ed.) *The Origins of British Social Policy,* Croom Helm.

Hay, R. (1977) 'Employers and social policy: the evolution of welfare legislation 1905—14', *Social History,* Vol. 4, January, pp. 435—55.

Hayburn, R. (1972) 'The police and the hunger marchers', *International Review of Social History,* Vol. 17, pp. 625—44.

Hayek, F. von (1960) *The Constitution of Liberty* Routledge and Kegan Paul.

Hennock, E. P. (1976) 'Poverty and social theory in England: the experience of the 1880's', *Social History*, Vol. 1, No. 1, pp. 67—91.

Henriques, U. R. Q. (1979) *Before the Welfare State: Social Administration in early Industrial Britain* Longman.

Hess, J. (1981) 'The social policy of the Attlee government', in W. Mommson and W. Mock (eds) *The Emergence of the Welfare State in Britain and Germany 1850—1950* Croom Helm.

Hill, C. (1969) *Society and Puritanism in Pre-Revolutionary England* Panther Books (first published 1964).

Hill, M. (1972) 'Are the workshy a myth?' *New Society,* 30 July.

Hills, A. (1980) 'How the press sees you', *Social Work Today,* Vol. 11, No. 36, pp. 19—20.

Himmelfarb, G. (1973) 'The culture of poverty', in H. Dyos and M. Wolff (eds) *The Victorian City* Routledge and Kegan Paul.

Hindle, W. (1937) *The Morning Post 1772—1937* George Routledge and Sons.

Hines, C. and Searle, G. (1979) *Automatic Unemployment* Earth Resources Research Ltd.

Hinton, J. (1973) *The First Shop Stewards Movement* Allen and Unwin.

Hirsch, F. and Gordon, D. (1975) *Newspaper Money* Hutchinson.
Hirschhorn, L. (1979) 'The theory of social services in disaccumulationist capitalism', *International Journal of Health Services,* Vol. 9, No. 2, pp. 295—311.
History of the Times, The (1935) Vol. 1 *'The Thunderer' in The Making 1785—1841* The Times Publishing Co.
Hogg, Q. (1947) *The Case for Conservatism* Harmondsworth, Penguin.
Holman, R. (1973) 'Poverty: consensus and alternatives', *British Journal of Social Work,* Vol. 3, No. 4, pp. 431—46.
Holman, R. (1978) *Poverty: Explanations of Social Deprivation* Martin Robertson.
Holton, R. H. (1974) *'Daily Herald* v. *Daily Citizen* 1912—1915', *International Review of Social History,* Vol. 19, pp. 347—76.
Holton, R. H. (1976) *British Syndicalism 1900—1914* Pluto Press.
Hopkin, D. (1978) 'The socialist press in Britain 1890—1910', in G. Boyce, J. Curran, P. Wingate *Newspaper History* Constable.
Horan, P. and Austin, P. L. (1974) 'The social bases of welfare stigma', *Social Problems,* Vol. 21, pp. 648—57.
Howkins, A. and Saville, J. (1979) 'The nineteen thirties: a revisionist history', *Socialist Register,* pp. 89—100, Merlin Press.
Hubbard, J. C., Defleur, M. and Defleur, L. (1975) 'Mass media influences on public conceptions of social problems', *Social Problems,* Vol. 23, No. 1, pp. 22—34.
Huber, J. and Form, W. H. (1973) *Income and Ideology: An Analysis of the American Political Formula* New York, The Free Press.
Hughes, J. (1978) 'A rake's progress', in Barratt Brown *et al.* (eds).
Hutchison, T. W. (1953) *A Review of Economic Doctrines: 1870—1929* Oxford, Clarendon Press.
Inglehart, R. (1977) *The Silent Revolution: Political Change Among Western Publics* USA, Princeton University Press.
Inglis, B. (1972) *Poverty and the Industrial Revolution* Panther Books.
International Labour Organisation (1979) *The Cost of Social Security* Geneva, International Labour Organisation.

Jackson, I. (1971) *The Provincial Press and the Community* Manchester, Manchester University Press.
Jahoda, M. (1979) 'The impact of unemployment in the 1930's and the 1970's', *Bulletin of the British Psychological Society,* Vol. 32, pp. 309—14.
Jenkins, C. and Sherman, B. (1979) *The Collapse of Work* Eyre Methuen.
Jessop, B. (1974) *Conservatism, Traditionalism and British Political Culture* Allen and Unwin.
Jessop, B. (1977) 'Remarks on some recent theories of the capitalist state', *Cambridge Journal of Economics,* Vol. 1, No. 4, pp. 353—73.
Jessop, B. (1980) 'The transformation of the state in post-war Britain', in R. Scase (ed.) *The State in Western Europe* Croom Helm.

Jolly, R. (1977) 'Redistribution with sloth—Britain's problem?', *Bulletin of the Institute for Development Studies*, (Sussex University), Vol. 9, No. 2, pp. 12—16.

Jones, C. (1977) *Immigration and Social Policy in Britain* Tavistock.

Jones, C. and Novak, T. (1980) 'The state and social policy', in P. Corrigan (ed.) *Capitalism, State Formation and Marxist Theory* Quartet Books.

Jordan, Bill (1973) *Paupers: The Making of the New Claiming Classes* Routledge and Kegan Paul.

Jordan, Bill (1974) *Poor Parents: Social Policy and the Cycle of Deprivation* Routledge and Kegan Paul.

Jordan, W. K. (1959) *Philanthropy in England* Allen and Unwin.

Joseph, Sir Keith (1975) 'The cycle of deprivation', in E. Butterworth and R. Holman (eds) *Social Welfare in Modern Britain* Fontana/Collins.

Joseph, Sir Keith (1966a) *A New Strategy for Social Security* Conservative Political Centre

Joseph, Sir Keith (1966b) *Social Security: The New Priorities* Conservative Political Centre.

Keating, P. (1976) *Into Unknown England 1866—1913* Fontana/Collins.

Keegan, W. and Pennant-Rea, R. (1979) *Who Runs the Economy? Control and Influence in British Economic Policy* Maurice Temple Smith.

Keenan, A. and Dean, P. (1980) 'Moral evaluations of tax evasion', *Social Policy and Administration*, Vol. 14, No. 3, pp. 209—20.

Kellner, P. and Crowther-Hunt, Lord (1980) *The Civil Servants: An Inquiry into Britain's Ruling Class* Macdonald General Books.

Kerbo, H. (1975) 'The stigma of welfare and a passive poor', *Sociology and Social Research*, Vol. 60, No. 2, pp. 173—87.

Kerr, H. (1981) 'Labour's social policy 1974—1979', *Critical Social Policy*, Vol. 1, No. 1, pp. 5—17.

Kincaid, J. C. (1973) *Poverty and Equality in Britain* Harmondsworth, Penguin Books.

King, A. (1975) 'Overload: problems of governing in the 1970's', *Political Studies*, Vol. 23, Nos 2—3, pp. 284—96.

Klein, R. (1974) 'The case for elitism: public opinion and public policy', *Political Quarterly*, Vol. 45, pp. 406—17.

Knight, B. J. and West, D. J. (1977) 'Criminality and welfare dependency in two generations', *Medicine, Science and Law*, Vol. 17, No. 1, pp. 64—7.

Knight, L. (1975) 'Communication: a class of its own', *Community Care*, No. 72, 13 August, pp. 16—18.

Labour Party (1963) *New Frontiers for Social Security* National Executive Committee.

Laclau, E. (1977) 'Towards a theory of populism', in *Politics and Ideology in Marxist Theory* New Left Books.

Lang, K. and Lang, G. (1955) 'The inferential structure of communications: a study in unwitting bias', *Public Opinion Quarterly*, Vol. 19, pp. 168—83.

Laver, R. H. (1971) 'The middle class looks at poverty', *Urban and Social Change Review,* 5, pp. 8—10.

Layard, R., Piachaud, D., Stewart, M. (1978) *The Causes of Poverty* Background Paper No. 5 (to Report No. 6: *Lower Incomes*) for Royal Commission on the Distribution of Income and Wealth, HMSO.

Lee, A. J. (1976) *The Origins of the Popular Press 1855—1914* Croom Helm.

Lee, A. J. (1978) 'The structure, ownership and control of the press 1855—1914', in G. Boyce, J. Curran, P. Wingate (eds) *Newspaper History,* Constable.

Leeson, R. A. (1979) *Travelling Brothers* George Allen and Unwin.

Lippmann, W. (1922) *Public Opinion* G. Allen and Unwin

Lis, H. and Soly, H. (1979) *Poverty and Capitalism in Pre-Industrial Europe* Sussex, Harvester Press.

Lister, R. (1974) *Take Up of Means Tested Benefits* Poverty Pamphlet No. 18, Child Poverty Action Group.

Lister, R. (1976) 'Take up: the same old story', *Poverty,* No. 34, pp. 3—8.

Lister, R. (1978) *Social Assistance: The Real Challenge* Poverty Pamphlet No. 38, Child Poverty Action Group.

Lister, R. (1979) *The No-Cost No-Benefit Review* Poverty Pamphlet No. 39, Child Poverty Action Group.

Lister, R. (1980) 'Family policy', in Bosanquet and Townsend (eds).

Lister R. and Field, F. (1978) *Wasted Labour* Poverty Pamphlet No. 33, Child Poverty Action Group.

Locke, J. (1697) *A Report of the Board of Trade to the Lords Justices respecting the Relief and Employment of the Poor* Tegg.

London, J. (1977) *The People of the Abyss* The Journeyman Press (first published 1903).

Lubenow, W. C. (1971) *The Politics of Government Growth: Early Victorian Attitudes to State Intervention 1833—1848* Newton Abbot, David and Charles.

Luckhaus, L. (1980) 'Towards an explanation of the welfare scrounger', unpublished dissertation for MA, Socio-legal Studies, University of Sheffield.

Lummis, T. (1971) 'Charles Booth: Moralist or social scientist', *Economic History Review,* Vol. 24, pp. 100—5.

Lythgoe, P. (1979) 'The social security snowball', *The Media Reporter,* Vol. 3, No. 1, pp. 20—3.

McDonnell, K. (1978) 'Ideology, crisis and the cuts', *Capital and Class,* 4, Spring, pp. 34—69.

McGregor, O. R. (1957) 'Social research and social policy in the nineteenth century', *British Journal of Sociology,* Vol. 8, pp. 146—157.

McKay, R. and Barr, B. (1976) *The Story of the Scottish Daily News* Edinburgh, Canongate Publishing.

Mackenzie, N. and Mackenzie, J. (1979) *The First Fabians,* Quartet Books (first published 1977).

Macleod, I. and Powell, J. Enoch (1952) *The Social Services: Needs and Means* Conservative Political Centre.

Macleod, R. M. (1968) *Treasury Control and Social Administration* George Bell and Sons Ltd.

MacNicol, J. (1978) 'Family allowances and less eligibility', in P. Thane (ed.) *The Origins of British Social Policy* Crom Helm.

MacNicol, J. (1981) *The Movement for Family Allowances 1918—1945* Heinemann Educational.

McQuail, D. (1977) 'Social welfare and social policy content in national daily newspapers 1975', Part D in *Analysis of Newspaper Content,* Research Series 4 of the Royal Commission on the Press, Cmnd. 6810—4, pp. 215—41, HMSO.

Marshall, D. (1926) *The English Poor in the Eighteenth Century* Routledge.

Marshall, T. H. (1950) *Citizenship and Social Class and other Essays* Cambridge University Press.

Marshall, T. H. (1965) *Social Policy* Hutchinson.

Marwick, A. (1967) 'The Labour Party and the welfare state in Britain 1900—1948', *American Historical Review,* Vol. 73, No. 2, pp. 380—403.

Marx, K. (1973) *Grundrisse: Foundations of the Critique of Political Economy* Harmondsworth, Penguin Books (first published 1939).

Mason, J. (1978) 'Monthly and quarterly reviews 1865—1914', in G. Boyce, J. Curran, P. Wingate (eds) *Newspaper History* Constable.

Masson, P. 'The Effects of Television on Other Media' in J. Halloran (Ed) *The Effects of Television* Panther.

Matza, D. (1966) 'The disreputable poor', in N. J. Smelser and S. M. Lipset (eds) *Social Structure and Social Mobility* Chicago, Aldine Press.

Mawby, R., Fisher, C. and Parkin, A. (1979) 'Press coverage of social work', *Policy and Politics,* Vol. 7, No. 4, pp. 357—76.

Meacher, M. (1974) *Scrounging on the Welfare* Arrow Books.

Mearns, A. (1970) *The Bitter Cry of Outcast London* Leicester University Press (first published 1883).

Middlemas, K. (1979) *Politics in Industrial Society: The experience of the British system since 1911* Andre Deutsch.

Miliband, R. (1972) *Parliamentary Socialism* Merlin Press.

Mill, J. S. (1910) *Considerations on Representative Government* J. M. Dent and Sons Ltd (first published 1861).

Miller, S. M. (1978) 'The recapitalisation of capitalism', *International Journal of Urban and Regional Research,* Vol. 2, No. 2, pp. 202—12.

Minkin, L. (1978) *The Labour Party Conference: A Study in the Politics of Intra-party Democracy* Allen Lane.

Moore, P. (1980) 'Counter-culture in a social security office', *New Society,* Vol. 53, No. 921, pp. 68—9.

Moore, P. (1981) 'Scroungermania again at the D.H.S.S.', *New Society,* 22 January, pp. 138—9.

Moorhouse, H. F. (1976) 'Attitudes to class and class relationships in Britain', *Sociology,* Vol. 10, No. 3, pp. 469—96.

More, Sir Thomas (1516) *Utopia*, in Vol. 4 *Complete Works*, Yale University Press, 1965.

Morris, P. *et al.* (1973) 'Public attitudes to problem definition and problem solving', *British Journal of Social Work*, Vol. 3, No. 3, pp. 301—20.

Moser, C. C. and Kalton, G. (1971) *Survey Methods in Social Investigation* Heinemann Educational Books.

Mosley, H. (1978) 'Is there a fiscal crisis of the state?' *Monthly Review*, May, pp. 34—45.

Mountjoy, P. R. (1978) 'The working-class press and working-class conservatism', in G. Boyce, J. Curran, P. Wingate (eds) *Newspaper History* Constable.

Müller, W. and Neusüss, C. (1978) 'The "welfare-state illusion" and the contradiction between wage-labour and capital', in J. Holloway and S. Picciotto (eds) *State and Capital: A Marxist Debate* Leeds, Edward Arnold.

Murdock, G. and Golding, P. (1974) 'For a political economy of mass communications', in R. Miliband and J. Saville (eds) *Socialist Register* Merlin Press, pp. 205—34.

Murdock, G. and Golding, P. (1977) 'Beyond monopoly: mass communications in an age of conglomerates', in P. Beharrell and G. Philo (eds) *Trade Unions and the Media* Macmillan.

Murdock, G. and Golding P. (1978) 'The structure, ownership, and control of the press 1914—1976' in G. Boyce, J. Curran, P. Wingate (eds) *Newspaper History* Constable.

Murphy, D. (1976) *The Silent Watchdog* Constable.

National Consumer Council (1976) *Means Tested Benefits: A Discussion Paper* National Consumer Council.

Neuburg, V. (1977) *Popular Literature* Harmondworth, Penguin Books.

Norris, M. (1978) 'Those we like to help', *New Society*, Vol. 45, No. 822, p. 18.

Nozick, R. (1974) *Anarchy, State and Utopia* Oxford, Blackwell.

O'Connor, J. (1973) *The Fiscal Crisis of the State* New York, St Martin's Press.

Office of Population Censuses and Surveys (1978) *Demographic Review 1977* HMSO.

Organisation for Economic Co-operation and Development (1976) *Public Expenditure on Income Maintenance Programmes* Paris, OECD.

Ormerod, P. (1980) 'The Economic Record', in Bosanquet and Townsend (eds).

Orwell, G. (1937) *The Road to Wigan Pier* Victor Gollancz.

Page, R. (1971) *The Benefits Racket* Tom Stacey.

Pakenham, Lord (1953) *Born to Believe* Jonathan Cape.

Parker, J. (1972) 'Welfare', in Halsey (ed.).

Parker, J. (1975) *Social Policy and Citizenship* Macmillan.

Parkin, F. (1972) *Class Inequality and Political Order* Paladin.

Peek, F. (1883) *Social Wreckage: A Review of the Laws of England as they affect the Poor* Wm. Isbister Ltd.

Peek, F. (1888) *The Workless, the Thriftless and the Worthless* Wm. Isbister Ltd.

Pelling, H. (1968) 'The working class and the origins of the welfare state', in *Popular Politics and Society in Late Victorian Britain* Macmillan.

Perkin, H. (1969) *The Origins of Modern English Society 1780—1880* Routledge and Kegan Paul.

Phillips, M. (1979) 'Social workers and the media: a journalist's view', *Social Work Today,* Vol. 10, No. 22, p. 12.

Piachaud, D. (1974) 'Attitudes to pensions', *Journal of Social Policy,* Vol. 3, No. 2, pp. 137—46.

Piachaud, D. (1978) 'Inflation and income distribution', in F. Hirsch and J. Goldthorpe (eds) *The Political Economy of Inflation* Oxford, Martin Robertson.

Piachaud, D. (1980) 'Social security', in Bosanquet and Townsend (eds).

Plant, R., Lesser, H., Taylor-Gooby, P. (1980) *Political Philosophy and Social Welfare* Routledge and Kegan Paul.

Pollard, S. (1960) 'Nineteenth-century co-operation: from community building to shopkeeping', in A. Briggs and J. Saville (eds) *Essays in Labour History* Macmillan.

Pollard, S. (ed.) (1970) *The Gold Standard and Employment Policies Between the Wars* Methuen.

Pond, C. (1978) 'Prices and prejudice', *Low Pay Unit Bulletin,* No. 22/23, pp. 1—6.

Pond, C. (1979) 'Low pay in the 80's (1880 and 1980)', *Low Pay Unit Bulletin,* No. 30, December, pp. 1—4.

Poor Law Report (1834) edition edited by S. G. and E. O. A. Checkland, Harmondsworth, Penguin Books, 1974.

Popay, J. (1977) *Fiddlers on the Hoof: Moral Panics and Social Security Scroungers* Unpublished MA paper, University of Essex.

Poulantzas, N. (1978) *State, Power, Socialism* New Left Books.

Pound, J. (1971) *Poverty and Vagrancy in Tudor England* Longman.

Poynter, J. R. (1969) *Society and Pauperism: English Ideas on Poor Relief 1795—1834* Routledge and Kegan Paul.

Rathbone, E. (1924) *The Disinherited Family* Allen and Unwin (republished 1949 as *Family Allowances*).

Redpath, A. (1979) 'Public attitudes toward the unemployed, Paper given at SSRC Workshop, University College, London, September.

Ritchie, J. and Wilson, P. (1979) *Social Security Claimants* Office of Population Censuses and Surveys, Social Survey Division.

Ritt, L. (1959) 'The Victorian conscience in action: the National Association for the Promotion of Social Science 1857—1886',

Unpublished PhD, Columbia University, Reprint by University
Microfilms Inc., 1976.

Roberts, D. (1960) *Victorian Origins of the British Welfare State* New
York, Yale University Press.

Roberts, M. (1980) 'Giving the public the right image', *Community Care,*
27 March, pp. 16—17.

Robson, W. A. (1976) *Welfare State and Welfare Society* George Allen
and Unwin.

Rodman, H. (1963) 'The lower class value stretch', *Social Forces,* Vol. 42,
No. 2, pp. 205—15.

Rollett, C. and Parker, J. (1972) 'Population and family', in Halsey (ed.).

Rose, H. (1978) 'Towards a political economy of welfare, Paper given to
Research Committee on Poverty, Welfare and Social Policy, International Sociological Association, Uppsala, August.

Rose, M. E. (1972) *The Relief of Poverty 1834—1914* Macmillan.

Rose, M. E. (1976) 'Settlement, removal and the new poor law', in Fraser
(ed.).

Rose, M. R. (1971) *The English Poor Law 1780—1930* Newton Abbot,
David and Charles.

Rose, N. (1980) 'Socialism and social policy: the problems of inequality',
Politics and Power, No. 2, pp. 111—35.

Rose, R. (ed.) (1980) *Challenge to Governance: Studies in Overloaded
Politics* Sage Publications.

Rowntree, B. S. (1913) *Poverty: a study of town life* Thomas Nelson and
Sons (first published 1901).

Rowntree, B. S. (1941) *Poverty and Progress: A Second Social Survey of
York* Longmans.

Rowntree, B. B. and Lavers, G. R. (1951) *Poverty and the Welfare State*
Longmans.

Royal Commission on the Distribution of Income and Wealth (1978a)
Lower Incomes Report No. 6, Cmnd. 7175, HMSO.

Royal Commission on the Distribution of Income and Wealth (1978b)
Selected Evidence for Report No. 6 HMSO.

Royal Commission on the Distribution of Income and Wealth (1979)
Fourth Report on the Standing Reference Report No. 7, July, Cmnd.
7595, HMSO.

Royal Commission on the Poor Law (1909) *Report* Cmnd. 4499, HMSO.

Royal Commission on the Press 1947—1949 (1949) *Report* Cmnd. 7700,
HMSO.

Royal Commission on the Press (1977a), *Attitudes to the Press,* Research
Series 3, Cmnd. 6810—3, HMSO.

Royal Commission on the Press (1977b) *Final Report* Cmnd. 6810,
HMSO.

Royal Commission on the Taxation of Profits and Incomes (Radcliffe
Commission) (1954) *Second Report* Cmnd. 9105, HMSO.

Runciman, W. G. (1972) *Relative Deprivation and Social Justice*
Harmondsworth, Penguin Books.

Ryan, P. (1976) 'The poor law in 1926', in M. Morris (ed) *The General Strike* Harmondsworth, Penguin Books.

Ryan, P. A. (1978) ' "Poplarism" 1894—1930', in P. Thane (ed.) *The Origins of British Social Policy* Croom Helm.

Ryan, W. (1971) *Blaming the Victim* Orbach and Chambers.

Rytina, J., Form, W. H., Pease, J. (1970) 'Income and stratification ideology: beliefs about the American opportunity structure', *American Journal of Sociology*, January, pp. 703—16.

Salman, E. G. (1886) 'What the working classes read', *Nineteenth Century*, Vol. XX, pp. 108—17.

Saville, J. (1957) 'The welfare state', *New Reasoner*, 3, Winter, pp. 5—25.

Scannell, P. (1980) 'Broadcasting and the politics of unemployment 1930—35', *Media, Culture and Society*, Vol. 2, No. 1, pp. 15—28.

Schiltz, M. (1970) 'Public attitudes towards social security 1935—1965', *Research Report*, No. 33, US Dept. of Health, Education and Welfare, Social Security Administration, Washington.

Schlackman Research Organisation (1978) 'Report on research on public attitudes towards the supplementary benefits scheme', Report submitted to Central Office of Information, mimeo.

Schlesinger, P. (1978) *Putting Reality Together: BBC News* Constable.

Schlozman, K. L. and Verba, S. (1979) *Injury to Insult: Unemployment, Class and Political Response* Cambridge, Mass. and London, England, Harvard University Press.

Searle, G. R. (1971) *The Quest for National Efficiency* California, University of California Press.

Sedgemore, B. (1980) *The Secret Constitution* Hodder.

Seldon, A. (1967) *Taxation and Welfare* Research Monograph No. 14, Institute of Economic Affairs.

Seldon, A. and Gray, H. (1967) *Universal or Selective Social Benefits* Research Monograph No. 8, Institute of Economic Affairs.

Semmel, B. (1960) *Imperialism and Social Reform: English Social—Imperial Thought, 1895—1914* George Allen and Unwin.

Senior, N. W. (1841) *Remarks on the Opposition to the Poor Law Amendment Bill by a Guardian* John Murray.

Seymour-Ure, C. (1969) 'Policy-making in the press', *Government and Opposition*, Vol. 4, No. 4, pp. 425—525.

Seymour-Ure, C. (1974) *The Political Impact of Mass Media* Constable.

Shaw, M. and Miles, I. (1979) 'The social roots of statistical knowledge', in J. Irvine, I. Miles, J. Evans (eds) *Demystifying Social Statistics* Pluto Press.

Showler, B. and Sinfield, A. (1981) *The Workless State* Oxford, Martin Robertson.

Sims, G. R. (1883) *How the Poor Live*, with illustrations by Frederick Barnard, Chatto and Windus.

Sinfield, A. (1978) 'Analyses in the social division of welfare', *Journal of Social Policy*, Vol. 7, No. 2, pp. 129—56.

Skidelsky, R. (1970) *Politicians and the Slump* Harmondsworth, Penguin Books.

Skidelsky, R. (1981) 'Keynes and the Treasury view: the case for and against an active unemployment policy 1920—39', in W. Mommsen and W. Mock (eds) *The Emergence of the Welfare State in Britain and Germany 1850—1950* Croom Helm.

Slack, P. (1972) 'Poverty and politics in Salisbury 1597—1666', in P. Clarke and P. Slack (eds) *Crisis and Order in English Towns 1500—1700* Routledge and Kegan Paul.

Sleigh, J., Boatright, B., Irwin, P., Stanyon, R. (1979) *The Manpower Implications of Micro-Electronic Technology* Department of Employment.

Smigel, E. O. (1953) 'Public attitudes toward 'chiseling' with reference to unemployment compensation', *American Sociological Review,* Vol. 18, No. 1, pp. 59—67.

Smiles, S. (1875) *Thrift: A Book of Domestic Counsel* John Murray.

Smiles, S. (1910) *Self-Help: With Illustrations of Conduct and Perseverance* John Murray (first published 1859).

Smith, A. C. H., Immirzi, E., Blackwell, T. (1975) *Paper Voices: The Popular Press and Social Change 1935—1965* Chatto and Windus.

Smith, S. (1883), Social Reform, *Nineteenth Century,* Vol. XIII, May, pp. 896—912.

Smith, S. M. (1980a) *The Other Nation: the poor in English novels of the 1840's and 1850's* Oxford University Press.

Smith, S. M. (1980b) ' "Savages and martyrs": images of the urban poor in Victorian literature and art', in I. B. Nadel and F. S. Schwarzbach (eds) *Victorian Artists and the City* New York, Pergamon Press.

Stedman Jones, G. (1974) 'Working class culture and working class politics in London 1870—1890: Notes on the remaking of the English working class', *Journal of Social History,* Summer.

Stedman Jones, G. (1976) *Outcast London: A Study in the relationship between classes in Victorian Society* Harmondsworth, Penguin Book (first published in 1971, Oxford University Press).

Stevenson, O. (1973) *Claimant or Client? A Social Worker's View of the Supplementary Benefits Commission* George Allen and Unwin.

Stringer, J. K. and Richardson, J. (1980) 'Managing the political agenda: problem definition and policy making in Britain', *Parliamentary Affairs,* Vol. 33, Winter, pp. 23—39.

Supplementary Benefits Commission (1978) *Take-Up of Supplementary Benefits* SBC Administration Paper No. 7, Department of Health and Social Security.

Supplementary Benefits Commission (1980) *Report for the year ended 31 December 1979* Cmnd. 8033, HMSO.

Tarling, R. and Wilkinson, F. (1977) 'The inflationary impact of incomes policy', *Cambridge Journal of Economics,* Vol. 1, No. 4, pp. 395—414.

Tawney, R. H. (1964) *Equality* Unwin Books (first published 1931).

Taylor, A. J. P. (1970) *English History 1914—1945* Harmondsworth, Penguin Books (first published 1965).

Taylor-Gooby, P. F. (1976) 'Rent benefits and tenants attitudes', *Journal of Social Policy*, Vol. 5, No. 1, pp. 33—48.

Thane, P. (1978) 'Women and the poor law in Victorian and Edwardian England', *History Workshop*, 6, Autumn, pp. 29—51.

Thompson, D. (1958) 'The welfare state', *New Reasoner*, 4.

Thompson, D. (1960) 'Farewell to the welfare state', *New Left Review*, No. 4, July/August, pp. 39—42.

Thompson, E. P. (1968) *The Making of the English Working Class* Harmondsworth, Penguin Books (first published 1963).

Thompson, E. P. (1971) 'Mayhew and the Morning Chronicle', in Thompson and Yeo (eds).

Thompson, E. P. (1977) *William Morris: Romantic to Revolutionary* Merlin Press (first published 1955).

Thompson, E. P. and Yeo, E. (1971) *The Unknown Mayhew* Merlin Press.

Tierney, B. (1959) *Medieval Poor Law: A Sketch of Canonical Theory and its Application in England* Berkeley, University of California Press.

Timms, N. and Watson, D. (eds) (1978) *Philosophy in Social Work* Routledge and Kegan Paul.

Titmuss, R. (1958) 'The social division of welfare', in *Essays on the Welfare State* George Allen and Unwin.

Titmuss, R. M. (1962) *Income Distribution and Social Change* George Allen and Unwin.

Titmuss, R. (1974) 'The limits of the welfare state', *New Left Review*, 27, September/October, pp. 28—37.

Townsend, P. (1978) 'The problem: an overview', in Barratt Brown *et al.* (eds).

Townsend, P. (1979) *Poverty in the United Kingdom* Harmondsworth, Penguin Books.

Troyna, B. (1980) *The Mass Media and White Consciousness* Report to the Commission for Racial Equality.

Tunstall, J. (1971) *Journalists at Work* Constable.

Turnbull, M. (1973) 'Attitude of government and administration towards the 'hunger marches' of the 1920's and 1930's', *Journal of Social Policy*, Vol. 2, No. 2, pp. 131—42.

Wadsworth, A. P. (1954/5) 'Newspaper circulations, 1800—1954', *Transactions of Manchester Statistical Society*, pp. 1—40.

Walker, D. (1976) 'Are social workers badly treated by the newspapers?' *Social Work Today*, Vol. 7, No. 9, pp. 292—3.

Walley, J. (1972) *Social Security: Another British Failure* Charles Knight.

Watt, D. (1968) 'Criticism of the welfare state grows' *Financial Times*, 20 September.

Waxman, C. I. (1977) *The Stigma of Poverty* New York, Pergamon Press.

Webb, A. (1980) 'Television as a news and information source', mimeo, University of Leicester.

Webb, B. (1948) *Our Partnership* Longmans, Green and Co.

Webb, S. and Webb, B. (1927) *English Poor Law History* Longmans, Green.

Webb, S. and Webb, B. (1909) *The Minority Report of the Poor Law Commission* Longmans, Green.

Weber, M. (1948) 'The social psychology of the world religions', in H. Gerth and C. Wright Mills (eds) *From Max Weber* Routledge and Kegan Paul.

Wedderburn, D. (1965) 'Facts and theories of the welfare state', *Socialist Register,* pp. 127—46, Merlin Press.

Westergaard, J. (1978) 'Social policy and class inequality', *Socialist Register,* pp. 71—99, Merlin Press.

Whale, J. (1977) *The Politics of the Media,* Manchester, Manchester University Press.

Whitfield, J. and Jordan, B. (1979) 'Claimants in action', in M. Loney and M. Allen (eds) *The Crisis of the Inner City* Macmillan.

Wilensky, H. (1976) *The 'New Corporatism': Centralisation and the Welfare State* Sage.

Wilkins, L. (1964) *Social Deviance: Social Policy, Action and Research* Tavistock.

Williams, F. (ed.) (1977) *Why the Poor Pay More* Macmillan.

Williams, R. (1980) 'Base and superstructure in Marxist cultural theory', in *Problems in Materialism and Culture* Verso (first published 1973).

Williamson, J. B. (1974) 'Beliefs about the welfare poor', *Sociology and Social Research,* Vol. 58, pp. 163—75.

Wilson, H. (1971) *The Labour Government 1964—1970* Weidenfeld and Nicolson/Michael Joseph.

Wilton, G. (1980) 'What they think of you', *Social Work Today,* Vol. 11, No. 36, pp. 14—17.

Wintour, C. (1972) *Pressures on the Press* Deutsch.

Winyard, S. (1979) 'Insuring inequality', *Low Pay Unit Bulletin,* No. 26/27, pp. 14—16.

Wohl, A. S. (1970) Introduction to A. Mearns *The Bitter Cry of Outcast London* Leicester, Leicester University Press.

Woodward, D. (1980) 'The background to the Statute of Artificers: the genesis of labour policy 1558—63', *Economic History Review,* XXXIII, No. 1, pp. 32—44.

Wootton, B. (1978) 'Uses of sociology', *New Society,* Vol. 43, No. 805, pp. 553—4.

Wright, E. O. (1980) 'Class and occupation', *Theory and Society,* Vol. 9, pp. 177—214.

Wright, T. (1970) *The Great Unwashed* Frank Cass reprint (first published 1868, Tinsley Bros).

Yeo, E. (1971) 'Mayhew as a social investigator', in Thompson and Yeo (eds).

Yeo, S. (1980) 'State and anti-state: reflections on social forms and struggles from 1850' in P. Corrigan (ed.) *Capitalism, State Formation and Marxist Theory* Quartet Books.

Yokelson, D. (ed.) (1975) 'Public attitudes toward poverty and the characteristics of the poor and near-poor', in *Collected Papers on Poverty Issues,* Vol. III, Hudson Institute, Croton-on-Hudson.

Young, A. F. and Ashton, E. T. (1956) *British Social Work in the Nineteenth Century* Routledge and Kegan Paul.

Young, J. (1971) *The Drugtakers* Paladin.

Young, R. (1979) 'Social workers and the media: a social services view', *Social Work Today* 30 January, pp. 10–11.

Index

273